THE DEATH AND LIFE
OF *GENTRIFICATION*

PRINCETON STUDIES IN CULTURAL SOCIOLOGY

Clayton Childress, Angèle Christin, Paul DiMaggio,
Michèle Lamont, Iddo Tavory, and Viviana A. Zelizer,
Series Editors

For a full list of titles in the series, go to https://press.princeton.edu/series
/princeton-studies-in-cultural-sociology .

The Death and Life
of *Gentrification*

A NEW MAP OF A PERSISTENT IDEA

JAPONICA BROWN-SARACINO

PRINCETON UNIVERSITY PRESS

PRINCETON & OXFORD

Published by Princeton University Press
41 William Street, Princeton, New Jersey 08540
99 Banbury Road, Oxford OX2 6JX

press.princeton.edu

GPSR Authorized Representative: Easy Access System Europe - Mustamäe tee 50, 10621 Tallinn, Estonia, gpsr.requests@easproject.com

All Rights Reserved

ISBN 9780691244358
ISBN (e-book) 9780691244365

Library of Congress Control Number: 2025936042

British Library Cataloging-in-Publication Data is available

Editorial: Rachael Levay and Tara Dugan
Production Editorial: Terri O'Prey
Jacket Design: Karl Spurzem
Production: Erin Suydam
Publicity: Maria Whelan and Kathryn Stevens
Copyeditor: Leah Caldwell

Jacket images: Bryan Pocius / Wikimedia Commons

This book has been composed in Arno

Printed in the United States of America

10 9 8 7 6 5 4 3 2 1

For Louisa, Ezra, and Arlo, and for Jana

CONTENTS

THE DEATH AND LIFE
OF *GENTRIFICATION*

Introduction

TODAY, MANY rely on *gentrification* to evoke a variety of feelings, meanings, and messages. People use *gentrification* to communicate ideas unrelated to neighborhood change. Indeed, there are increasing references to how individuals, politics, and even food and flags "gentrify."

The liberal use of *gentrification* in everyday discourse is unmistakable. According to the *New York Times*, Burning Man has "gentrified" (Jones et al. 2023), and, according to *New Yorker* writers, so too has polyamory and penile enhancement.[1] Ava Kofman writes for the *New Yorker*: "Prominent urologists had long seen penile enlargement as the remit of cowboys and regarded Elist [a urologist] as such, insofar as they regarded him at all. As part of Penuma's *gentrification campaign*, Elist got the F.D.A. to explicitly clear his implant for the penile region in 2017 . . . his company also began to recruit 'key opinion leaders,' . . . to advise the company and join its new board" (2023, 30; my emphasis).[2]

In Kofman's rendering, to "gentrify" is to take something once unrarified and to render it elite. The *New York Times* writes similarly of how the Burning Man festival has changed: "Many said the unexpected rain had brought out the gritty, self-reliant roots of a festival that has sometimes been *criticized for gentrifying* into a destination party for tech moguls and social-media influencers" (Jones et al. 2023; my emphasis).[3] Here, grit is exchanged for glamour, and the economic and media elite replace the everyday artist.

I encountered these examples of *gentrification* as a metaphor not as I researched this book, but, rather, as part of my ordinary, daily news

1

media diet. To be sure, I am a member of what the sociologist Wendy Griswold terms the "reading class."[4] That is, I am more likely than some others to consume sources like the *New Yorker* and the *New York Times* that deploy *gentrification* to communicate the elite appropriation of the everyday, average, and humble, and that, crucially, subtly position that appropriation—or "gentrification"—as negative. At least in the corner of the world that I—a forty-something Boston professor—occupy, this symbolic deployment of *gentrification* is unmistakable, and even unavoidable.

This book is an exploration of that symbolic deployment. It explores what *gentrification* means today and charts its new, symbolic life across a variety of realms of contemporary popular culture, scholarship, and activism. The book also offers an argument about how and why *gentrification* has entered the mainstream. I believe that this work is crucial and timely because we live with *gentrification* now. Not just in cities across the globe, and not even just in our rural hamlets, but also in our cultural life. *Gentrification* is an idea that we have latched on to; it is a lens through which some present the world and through which some of us, increasingly, interpret things—from sandwiches to sculpture to our own selves.[5]

More and more people are familiar with what the Showtime series *The Curse* calls the "G Word." At the same time, more and more people increasingly assign a collection of different meanings to the term— meanings that both play off of and extend beyond brick-and-mortar, or what I refer to as "literal gentrification," following the example of Sarah Schulman, the author of *The Gentrification of the Mind* (2012).[6] Most prominently, these include generalized upscaling; the appropriation by elites of something that once belonged to the working class, particularly to working-class ethnic and racial minorities; the loss of "authenticity" and of community; and involuntary change. This book reveals how *gentrification* has come to occupy space rendered vacant by the absence of a shared language for directly addressing structural inequalities and concomitant social changes. That is, the pages that follow document how cultural actors rely on *gentrification* to help them communicate messages about how unequal opportunity structures shape our lives, as well as about the feelings of loss that many associate with social change.

We will see that *gentrification* is at the nexus of contemporary cultural currents. It captures enduring ambivalence and anxiety about social change, as well as about navigating social heterogeneity (can we all live together?!). *Gentrification* knits those long-standing concerns together with pressing worries of our times about deepening inequalities and attendant social divisions and conflict. Recognizing these currents helps us to understand how and why *gentrification* works well as a communication device. It also reveals how *gentrification* is a window into the problems that weigh on cultural producers and that they turn to *gentrification* to explore, if not to solve.

Literal gentrification continues apace. In my own city of Boston, nearly everyone, from the poor to the upper-middle class, grapples, in distinct ways and to varying degrees, with the consequences of several decades of intensive reinvestment and subsequent severe affordable housing shortages, sky-high rents, and commercial vacancies borne of unaffordable storefront leases.[7] As chair of my department, I must tell faculty job candidates how professors navigate a remarkably expensive housing market, and I field emails from new graduate students stymied by the search for an affordable place to live. Here, we are so in the grasp of literal gentrification, or the kind of brick-and-mortar upscaling and demographic turnover that is so recognizable in so many contemporary cities, that hardly a day goes by when, setting my own scholarship aside, I do not think of literal gentrification and of how it shapes life around me.

But this book calls on us to acknowledge how the symbolic power of the term has stripped it of the original meaning sociologist and urban planner Ruth Glass assigned *gentrification* in 1964 when she coined the phrase. Glass defined *gentrification* as the movement of the middle classes into working-class city neighborhoods. According to Glass, the middle class renovated existing housing stock, raising prices, and, subsequently, displaced the original, working-class residents.[8]

"One by one," Glass famously wrote, "many of the working class quarters of London have been invaded by the middle classes—upper and lower Shabby, modest mews and cottages—have been taken over, when their leases have expired, and have become elegant, expensive residences. . . . Once this process of 'gentrification' starts in a district, it goes on rapidly until all or most of the original working class occupiers are displaced, and the whole social character of the district is changed" (Glass 1964). Eventually, the neighborhood becomes the domain of the gentry, with working-class residents, their businesses, and the "character" that both lent to the neighborhood (Glass 1964) increasingly vanished.

Today, the *New Yorker* and the *New York Times* echo Glass not only by using the term she coined, but also by using *gentrification* to convey changed social character or status. However, the changed character and status that they aim to communicate is not that of a city neighborhood, but rather that of a desert festival and a penile implant company. *Gentrification* has been loosed from its original meaning. We might say that *gentrification* has a new life as a metaphor.

Gentrification's New Life

Today, talk of *gentrification* is not limited to urban settings or issues; *gentrification* has a life that extends well beyond the traditional parameters of urban change. More and more, *gentrification* is used to evoke a broad set of transformations, from the personal to the collective and the political; from the spatial to the immaterial. A prominent example is the aforementioned *Gentrification of the Mind*, in which the author Sarah Schulman deploys "gentrification" as a metaphor to explain how, partially as a result of material changes, some urbanites' mentalities have changed (2012). *Gentrification* no longer narrowly refers to urban residential change; that specific connotation has perished in favor of more flexible and nimble evocations of the term that are increasingly detached from urban political-economic transformation.

References to *gentrification* are abundant, heterogenous, and cut across a range of realms, including literature, activism, artwork, scholarship, and everyday conversation. As an idea or term, *gentrification* is also increasingly flexible. The writers, artists, scholars, and activists whom this book features have come to wield *gentrification* to communicate a range of ideas, experiences, and processes. In other words, *gentrification* is a resource they leverage for a variety of purposes, from supporting social movements to calling together a sense of community to signaling that viewers ought to be critical of how a television character has transformed or upscaled.

As the four chapters that follow reveal, *gentrification* has become a staple shortcut for talking about a range of social issues and dynamics, including growing income inequalities. It has, equally, become a way of *talking around* or dodging issues pertaining to inequality that make many uncomfortable.[9] Sometimes, talk of *gentrification*, or communication that occurs in conversation, print, or other media that evokes *gentrification*, serves to avoid direct engagement on issues related to race, class, and sexualities; other times, it works in exactly the opposite manner, serving as a kind of signal or wink that inequalities are afoot.

This book provides a cultural map of the idea of *gentrification*; it reviews how *gentrification* operates in contemporary discourse and entertainment. It documents how cultural producers rely on *gentrification* to cultivate social ties; to describe the transformation of place-based communities forged in shared space; and to describe the evolution the self. It also reveals how *gentrification* is a tool that movement activists and scholars alike deploy to diagnose the structural roots of social inequalities and cultural appropriation. Put differently, this book explores the new territories that *gentrification* has taken, migrating from its original home in urban studies to the realms of art, television, literature, film, social media, and social movement activism.

If *gentrification* doesn't just mean literal gentrification anymore, what does it mean? Above all else, *gentrification* has been reborn as a catch-all term to indicate elite appropriation of something significant to a lower status group, and the transformation of a person, group, or object to a more elite or rarified version. *Gentrification* also often implies that something "authentic" has been lost, in favor of something more upscale. In this sense, when cultural producers rely on *gentrification* as a metaphor, they often do so to leverage subtle criticism of how something has changed or to communicate a sense of loss that they believe such change produces.

While scholars increasingly attend to how *gentrification* operates in novels, television shows, or in the media, few take a bird's eye view of *gentrification* as a symbol to which a variety of actors assign meaning and leverage for their own purposes across a variety of domains of contemporary life.[10] This book looks across genre and form to document the heterogeneous manner in which *gentrification* operates as a metaphor, as well as patterns apparent across a broad assemblage of usages. I do not, as my terrific colleagues in the humanities do, trace in fine detail precisely how plot lines and character development rely on *gentrification*. Instead, my analysis is sociological or, one might say, more meta; I look across genres and fields to provide a portrait of *gentrification's* new life and to document what *gentrification* reveals about how contemporary cultural producers frame social issues, such as racial and economic inequalities, segregation, and the problems of contemporary neoliberalism and corporate capitalism.

Scholars of brick-and-mortar gentrification have not yet directly acknowledged the vivid, independent life of *gentrification*.[11] I write this book from the vantage point of a longtime scholar of literal gentrification. I have, for almost a quarter of a century, studied gentrification on the ground via ethnographic research. I have also mapped scholarly debates about literal gentrification, and examined newspaper coverage of brick-and-mortar gentrification. As a result, I am keenly attentive to how usages of metaphorical *gentrification* relate to scholarly representations of literal gentrification, and I aim to start a conversation about the implications of *gentrification's* new life as a metaphor for the study of literal gentrification, as well as for the development of policies that might help us to predict and address its consequences for residents and for the places in which they live.[12]

I am also a cultural sociologist drawn to questions of how meanings and concepts take shape and influence social life. As a result, while I bring the conversation back to literal gentrification more than some humanists might do, this book does not advocate for a single shared definition of *gentrification* that is narrowly wedded to how urbanists conceive of the term.[13] Above all else, this book is guided by my abiding curiosity about *gentrification's* new life, and, secondarily, by questions about the implications that new life has for its old one.

In the chapters that follow, I draw attention to *three primary ways* in which *gentrification* is deployed, relying on examples from a range of cultural forms. These are just a few items from an archive that I have collected—at first by accident, and then with intention. My concern is not that they are representative, nor that they capture the full range of variation in how *gentrification* works as a symbolic device. Instead, I rely on them as illustrative examples of the patterns evident in my archive of cultural objects, from art to songs to television series to novels, that rely on *gentrification* as a metaphor or communication device.[14] I also hope that they operate as a call for others to constitute an even broader and more heterogeneous archive. I aim for this to be the start of a conversation and for the examples that I rely on to serve as benchmarks for readers as they contemplate the broader landscape in which *gentrification* operates as a symbol and device.

First, some deploy *gentrification* to *rebuild community*, such as artists who use anti-gentrification installations to express nostalgia for White working-class communities and dyke bar commemorators who use talk of *gentrification* to regenerate community without relying on extant identity politics.[15] *Gentrification* works in this way because it evokes vulnerability and marginality; gentrification harms, largely by displacing and disrupting a way of life.[16] For some, talk of the threat of *gentrification* or nostalgia for how a community was before literal gentrification works to help a group remember what it shares—or once shared—and therefore to find the common ground on which identity-based community rests. *Gentrification* can denote a sense of shared loss that has the potential to be generative of a sense of commonality or "groupness."

Second, cultural producers rely on *gentrification* to *express and examine the transformation of the self*.[17] These accounts present individuals from traditionally marginalized groups who have achieved mobility, such as a Black playwright, and they position the "gentrification" of the self as severing one's original authenticity. In this rendering, to "gentrify" is to become upscale and to become less real and less connected to one's natal community. Like a refurbished home, the new self bears a resemblance to its original state, but it has been remade for a more elite audience. Here, *gentrification* again denotes loss, but a loss borne by an individual, specifically by the "gentrifying" subject who leaves community, authenticity, and originality behind as they become more upscale.

Third, *gentrification serves as a shorthand for the systemic roots of social problems and issues.* A variety of actors deploy *gentrification* in this manner, from Black Lives Matter activists to journalists and academics; these cultural producers rely on talk of *gentrification* to underline the problems of late-stage capitalism and neoliberalism. Even gentrification scholars sometimes rely on *gentrification* as a metonym to build arguments about endemic racial and economic inequalities and cultural appropriation. When *gentrification* is used in this manner it works as a metaphor for—and sometimes simultaneously as an illustration of—the structural roots of broad social problems and inequities.

I first explored the themes of this book in an article in the *American Journal of Sociology*, which traces how dyke bar commemorators in four US cities rely on talk of *gentrification* to bring disparate LBQT+ individuals together to reestablish community.[18] My ethnographic research revealed that commemorators neither aim to revive bars, nor to forestall literal gentrification. Instead, they use the memory of bars and talk of *gentrification* to create a sense of shared marginality among a heterogeneous collection of LBQT+ individuals. Disdain for literal gentrification and nostalgia for bars serve as a "social glue" that facilitates connection and commonality, despite differences along the lines of race, class, age, and gender.[19]

This drew my attention to *gentrification* as a symbolic device. When commemorative activists placed literal gentrification front and center—despite the fact that they did not aim to advocate against literal gentrification—the research questions that are central to *The Death and Life of* Gentrification emerged: What does *gentrification* mean today, within and beyond the academy?[20] How does that meaning vary? How do activists and cultural producers use talk of *gentrification*; what work does it accomplish for them?

The pages that follow chronicle how *gentrification* functions in contemporary culture, at least as it appears in my archive—or the collection of cultural objects that rely on *gentrification* as a communication tool that I analyze in the book's chapters. They also explore how six decades of fractious scholarship have contributed to the ambiguity that freed *gentrification* to become a device that activists, novelists, playwrights, and screenwriters deploy, as well as how abundant deployment of *gentrification* as a metaphor begets more of the same, creating new opportunities for the meaning and role of *gentrification* to proliferate and to coalesce around several dominant usages.[21] Finally, I discuss the consequences of this abundant usage of *gentrification* for scholars and policymakers.

While humanities scholars are increasingly attentive to *gentrification* as a storytelling device, perhaps in the interest of maintaining scientific authority and a related commitment to treating literal gentrification as a measurable empirical process, scholars of gentrification as a brick-and-mortar process have habitually looked away from *gentrification* as a concept or symbol to which a variety of actors assign meaning and leverage for their own purposes.[22] We have devoted too little attention to *gentrification*'s vivid, independent life.

How *Gentrification* Was Reborn

The Death and Life of Gentrification maps how and why *gentrification* is so easily adopted for a wide array of aims. First and foremost, both literal gentrification and *gentrification* as a term are *abundant and enduring*. This ubiquity and familiarity render the term increasingly recognizable and retrievable.

Second, gentrification is *deeply associated with the "urban,"* which is, in its own right, weighty and charged. Because of its association with the city, *gentrification* is especially evocative of urban racial and economic inequalities and sexual heterogeneity; it has become a shorthand that allows us to, in some cases, efficiently reference these subjects, and, in others, to dodge direct conversation about them, while, at the same time, indirectly signaling their relevance. As literal gentrification has advanced in recent decades in many neighborhoods that were historically home to racial minorities, the notion that literal gentrification is a process of racial turnover or replacement—with White gentrifiers replacing Black and Latinx residents, for instance—has become widespread.[23] This partially enables *gentrification*, as a term, to evoke ideas about race, racism, and displacement. In this sense, *gentrification* can be a wink. We might say, for instance, that San Francisco's Mission neighborhood has *gentrified* rather than explicitly acknowledging the substantial displacement of Latinx populations and an influx of White tech workers. In other words, *gentrification* evokes racial, economic, and sexual differences and related inequalities that we associate with the urban; by using the term one can gesture to these issues without talking about them directly.

Third, *gentrification* evokes not only the urban but also *change itself*.[24] Because change is such a general and inclusive experience, this association renders *gentrification* a nimble and resonant concept. It is this conflagration with change that partially allows *gentrification* to evoke personal and collective transformations, from a person's evolving class status to changing sexual identities. Popular culture presents the "gentrified" self as bourgeois and inauthentic; thus, novels and TV series present upwardly mobile Latinx and African American women as "gentrified" and increasingly divorced from their cultural roots.

Fourth, *gentrification* is multivocal, in part because it is a concept that is hotly contested by experts; among literal gentrification experts there is much discord about literal gentrification's causes and consequences, and even about how to define and measure it.[25] The prolific and fractured scholarly literature, which seeps into the news media, helps liberate *gentrification* from any narrow meaning. Partially as a result, *gentrification* can be deployed to tell a range of stories and to accomplish an array of aims. As I've suggested above, this is not the only reason that *gentrification* operates as a metaphor, but it is one piece of the explanation for why we can find *gentrification* on our television screens, in the novels that we read, in the songs that we listen to, and on Reddit.

Gentrification has become a holding container—for scholars and everyday actors alike—for so many anxieties and hopes and political positions that it has come to mean, more and more, very little. Consider, for instance, that some scholars define literal gentrification as Ruth Glass did in 1964: as the movement of the professional classes into working-class neighborhoods. Consider, that, at the same time, others define it specifically as a process of racial turnover, with White gentrifiers moving into the neighborhoods of racial minorities.[26] This way of thinking about literal gentrification has proliferated in recent years, as the gentrification of Black, Latinx, and other racial minority neighborhoods has intensified (after several decades of upscaling in White immigrant neighborhoods); this is, in a sense, literal gentrification's new "frontier," and definitions of brick-and-mortar gentrification are adjusting in real time as the frontier moves.[27] Consider that some, like Glass, insist there is no literal gentrification without displacement. Consider that others contend that in some instances, literal gentrification occurs without engendering significant, direct displacement.[28] As these impasses illustrate, literal gentrification is, conceptually, a moving target—within the academy, and, as this book reveals, well beyond it. Consider also that positions on these academic debates relate not just to how one thinks about *gentrification*, but also to how one thinks about a broader set of dynamics and concepts, such as the role of racial inequalities in shaping cities.

But that is not all. In October of 2023, with my colleague, the geographer Loretta Lees, I organized an international conference on literal gentrification at Boston University. Some of our keynote speakers—at a conference titled "Gentrification and Displacement"—suggested that they are not comfortable with the term *gentrification*. They are not alone in this. This view is particularly abundant among scholars of the Global South, some of whom resist applying a Global North concept to explain a region that experienced intensive colonization.[29] But discomfort with the term is by no means limited to such scholars. This theme cut across the conference.

Some scholars prefer to speak and write of colonization; they regard literal gentrification as an extension of an enduring imperialist project. Others prefer financialization, intentionally connecting literal gentrification to broader processes of capital accumulation. Still others suggest that racial capitalism works as well as anything else to describe what has been called *gentrification*.[30] By stepping back from *gentrification* they situate neighborhood upscaling in a broader set of processes and dynamics—and gesture more overtly to the broad causes of neighborhood reinvestment and displacement. In this rendering, literal gentrification is a symptom, rather than a direct cause, of enduring racial and economic inequalities, capitalist dynamics, and many decades of urban planning and policy. Thus, some scholars who study literal gentrification are ambivalent about the term *gentrification*, in part because they worry that it distracts from underlying processes and histories that facilitate what Ruth Glass termed *gentrification*.

I agree with many of these scholars that one of the problems of *gentrification*, as an idea, is that it evokes the end of a process, the tip of the iceberg, if you will, rather than the full history and set of forces that will literal gentrification into being.

I don't say this lightly. I have spent much of the last two and a half decades writing and thinking about literal gentrification. I impugn myself, as much as anyone else, when I write these words. As I gestured to above, and as other scholars argue, we omit oceans upon oceans when we call literal gentrification the cause of anything, which is why contemporary scholars increasingly rely on racial capitalism, colonialism, or financialization to explain the dominance of literal gentrification.[31]

I suspect that there is a relationship between the broad adoption of *gentrification* in popular culture and the two features of gentrification scholarship that I highlighted above: the enduring debates that characterize the literature on literal gentrification and ambivalence among *gentrification* scholars about allegiance to the term and concept of literal gentrification. When experts on a concept become ambivalent about that concept and openly debate its meaning and significance, that ambivalence and those debates are unlikely to stay in a vacuum.[32] The reader will find that I believe they have bearing on *gentrification*'s new life.

But just how much bearing do they have? How can we be certain about which came first—scholarly debates about *gentrification* or popular adoption of *gentrification* as a metaphor? Do scholars become increasingly ambivalent about terms once they are taken up by the masses and lose some of their specificity? Perhaps. Do endless academic debates about literal gentrification—what it means, when to apply the term, whether gentrification is singular or multiple—help to create a certain haziness about *gentrification* that has freed the term for expansive and creative popular adoption? Perhaps. I won't make a neat causal argument, claiming that this ambivalence has a clear root or time stamp, but I return to these questions again in the conclusion.[33] Throughout the book, I entertain the possibility that scholars and other cultural producers are, directly and indirectly, co-creating *gentrification*'s new life.

Still, I want be clear that scholarly debate is not the only explanation for *gentrification*'s new life. *Gentrification*'s strong association with other powerful concepts, such as the urban and change, also plays a crucial role. Moreover, the ubiquity and durability of brick-and-mortar gentrification renders the term highly recognizable and retrievable. And the more we rely on *gentrification* as a metaphor, the more available the term becomes for adoption and, with it, evolution.

However, as a scholar of literal gentrification and as one who has devoted significant attention to scholarly debate on the subject, I have an obligation to consider how academic debates about literal gentrification are at play in *gentrification*'s new life as a metaphor. Nonetheless, I would not want the reader to mistake the fact that I task myself with considering the influence of literal gentrification on metaphorical *gentrification* as constituting the book's core argument, nor as an effort to narrowly impugn scholars of literal gentrification for the term's new role.

I should also be clear that I believe that conceptual messiness about how to define and explain literal gentrification is useful. It is useful, in no small part, because it pulls back the covers on how literal gentrification emerged from a long-standing and interconnected web of policies, practices, and planning, and how gentrification is but one face of contemporary capitalism and other political and economic processes and dynamics that shape the unequal world in which we live. In general, scholarly debates are generative because they refine and advance ideas. At the same time, this conceptual messiness, however clearsighted it is, may, alongside the other factors that I mention above, have helped to open the door for *gentrification*'s rebirth as a symbolic device.

Gentrification Hits Newstands

As I mentioned at the outset, over the last several years I have, by chance, stumbled upon news media reports that rely on *gentrification* as a metaphor. That is, they evoke *gentrification* not to capture brick-and-mortar gentrification, but to encapsulate a different kind of transformation.

To get an idea of the scope and contours of such reporting, with a team of student researchers I conducted a targeted search of a decade of references to the "gentrification of" in a database of articles from eight major US newspapers, eliminating references to the "gentrification of" neighborhoods so that I could zero in on references to the "gentrification" of things that have little to do with literal gentrification. What does *gentrification* mean today? How do some people use *gentrification* to talk about things that have little to do with cities or brick-and-mortar upscaling? Answering these questions will provide us with a shared landscape of the range of meanings and purposes that cultural producers assign to *gentrification* and, from the book's outset, will provide the reader with a sense of the breadth and diversity of usages of *gentrification*—as well as of some of the patterned ways in which cultural producers deploy the term.

As is true of much of this book, I won't offer a full recap of that research, such as the frequency of references per newspaper or over time (although our analysis did capture those patterns). Instead, I provide illustrative examples of the patterned ways in which the news media relies on *gentrification* to describe the transformation of entities that are not urban neighborhoods. I do so to sketch a portrait of just how abundant and broad-ranging this liberal use of *gentrification* is, as well as to signal the work that *gentrification* accomplishes as a communication device.

As the rest of the book will reveal, the patterns apparent in newspaper coverage extend beyond print media—to Reddit, literature, scholarship, television shows, documentary, and sculpture. I begin with newspaper coverage to introduce the patterned deployment of *gentrification* as a metaphor that this book's chapters trace and develop. There is more and more talk of *gentrification*, but that talk is, less and less, merely about literal gentrification. Instead, literal gentrification has become a powerful reference point that enables *gentrification* to serve as an abundant and powerful metaphor.

Journalists use *gentrification* to describe the upscaling and appropriation of a broad range of entities, particularly those that once belonged to racial minorities. Take a *Boston Globe* article that quotes a Twitter post:

"'Dunkin' Donuts 'inventing' donut fries is the gentrification of the churro'" (Nanos 2018).[34] In another article, the *Globe* writes, "Thus began the gentrification of cable."[35] In a *New York Times* op-ed, Ginia Bellafante asks, "Must We Gentrify the Rest Stop?"[36] For its part, in a long article on changes to military commissaries, the *Chicago Tribune* makes a casual claim about *gentrification*, writing: "The gentrification of the commissaries began in the name of efficiency" (Chandrasekaran 2013).[37]

This is not the only example in which it is food—or the venues that sell food—that "gentrify." A *Chicago Tribune* journalist writes that "the real story in barbecue in the last several years has been the gentrification of the genre—spareribs and long smoked brisket repositioned as totems of the artisanal food movement" (Gold 2013).[38] A *New York Times* article laments "the gentrification of the sandwich" (Rosenberg 2016).[39] Similarly, another article captures anxiety about the upscaling of a longtime, affordable New York food market: "Alarms went off after the *Times* reported on the planned makeover [of Grand Central Market]. . . . The news bounced around the blogosphere, drawing complaints about the loss of authenticity. *Times* staff writer Joseph Serna denounced the gentrification of the 'people's market'" (Holland 2013).[40]

It is not just food that "gentrifies." Reflecting on an upscale marijuana dispensary near a remodeled Erotica Museum with "a sleek steel and stone exterior," the author of a *Los Angeles Times* article suggests that the museum, together with the fancy dispensary, embodies, "the gentrification of vice" (Montero 2018).[41] Echoing this, a *Los Angeles Times* theater critic suggests that the themes of a show include "the gentrification of cannabis" (Lloyd 2019).[42] Seven years earlier, the *New York Times* referred to "the gentrification of contemporary art" (Cotter 2012)[43] and, a year after that, "the gentrification of conventional pickups, including Chevy's own Silverado" (Tingwall 2013).[44] According to the same paper, the self can "gentrify,"[45] as can addiction (Roller 2016).[46]

Music "gentrifies," too. A *Boston Globe* article describes an "idealistic community grappling with a 21st-century gentrification of concert going" (Borrelli 2015).[47] Another says, "It's largely thanks to a global commercial interest in [Puerto Rico's] musical output, namely reggaeton, that Bad Bunny was able to launch his career in the first place; as a result, many a mainstream pop heartthrob has been rebranded in the image of Bunny and other Caribbean artists, furthering the gentrification of their sounds" (Exposito 2022).[48] Here, something specific and special to a particular group becomes available for consumption by a broader group, and, in so doing, becomes less exceptional. There is loss associated with becoming more upscale and mainstream, or so this deployment of *gentrification* suggests.

Building on this sense of lost exceptionality, newspaper accounts suggest that when entities "gentrify," they become more upscale, less distinctive, and less authentic. Consider a *Chicago Tribune* article, in which the author engaged in a conversation about English pubs: "'But, wait, I said, there's no gentrification of the English pub?' Wright: 'Absolutely, there is! Our joke about them looking the same now is right. Our pubs are being streamlined, like your bars. The rough edges are coming off . . . The signage, menus, all exactly the same. It's sad. . . . Pubs, down to their names, once had a florid eccentricity. Occasionally, an actual historical link. Now it all seems pulled out of a hat somewhere else'" (Borrelli 2013).[49] Pubs, like neighborhoods, are losing their distinction—but not because the places where pubs are located are literally gentrifying. In this rendering, to "gentrify" is to upscale regardless of how the city itself is transforming. Corporatization and literal gentrification are synonymous, and the end result is stultifying sameness and a loss of authenticity. Here, *gentrification* again communicates how change produces feelings of loss, this time of distinction and authenticity.

Sometimes media accounts build connections between literal gentrification and the "gentrification" of culture. For example, an article in the *Boston Globe* draws parallels between the literal gentrification of the seaside resort, Provincetown, and the "gentrification" of gay culture: "Ten years before the Supreme Court ruling, and just one year after marriage equality arrived in Massachusetts, Andrew Sullivan famously lamented 'The End of Gay Culture' (or, more specifically, the gentrification of Provincetown) in *The New Republic*, bemoaning the erosion of 'distinctive gayness' in the wake of a fresh wave of acceptance" (Brodeur 2015).[50] However, my research reveals that this type of usage—which evokes the brick-and-mortar gentrification of a specific place as occurring in tandem with cultural "gentrification"—is rare. Much more frequently, journalists deploy *gentrification* as a metaphor to describe the transformation of entities that changed independently of place-upscaling.

Occasionally, those who deploy *gentrification* as a metaphor take pains to be clear about the specific meaning they assign to the term. Take, for instance, a 2018 *Chicago Tribune* op-ed about collard greens. The author, Clarence Page, writes, "Collard greens are 'the new kale.' So say the chic eaters. But some concerned cultural guardians fear a new social and economic menace: 'food gentrification.' *Gentrification, simply defined, is when something that you used to buy because it was cheap suddenly turns fashionable—which makes it too expensive for its original consumers to afford"* (Page 2014; my emphasis).[51] Another *Tribune* article takes similar pains to explain why *gentrification* works to explain the problem of chefs seeking culinary awards. "There's also the potential gentrification of fine-dining (the *tweaks made to conform to a better rating*); the chefs who grow *more business oriented*" (Borrelli 2014; my emphasis).[52]

While this type of specificity about the meaning that journalists assign to *gentrification* is relatively rare, certain assumptions about *gentrification*— and why it works as a symbolic device—are apparent in other journalists' accounts. For instance, a *New York Times* article reveals the author's presumption that the reader will recognize that *gentrification* harms; the author deems the absence of harm to be noteworthy, writing: "The gentrification of Kickstarter doesn't seem to be hurting its original inhabitants" (Lapidos 2013).[53] Somewhat more subtly, the author of an article on the creation of a charter school in a Los Angeles neighborhood in which parents are dissatisfied with the quality of public schools seems to assume the reader will recognize that literal gentrification is known to generate conflict: "But it's a *charged situation*, the educational equivalent of the gentrification of housing" (Banks 2012; my emphasis).[54]

In these elaborations on what they mean by *gentrification*, we see that journalists ascribe certain meaning to the term. They tend to assume, for instance, that literal gentrification—and therefore its metaphorical extension—is charged or is a site of conflict; that it harms the original inhabitants, owners, creators, or users; that it operates in pursuit of profit, at the cost of authenticity and other intangible values; and that it takes something affordable and places it out of reach for the average person. They also imply that something, usually authenticity, community, accessibility, or distinction, is lost when something "gentrifies."

Crucially, more often than not, journalists don't bother to spell these associations out for readers; they assume their audience is in the know about literal gentrification and the harm it causes. This illustrates at least some contemporary cultural producers' confidence in *gentrification*'s resonance and retrievability.

On *Gentrification*'s Utility

The certainty that literal gentrification is a problem—and a recognizable one at that—is part of why *gentrification* works as a communication device for journalists and for the activists, academics, artists, and others whom this book engages. *Gentrification* also works as a device because it is evocative of feelings of loss and of appreciation for "authenticity." As is clear in newspaper articles, by evoking *gentrification* journalists effectively tip their hat at a (loosely defined) political and moral position; one that roots for the underdog and decries systems of power, whether corporate or governmental, that favor the elite. However, *gentrification* also has symbolic purchase because it is a nimble word; *gentrification* is a noun that implies action, specifically change, and it is a word that can be used to describe the transformation of a broad diversity of people, places, things, and even ideas. *Gentrification* is catchy (both in the literal sense, and as a term). As the chapters to follow reveal, *gentrification* is also adaptable and flexible, in part because scholarly debate and discord have rendered it so, and because literal gentrification is so prolific and recognizable and emotionally and politically evocative. In short, *gentrification* is multivocal, recognizable, and highly resonant. For all of these reasons, in the current zeitgeist (Krause 2019) the term solves problems for those who deploy it, whether by providing a metaphor that captures the meaning they wish to evoke, or by serving as an efficient metonym for a tough-to-communicate idea (McDonnell et al. 2017, 7).[55] As with certain other terms and ideas, *gentrification*'s problem-solving utility only expands the more we put it into circulation.[56]

Personally, I am not certain that this adoption of *gentrification* as a symbolic device is a bad thing—as long as we acknowledge the conceptual messiness that this adoption creates and do the work of unpacking it. This is a theme that I explore in the book's conclusion. For now, I will note that if we acknowledge and harness the idea that *gentrification* doesn't just mean neighborhood upscaling anymore, we can garner insights about myriad facets of social life, not just those pertaining to cities and not just pertaining to literal gentrification. This endeavor is also valuable because it pulls back the cover on assumptions about literal gentrification, such as we've already seen, about how it causes harm to the marginal, threatens authenticity, and is, at heart, a conformist practice that reduces the variety and novelty of individuals and communities. By tracing how cultural producers rely on metaphorical *gentrification*, we see, for instance, how frequently they associate literal gentrification with loss and the specific types of change they believe to be generative of loss. At the same time, it sheds light on so much more, such as how cultural producers frame the upward mobility of racially and economically marginalized individuals; how some grapple with what it means for sexual and gender minorities to gain new legal, cultural, and political victories; and the confidence of a growing body of movements in the effectiveness of a metonym that gestures to some of the problems of capitalism. In short, we have much to learn by tracing how cultural producers deploy *gentrification* in a variety of contexts.

That's just what this book aims to do. It traces what cultural producers mean by *gentrification* and documents how they deploy it. In so doing, we learn much about what worries contemporary actors today, how they understand themselves, conceptualize community, and what facets of contemporary life they regard as fragile and in need of protection (from "gentrification"). Looking at how people rely on talk of *gentrification* is a window into contemporary orientations to change, capitalism, racial inequalities, sexual and gender identities, and other social issues.

We learn, for instance, that contemporary social actors seek external explanations for how they and the communities they are a part of change and evolve. We also learn that some are ambivalent about or even downright uncomfortable with the upward mobility of traditionally marginalized individuals. Still others worry that such mobility and other sources of increased heterogeneity will weaken communities predicated on shared traits. More generally, by closely reading how people rely on *gentrification*, we discover the degree to which many struggle with processing and accepting all kinds of social change, particularly changes that upend the social order and that are not equally distributed across members of a social group. *Gentrification* works to express and encapsulate all of these anxieties. If it sounds like we ask a lot of *gentrification*, that's because we do.

Could we garner insights about contemporary anxieties, yearnings, and ambivalences by looking at any term? After all, *gentrification* is not the first, nor will it be the last, academic term adopted by those outside of the academy with the aim of solving certain problems or carrying certain related meanings (Hallett et al. 2019; McDonnell et al. 2017).[57] Others have written about how media elites and others take up academic concepts, such as social capital, precarity, and the creative class, popularizing them, and, sometimes, altering their meaning (Hallett et al. 2019; Lamont 1987). This book does not, as some works do, compare and contrast the careers of a set of academic concepts; that is, I do not systematically compare *gentrification* to other scholarly terms that have entered the mainstream, nor do I mean to suggest that *gentrification* is the only academic concept that has a new life. My goal, instead, is to specifically explore *gentrification*'s position in the public sphere.

Yet, for reasons I have already mentioned, without formally comparing the term to others, I argue that *gentrification* possesses qualities that make it available for adoption by cultural producers and resonant for a broad audience.[58] These reasons include, but are not limited to, close associations between *gentrification* and other charged concepts such as *urban* and *change*; the ambiguity of scholarly definitions of literal gentrification; the fact that the term, as a word, evokes a process ("ion"); and the reality that literal gentrification is so widespread and so recognizable in a wide array of settings. In addition, literal gentrification is commonly regarded as a social problem that harms marginalized groups and affects quality of life for many, rendering the term politically and emotionally charged—without gesturing to a specific political position or emotion. Finally, *gentrification* seems to entertain more than most academic concepts that get batted around by the mainstream media. After all, *gentrification* is evident in television series' titles, newspaper headlines (that aren't about literal gentrification), song lyrics, and catchy protest chants. I suspect this is because *gentrification*, unlike an academic concept like *social capital* or the *creative class*, implies interaction, conflict, and a process that unfolds over time; it is even suggestive of character types (longtimers and gentrifiers) and of a semi-predictable plotline (invasion, resistance, and, sadly, inevitable transformation).[59] We might say that *gentrification* was made for television. Again, I build this argument not because I have systematically compared *gentrification* to other terms, but from my close reading of how the term operates in my archive.

Perhaps it is not a coincidence then that the way that *gentrification* is used bears some resemblance to the adoption of *colonization* and *decolonization* as metaphors. This is a trend that has been quite famously— and, in my estimation, rightly—critiqued.

Eve Tuck and K. Wayne Yang point out that *colonization* is frequently used "as a metaphor for oppression" (2012, 20).[60] They go on to suggest that "decolonization" has also been adopted as a metaphor, writing that "'internal colonization' reduces to 'mental colonization,' logically leading to the solution of decolonizing one's mind and the rest will follow" (2012, 20).

Tuck and Yang regard the abundant metaphorical adoption of *colonization* and *decolonization* as deeply problematic, for this adoption fundamentally alters the meaning of the original concepts, partially stripping them of their significance and power. They write that "decolonization specifically requires the repatriation of Indigenous land and life. Decolonization is not a metonym for social justice" (2012, 21).

Thus, *gentrification* may be particularly ascendant as a metaphor right now, however, if we take a longer view, we can see that *gentrification* belongs with a few other highly evocative and politicized terms, such as *colonization* and *decolonization*. This class of terms has been liberally deployed to advance a range of causes, some of which take us far from the meaning of the term as first conceived. While, in contrast to Tuck and Yang, I take a more curious than critical position on how *gentrification* operates in contemporary American culture, throughout the book's chapters and in its conclusion, I ask the reader to think with me about some of the risks inherent in *gentrification*'s new life.

On Metaphor, Metonym, Heuristic, and Parable: A Primer on the New Language of *Gentrification*

At a talk in late 2023, the historian Jules Gill-Peterson made a passing reference to the "gentrification of lesbians" in the 1980s. Sitting in the audience, I assumed she did so to signal that in the 1980s, because of reduced barriers to women's labor force participation and broader access to higher education, some (mostly White) lesbian couples experienced newfound access to the middle class. Notably, Gill-Peterson used the term *gentrification* unselfconsciously and did not pause to ensure that an audience who had gathered to hear a talk on transgender history was certain of her intended meaning. I can only presume that, like so many we will encounter in this book, Gill-Peterson was confident that the audience, which was composed of faculty and students at Boston University, would be familiar with *gentrification*.

This is significant, because Gill-Peterson was not using the term to refer to literal gentrification. Thus, at least to this audience member, it seemed that Gill-Peterson was confident not only that the audience would have a working image of literal gentrification, but that the audience would also understand her use of the term to refer to the transformation of a traditionally marginalized social group to a higher economic position.

What did Gill-Peterson mean by *gentrification*? Why did she adroitly use it to describe lesbians? On first glance, it seems that the historian was deploying the term as a metaphor to illustrate parallels between neighborhood gentrification and the upscaling of lesbians as they achieved economic mobility. On closer examination, though, we can see she was also using *gentrification* as a *metonym* for upscaling—a core feature of both neighborhood gentrification and of the type of personal upward mobility her language conjured. After all, her sentence would have communicated much of the same meaning if she had said that "lesbians became more upscale" in the 1980s as they entered the professional classes—or became members of the gentry—in greater numbers. In this instance, *gentrification* and *upscaling* work interchangeably.

But to say that lesbians became more upscale in the 1980s would carry a lot less punch than to claim that they *gentrified*. To my ear, the claim that lesbians *gentrified* carries a modest critical edge. When neighborhoods gentrify, many (although not all) will agree, something is lost in the transition; usually, a grittiness and "authenticity" that some mourn once a neighborhood becomes upscale. Cue nostalgic recollections of Times Square pre-Disneyification; of Greenwich Village as a bohemian enclave; of Le Marais as a humble gay enclave. Such neighborhoods may be cleaner and more status-secure now that they are highly gentrified, but many would say they've lost a great deal of character and accessibility as a result.

As we will see in some of the chapters to come, Gill-Peterson—consciously or not—was, at least to my mind, evoking the trope of the lesbian who traded in her lesbian housing collective, protest signs, and natural foods co-op membership for a briefcase, a mortgage, and monogamy. For me, her words brought to mind a 1980s lesbian subject as tidy and unobjectionable as Boston's contemporary Back Bay, but also far less distinctive and engaging than the 1970s version of each. Metaphor and metonym bleed into each other here.

My point here has little to do with either the Back Bay neighborhood or 1980s lesbians. I offer this example to signal that the chapters to come zero in on the new language of *gentrification*.

As my description of Gill-Peterson's talk suggests, in the chapters that follow the reader will find that I closely attend to language. That is, I care very much about how cultural producers—whether a historian or a sculptor—talk about or present *gentrification*. I am not just interested in what they mean by *gentrification* but also in identifying the type of work that the word *gentrification* accomplishes. To get at this, I find it is helpful to think not only about the content of cultural producers' language, but also about its structure.

To be sure, I am not a literary scholar. Long ago, I imagined I might be an English major, but it has been more than twenty-five years since I became permanently rooted in sociology. Nonetheless, I find it useful to rely on certain literary terms to think about how *gentrification* works for cultural producers. I am not overly concerned with formal or elaborate definitions of the terms I turn to, such as metaphor, metonym, heuristic, and parable. However, I find such terms to be helpful for considering some of the similarities and differences in how people use *gentrification* as a symbolic device.

I've noticed patterns in how cultural producers deploy talk of *gentrification*. Most abundantly, and as we've seen above, they rely on *gentrification* as a *metaphor*—to draw out similarities between two things that are not obviously related to one another. I never once thought of *gentrification* as relevant to penile enhancement, for instance. But once Ava Kofman wrote about it in those terms for the *New Yorker*, I could see how evoking neighborhood upscaling shines a light on how an emerging medical procedure is on a path toward acceptance and respectability.[61] Likewise, before I read an article by Karen Halnon and Saundra Cohen, I hadn't thought of tattoos as "gentrifiable." Yet the authors so successfully rely on the metaphor of "gentrification" to underline how a traditionally working-class form—the tattoo—has been adopted by affluent people, that it permanently altered how I think about tattoos. When I walk by the tattoo shops in my gentrified neighborhood, I can't help but think about how tattoos have traveled from the working-class to the affluent, upscaling in the process.[62] Here, the use of *gentrification* as a metaphor made me see tattoos differently; I now recognize the tattoo as a cultural form that has crossed traditional class barriers, taking on new significance and meaning (and a heftier price tag!).

Still others rely on *gentrification* as a *metonym* that is interchangeable with certain other words. Here, *gentrification* typically stands in for upscaling, as we see above with 1980s lesbians. Often, although not always, this usage implies a critical edge or a subtle stance of judgment about what is lost when something or someone becomes more upscale.

Relatedly, some turn to *gentrification* as a heuristic or a kind of communicative shortcut that efficiently conveys meaning. For instance, the communications scholar Jessa Lingel can tell her reader that the internet has become more elitist and corporatized by simply suggesting it has undergone *gentrification*.[63]

There are certain lessons to be learned from each manner in which cultural producers leverage *gentrification*. From metonyms, we get a close view of the precise meaning *gentrification* holds for cultural producers. For instance, we might see, as I've suggested, that, for many, *gentrification* references a generalized upscaling—to take something previously associated with the working class and make it over for the affluent. By attending to metonyms, the book will reveal that upscaling is the dominant alternate meaning of *gentrification*. Sometimes, *gentrification* still refers to neighborhood upscaling, but sometimes *gentrification* simply refers to upscaling, bracketing neighborhood entirely.

Metonyms matter for an additional reason, too—which is that they reveal the degree to which, for many, the meaning of *gentrification* has drifted away from literal gentrification. I don't mean to suggest that *gentrification* has become entirely divorced from the urban; we will see that literal gentrification is still the most dominant point of reference. However, *gentrification* now evokes more than the urban; its meaning has become diffuse, circulating around upscaling almost as much as around the urban.

Another common way in which cultural producers evoke *gentrification* is as a *parable*. That is, they rely on *gentrification* to convey a moral lesson. Most often, the moral lesson that such stories convey is that to "gentrify" is to engage in a morally questionable act that can separate a person from their "true" community and their "true" self.[64] There is much to learn about how people evaluate the ethics of literal gentrification by paying attention to how they use *gentrification* as a parable. Here, especially, we see how many who deploy *gentrification* as a symbol presume their audiences will agree that *gentrification* is a bad thing; they present *gentrification* as a process that diminishes authenticity, uproots communities, and severs ties. By tracing how *gentrification* works as a parable, we have a powerful reminder that evocations of *gentrification* are almost never value-neutral. This is even more the case when it comes to evocations of metaphorical "gentrification" than of literal gentrification. Even some who regard literal gentrification in nuanced terms—as providing historically economically disinvested neighborhoods with certain valuable resources, while also problematically displacing long-time residents—will recognize that metaphorical "gentrification" presents the process in starker or more black and white terms. In the realm of metaphorical "gentrification," there is no gray zone when it comes to the morality of *gentrification*. In parables of *gentrification*, something precious is irrevocably lost as it changes.

For those of us who study literal gentrification on the ground, and even more so for those who organize to mitigate literal gentrification and to protect affordable housing, paying attention to these parables reveals a kind of tipping point when it comes to perceptions of literal gentrification. Plenty of cultural producers seem confident that they can present moral problems through the lens of *gentrification*, and that means they are reasonably confident that a large share of their audience will not only recognize *gentrification* as a concept, but that they will also recognize that literal gentrification is problematic—or at least that many regard it as problematic. We can learn a lot about cultural attitudes about literal gentrification from tracking how cultural producers leverage the term to accomplish other kinds of work, including to tell stories that offer moral lessons.

In short, we learn different things from the different ways in which *gentrification* operates as a communication device. I don't explore these usages in any formal sense, but I gesture to them throughout the book, because I think they are useful tools for thinking about the shape that *gentrification*—as an idea—takes in contemporary popular culture. By attending to how cultural producers talk and write about and otherwise depict *gentrification*, we see the precise communicative work that *gentrification* is doing and the meaning it carries today.

The meaning of *gentrification* is not totally random or endlessly heterogeneous either. If one narrow way of thinking of *gentrification*—as strictly referring to neighborhood upscaling—has died, several others now flourish. The book at once underlines the diversity of meanings of *gentrification* today and elucidates clusters of meaning and significance associated with *gentrification*. Throughout, I will signpost the most common clusters of meaning. These include, as we've begun to see, upscaling; the appropriation of something belonging to working-class racial and ethnic minorities by the affluent; the loss of authenticity; and the fracturing of community.

Notes on My Own Language

Gentrification

To create order in what might sometimes seem to be a sea of discursive heterogeneity and ambiguous meaning, I want to be clear from the beginning about how I approach the term *gentrification*. Throughout the book, I use *gentrification* in three primary ways. First, as the reader may have noticed, borrowing language from the author Sarah Schulman, I use "literal gentrification" to refer to neighborhood gentrification or to the economic and demographic makeover of neighborhoods along the lines of what Ruth Glass outlined in her original definition (2012).[65]

Schulman coined the phrase "literal gentrification" to distinguish between what she termed "the gentrification of the mind" and "literal gentrification" or the class turnover of Lower Manhattan. Making this distinction neat was imperative for Schulman, as, for her, literal gentrification and the "gentrification of the mind" exist in a causal relationship. Specifically, she argues that the literal gentrification of Manhattan called forth a "gentrification of the mind" or an upscaling and professionalization of creative and experimental populations who had to remake their lives to survive in an increasingly expensive and neoliberal city. Lesbian poets and gay artists, for instance, had to adapt to find a way to live in gentrified Manhattan; they sought degrees and professionalization to survive. Later, they relied on legal marriage to access health insurance and other forms of security in an increasingly neoliberal society that individuates protection and well-being. As result, their perspective changed; in Schulman's terms, their minds "gentrified." In this sense, Schulman has it both ways—she attends both to literal gentrification and to metaphorical "gentrification"—building an argument about how one (literal gentrification) produced the other ("gentrification of the mind"). Indeed, Schulman's book is a prominent example of the deployment of metaphorical *gentrification* to make a point that extends beyond literal gentrification and to evoke a sense of collective loss. In fact, Schulman's book may have inspired others to wield *gentrification* as a metaphor.[66]

While I follow Schulman by using the term *literal gentrification* to refer to the process that Ruth Glass first described, occasionally I use three other terms interchangeably to capture literal gentrification. I occasionally refer to literal gentrification as neighborhood upscaling, neighborhood gentrification, or as brick-and-mortar gentrification. I do so to signal that I am referring to a place-based process in which one class of people is replaced by another, more affluent, class of people, and to emphasize that literal gentrification produces material changes.

I contrast this with "gentrification"—that is, *gentrification* in quotation marks—by which I mean to refer to metaphorical *gentrification*. I will use "gentrification" to convey that the term is working as a symbolic device to describe the transformation of something that is *not* a neighborhood. We have already encountered several examples of this. We know that penile enhancement has "gentrified" and that, in the 1980s, lesbians did, too. We know that journalists are following the "gentrification" of collard greens and reggaeton and that some films and TV series offer parables that suggest that we ought to guard against our own, personal "gentrification."

Finally, when I mean to refer to *gentrification* as a word or a term, I italicize it. In so doing, I wish to remind the reader that *gentrification*, like any other term, does not have any inherent or stable meaning. It is, after all, not just a process, but also, in simplest terms, a word.

Many of the objects from my archive that we will encounter tell stories of metaphorical "gentrification" set against the backdrop of literal gentrification. Sometimes, like Schulman (2012), they present a relationship between the two things, suggesting that literal gentrification can lead to other "gentrifications." More often, I suspect that they situate metaphorical "gentrification" against the backdrop of literal gentrification because it makes their metaphorical usage more obvious; look, these two things are changing at once, even though change in one did not directly produce change in the other. This shines a light on how personal or community change shares some of the characteristics of literal gentrification. Take the Starz series *Vida* as an example. The idea that a Latinx character is "gentrifying" is all the more obvious because her personal upscaling is set against a neighborhood undergoing literal gentrification. Even if, in this instance (at least as presented by the show-runners) literal gentrification did not produce metaphorical "gentrifica-tion," the changes reflect back on one another, convincing us of the appropriateness of *gentrification* as a metaphor for the primary charac-ter's personal transformation.

Cultural Objects

This book analyzes what I will refer to as "cultural objects," from books to television shows to sculptures to academic articles. I borrow the term and concept from the sociologist Wendy Griswold. For Griswold—and for me—a cultural object is, in simplest terms, "shared significance em-bodied in form" (Griswold 1987, 4), or cultural material that we can see, touch, hear, feel, read, or otherwise engage. A cultural object does not have to be material, although often it is. Cultural objects include beliefs, doctrines, poems, songs, hairstyles, and quilts (Griswold 1987, 4–5). The cultural objects I analyze in this book include television shows, Reddit conversations, newspaper reports, memoirs, nonfiction monographs, novels, academic articles and books, songs, sculpture, and films. In a sense, *gentrification* is itself a cultural object—or a set of cultural ideas encapsulated in a term. Indeed, it would be fair to say that I rely on the analysis of a diverse set of cultural objects to better understand the cul-tural object at the heart of this book, which is, of course, *gentrification*. I seek to better understand *gentrification* not as a material process, but as an idea, to which many attach significance and meaning.

Cultural objects, of course, do not exist in a vacuum.[67] They are cre-ated by cultural producers living in a world full of myriad other cultural objects (Griswold 1997). Whatever meaning a cultural producer, whether a writer, a painter, or a musician, presumes to assign to cultural objects, the meaning they have is, in large part, shaped by how cultural receivers—or audiences—interpret them (Griswold 1997). Other cultural objects can shape audience reception, such as an advertisement in the midst of a television show or a set of beliefs that a person brings to their engagement with a sculpture or a book.[68] There is also a long pathway between the intentions of the creator of an object and the form the object ultimately takes. This is, in part, because so many different people and processes have a hand in the production of any cultural object. This book, for instance, has been read and commented on by my writing group; it has been the subject of questions and engagement at talks I've given; it has been edited and, later, copyedited. Whatever my original intentions were for this cultural object, it has been shaped along the way by many people, ideas, and institutions.[69] This long winding pathway, and the myriad individuals and institutions that influence the final shape a book takes, is brilliantly captured by Clayton Childress in *Under the Cover* (2017).

Some scholars busy themselves studying the intentions of cultural producers or the reception of cultural objects, or, in the case of Childress, they study all of these things. This book only engages such questions in a passing manner. I do not make claims about the intentionality of representations of *gentrification* in the cultural objects I analyze. I cannot state with any confidence that those who wrote the screenplays and memoirs that I feature, for instance, consciously thought of *gentrification* as a device to communicate a morality tale, nor can I determine whether producers or editors nudged authors or screenwriters to make such devices more prominent. I also cannot be certain that audiences have received or interpreted a film or book—or any other cultural object—in a specific manner, for I have not systematically studied reception.

To make those claims would be to speak beyond the archive that I have assembled and the questions that I have asked. For instance, I do not mean to claim that people self-consciously extend *gentrification* as a metaphor. Instead, I pursue questions about the circulation and diffusion of a concept. My aim is to present a reading of the cultural objects in my archive; to reveal how the objects I've assembled *can* be read or interpreted. Ultimately, I want to reveal what they, collectively, can communicate about *gentrification,* which is, after all, the cultural object of greatest interest to me. Put differently, this book doesn't seek to explain why cultural producers rely on *gentrification* or how institutions facilitate the adoption of *gentrification* as a metaphor. Rather, it aims to identify *how gentrification* works for those who deploy it. By that I mean that, by closely reading the objects in my archive, the book sheds light on the work that the term accomplishes in contemporary American culture.[70]

Why do cultural objects matter? As "externalized manifestations of ideas" (McDonnell 2023, 196) they are crucial vehicles for sharing meaning.[71] They help us to develop or revise beliefs and feelings about innumerable things (2023, 196). Beyond this, as Terence McDonnell argues, cultural objects matter because they shape action (2023). McDonnell cautions that too often everyday actors and scholars alike "forget how those objects have come to shape behavior. We ignore cultural objects' centrality to action" (2023, 196). Some cultural objects, like religious texts or political treatises, direct action in tremendously powerful ways. Like certain other charged cultural objects, *gentrification* has become increasingly institutionalized, and, as a result, is ever more available for adoption as a metaphor, potentially extending its ability to direct (or inhibit) action (McDonnell 2023). We encounter this possibility, for instance, when we consider the breadth and diversity of *gentrification* in newspaper coverage.

My wish is that this book will spur others to devote serious attention to questions about how the *idea of gentrification* shapes action—and inaction. If we cease thinking of *gentrification* as a single, concrete, and easily delineated urban process (i.e., as literal gentrification as first defined by Ruth Glass) and begin acknowledging that it is a cultural object, or shared significance embodied in a term, then planners, policymakers and everyday actors will be better positioned to respond to literal gentrification in a manner that is sorely needed. In the current moment, I suspect that many of us are responding, in myriad ways, to both literal and metaphorical "gentrification"; this muddies the water when it comes to evaluating what people make of literal gentrification and perhaps even stymies our collective ability to resist unmitigated urban upscaling.

My engagement with the archive I have assembled for this book leads me to believe that growing fuzziness about what *gentrification is* has made it difficult to assemble a coalition to advocate for policies that anticipate neighborhood upscaling, protect longtime residents, and secure affordable housing. At the same time, looking directly at the heterogeneous meanings assigned to *gentrification* leaves this scholar uncertain of the utility of continuing to treat literal gentrification as a reference to a single, discrete process, rather than as a concept that is a holding container for multiple instantiations of urban transformation—from a kind of generalized urban upscaling to financialization to the sustained effects of imperialist investment and divestment. My great hope is that by approaching *gentrification* as a cultural object, and by offering close readings of the cultural objects that inform ideas about *gentrification*, we will liberate ourselves to acknowledge the messiness and significance of the concept, and to move forward with great intentionality about how we approach *gentrification*—both as a metaphor and as a word that captures a brick-and-mortar urban process.

Why *Gentrification*'s Meaning Matters

On the one hand, this book is very different than any I have written before. My first two monographs relied on extensive ethnographic observation in geographically disparate places. My edited volume, *The Gentrification Debates*, and several subsequent articles, interpret academic research on literal gentrification. In contrast, this book originates in an observation about contemporary social life—that *gentrification* is deployed in ways that are increasingly distant from literal gentrification—but it relies on evidence in support of an argument rather than on a mountain of original data. The book is in conversation with academic debates about literal gentrification, but it centers cultural representations of *gentrification* to tell its story. I was called to write this different kind of book by my dyke bar commemoration research and, equally, by the deployment of *gentrification* as a symbol that I stumbled upon in the television series that I watch, the art that I consume, and the newspapers and novels that I read.

In another sense, though, *The Death and Life of* Gentrification closely aligns with how I have long approached the study of literal gentrification. My first book—an ethnography of four gentrifying communities— uncovered what scholars miss by looking away from the meanings that gentrifiers assign to literal gentrification.[72] Scholars had erroneously assumed that all gentrifiers embrace literal gentrification, not only welcoming the transformation of neighborhoods to upper-middle-class space, but also celebrating their role in that transformation. In so doing, they missed how variation in gentrifiers' attitudes about literal gentrification shapes their practices and the contours of daily life in gentrifying locales.

Just as my first book revealed, scholars ought not look away from the cultural life of *gentrification* if they wish to facilitate policy and planning that is responsive to conditions on the ground. Today, that cultural life is much broader than what happens in gentrifying neighborhoods. To understand what *gentrification* means, we must look beyond cities—to a series about a struggling family-owned taqueria; a memoir about the AIDS pandemic; Reddit comments; and activists' protest chants. The *Death and Life of* Gentrification does just that, and in so doing promises to advance knowledge not only of what *gentrification* means, but, also, of how academic scholarship filters into the public sphere, taking on new life and meaning.

What are the implications of all of this talk of *gentrification*? What are the consequences for the study of literal gentrification and for policy and planning aimed at mitigating the harms that it causes? I caution that reliance on *gentrification* as a metaphor risks taking us further afield from a concrete, shared meaning of literal gentrification, potentially troubling our ability to develop responsive and boundary-spanning policies and mitigation strategies. For instance, when *gentrification* is evoked to describe personal transformation rather than neighborhood change, it might trouble efforts to build public support for affordable housing and other strategies for ameliorating gentrification's effects. Moreover, this usage might heighten ambivalence and malaise about the systemic inequalities and injustices of which *gentrification* is symptom and tool. When *gentrification* is used, more and more, as a metaphor for transformations that have little or nothing to do with the city, it makes the term more evocative of feeling than generative of action. In a sense, it takes a process of material change and at once renders it increasingly meaningful and increasingly ephemeral. I revisit these and other potential consequences of the metaphorical usage of *gentrification* in the book's conclusion, including the possibility that we are deploying the term with such frequency and to convey such a broad range of meanings that the salience of *gentrification* may soon be at risk.

Yet, despite my misgivings, it makes no to sense to turn our back on *gentrification*'s new life in a variety of cultural domains. To date, we have missed how *gentrification* has become an increasingly common method for communicating ideas about social inequalities and social change. This lack of acknowledgment complicates proactive responses to literal gentrification by politicians, policymakers, and activists; we are ill-prepared for the weight and meaning everyday actors assign to *gentrification*, complicating efforts to engage residents in planning processes. It also exacerbates scholarly and popular debates about how to define and measure literal gentrification. Researchers rarely acknowledge how public discourse about *gentrification* might influence academic debates about literal gentrification. We have yet to consider whether increasingly diffuse popular definitions of *gentrification* influence how scholars define the term.

This book is a starting point. It marks the death of *gentrification* as an idea conceived in 1964 by Ruth Glass, and acknowledges its new, vast life as a weighty metaphor.

What Follows

I begin where this project did, with dyke bar commemorators in New York, New Orleans, San Francisco, and Chicago, who rely on talk of literal gentrification to communicate a sense of shared threat that, they hope, will help them to regenerate community. The book's second chapter continues to trace how cultural producers use *gentrification* to grapple with community change. Specifically, the chapter attends to cultural objects that offer accounts of how literal gentrification drives people apart, destroying place-based communities. I reveal how, in actuality, a documentary, sculpture, television series, and a film rely on *gentrification* as a metonym for how communities—whether that found at mid-century in Boston's Little Italy or today in Los Angeles's Boyle Heights—change and even fade away. Some of these accounts rely on narratives of literal gentrification and in so doing avoid engagement with how community members directly or indirectly contribute to the transformation of their ties, whereas others use *gentrification* as a metaphor for the myriad structural forces that pull people apart. From chapter 2 we learn that *gentrification*, deployed as a metonym for community dissolution, can either camouflage or shine a light on how broad systems and the inequalities they produce separate us from one another.

Next, in the book's third chapter, I consider how *gentrification* works as a metonym for personal upward mobility and how it also operates as a parable for the risks of such upscaling. I caution that the self that cultural producers depict as "gentrifying" is, at least in my archive, more often than not a person of color, a woman, and/or a sexual or gender minority. I ask the reader to consider with me the stakes of using *gentrification* to spotlight the transformation of certain traditionally marginalized subjects. I also call us to observe what this suggests about the increasing frame for literal gentrification as a problematic process that strips locales of authenticity.

Finally, in the book's fourth chapter I explore how *gentrification* communicates and advances causal arguments about the sources of social inequalities and other problems—from journalists' and scholars' broad critiques of neoliberal capitalism to denouncements of changing LGBTQIA+ politics and identities. I also demonstrate how some movements rely on *gentrification* as a rallying cry, even when they are unconcerned with literal gentrification. More and more, *gentrification* operates to organize and motivate activists and to communicate causal arguments about the structural sources of inequalities, appropriation, and other social problems.

In the conclusion, I weigh the role of a fractious and vast body of scholarship on literal gentrification in shaping *gentrification*'s new life as a metaphor. I also grapple with questions about how those who study literal gentrification, and who seek to develop policies to address it, ought to make sense of *gentrification*'s cultural life. What does it mean to study literal gentrification once we acknowledge the cultural significance of *gentrification*? How can we chart and attend to the intersecting influences of metaphorical and literal gentrification? Ultimately, I elaborate on the themes I have introduced of whether we ought to think of the death and life of *gentrification* as problematic or promising. Should we welcome *gentrification*'s new life, or mourn the passing of convergence around Ruth Glass's original rendering of the term?

1

Mourning the Dyke Bar

IN 2016, newspapers, websites, and blogposts began profiling the work of activists in several cities, including New York, San Francisco, Chicago, and New Orleans, who were commemorating dyke bars. The stories noted that lesbian bars, which have almost always had short lives, were closing at a particularly rapid pace.[1]

Atlas Obscura published an account of bar commemoration in New Orleans titled "The Lost Lesbian Bars of New Orleans."[2] Writing of the same project, a commemorator penned an essay for *Autostraddle*, a website that is geared toward lesbian, bisexual, and queer women and transgender and nonbinary (LBQT+) audiences, and reports on everything from queer-friendly vacation destinations to sex toys and politics. Reflecting on what they learned about the 1970s and 1980s by interviewing "elders," the commemorator, a queer-identified individual in their thirties who works for a New Orleans nonprofit, wrote, "Dyke bars during this period were spaces for identity formation, community building, political organizing, and celebration. All around the country these spaces are disappearing, or are already gone."[3]

It is worth noting that the commemorator, like many others, referred to the institutions that they remembered as *dyke* bars rather than as *lesbian* bars. In so doing, this commemorator and others like them gesture both to a specific time period (roughly the 1970s–1990s, when some lesbians pridefully reclaimed the derogatory term "dyke" as an identity label) and to dive bars with a specifically working-class ("dyke") clientele. Their commemorative projects conjure bars in which customers drink beer on bar stools or play pool, implicitly contrasting this with a *lesbian* bar in which one might sip chardonnay at a patio café table. Of course, in actuality, not all who identify as dykes are working class, nor are there many (middle-class) lesbian wine bars. Still, as we will soon find, for the stories of *gentrification* that bar commemorators tell, it is critical that their projects conjure *dyke bars*; that is, remembering working-class dive bars of the 1970s–1990s located in ungentrified urban neighborhoods permits them to offer their audiences an object vulnerable to literal gentrification.

Building on these themes, in 2016, many publications reported on Macon Reed's life-size recreation of a dyke bar in Brooklyn, *Eulogy for the Dyke Bar*. The installation, clad in vibrant blues and purples and complete with pool table, bar, and dartboard, drew crowds who gathered together in the installation to sip drinks such as "Butch Tears" and to listen to dyke-bar veterans in their fifties, sixties, and seventies share their bar stories.[4]

Fast-forward to 2019, when I began analyzing in earnest the interviews and field notes I had collected studying dyke bar commemoration in New York, New Orleans, Chicago, and San Francisco. An unmistakable theme cut across my transcripts and notes, and that theme was, much to my surprise, *gentrification*—metaphorical and literal. As I alluded to above, commemorators talked about literal gentrification with great frequency and ease. They spoke of it in our private interviews; at commemorative events; and in conversation with one another.

What did they say about literal gentrification?[5] Commemorators' talk of *gentrification* does not constitute a singular or neat narrative; some describe limited personal struggle with literal gentrification, others acknowledge that they are themselves gentrifiers. Some define literal gentrification as a process of racial turnover; others describe it in purely economic terms.[6] Few offered concrete explanations of what they meant by *gentrification*. And despite all of their talk of literal gentrification, few truly believed it was solely to blame for dyke bar closures.

This versatility and underspecificity about what *gentrification is* worked for commemorators. It worked because *gentrification* provides a flexible symbol for calling out a sense of shared fate and vulnerability among those who come together to remember the "hardscrabble" dyke, her bar, and neighborhood. This solves a problem that dyke bar commemorators wrestle with and that this chapter explores: namely, how to bring together a diverse set of LBQT+ individuals without presuming they share a singular identity, set of experiences, or a uniform social position.

Commemorators deploy talk of *gentrification* to help explain dyke bar closures. But that is not the only reason they evoke *gentrification*. Referencing literal gentrification works to establish a sense of collective threat that extends to the present day and that unites a diverse assemblage of LBQT+ individuals against the looming threat of neighborhood upscaling. Their events imply that literal gentrification threatens not only their institutions, but also the place of LBQT+ individuals in the city. Merging the ghosts of the working-class dyke and her bar and neighborhood with narratives of how gentrification continues to alter public life and territoriality for LBQT+ residents, commemorators call out a shared vulnerability that, together with a sense of shared lineage to an earlier lesbian feminist identity and politics, provides a basis for ties—in place of the identity politics that once bound certain lesbians to one another. In other words, they rely on *gentrification* to evoke a sense of shared experience and to establish a source of shared vulnerability. In lieu of other bases for common ground, and amid a collection of individuals who are deeply mindful of intersectionality, *gentrification* operates to signal shared experience and positionality. Here, *gentrification* operates as a metonym for shared vulnerability and marginality.

As I've begun to suggest, it was not *gentrification* that drew me to study dyke bar commemoration. Instead, the project originated in a kind of autobiographical, midlife curiosity. I was approaching forty when reports of dyke bar commemoration began to proliferate, and news coverage drew me in, especially accounts of efforts to commemorate bars in New Orleans. Just after college, I lived in New Orleans and occasionally frequented Charlene's, one of the city's long-standing dyke bars. I remember the bar's dimly lit interior, dominated by a pool table, jukebox, and a dark, wooden bar. Mostly, I recall the anxious feeling of waiting on Elysian Fields, a busy street between the French Quarter and warehouses along the Mississippi, to be admitted to the bar, as the door was locked and barred. That feeling of anxiety came from a few sources, including wondering whether I would be admitted to the bar (did I look too straight?!) and, at the same time, fearing violence or harassment from passersby before I was (was I legibly gay?!). But I also vividly recall how the whole room paused as each new patron crossed the threshold. At twenty-one, visiting Charlene's was exhilarating and terrifying; it seemed that I was, all at once, seeing backward and forward in time. The women, some in men's shirts and jeans, and others with big, permed blowouts, reminded me of an earlier era. Yet, with no idea of how rapidly the world was poised to change on LGBTQIA+ issues, I wondered if I was somehow glimpsing my own (middle-aged) future. At the time, I imagined I might forever anxiously await admittance to Charlene's and other bars of its ilk; this, I thought, was my fate.

Having come out at a New England women's college in the mid-1990s, I had rarely bothered with bars in other places that I'd called home, such as the Massachusetts towns of Northampton and Provincetown; a petite, White, cisgender woman with shoulder-length red hair and a habit of wearing dresses, in those cities my movement between heterosexual and queer worlds was, most of the time, fairly seamless. This was, in part, because of how the world saw me, presuming I was straight, but also because those places, compared to most, were exceptionally accepting of sexual difference. But in New Orleans, where friends sternly warned me to stay in the closet at work, and strangers sometimes confronted me when I held my girlfriend's hand, I was glad to find occasional refuge at Charlene's.

Given this, when the New Orleans troupe Last Call began fundraising to support their musical, *Alleged Lesbian Activities*, commemorating New Orleans's shuttered dyke bars, it piqued my interest; not because I anticipated that their work had anything to do with literal gentrification (that insight would come much later)—a topic I have long studied and written about—but because I was curious about how individuals who were half a decade or so younger than myself remembered bars that most of them had never frequented.

I soon also read about a group in New York, Dyke Bar Takeover, that organized Lost Dyke Bar Tours of Lower Manhattan, drawing on oral history interviews they conducted with those who once peopled now-shuttered bars. Later, I heard about efforts to commemorate San Francisco's Lexington Club, a pinnacle of lesbian nightlife in the Mission neighborhood in the 1990s and early 2000s, as well as of an archival exhibit of lost dyke spaces in Chicago, *Lost and Found*.

Armed with this information, I began researching these specific commemorative projects, seeking to observe commemorative events and interview their organizers in every US city where I could locate their work. Ultimately, I took the train from Boston to New York to walk East Village streets and hear accounts of shuttered 1970s bars, and boarded a plane to Chicago to visit a storefront in Logan Square, a neighborhood with a large Latinx population that, like other swiftly upscaling Chicago neighborhoods, includes a growing number of cocktail bars, coffee shops, and galleries. There, I attended a guided tour of *Lost and Found*, taking in a map of Chicago dyke bars from the 1970s and 1980s, and peering at lesbian newsletters and magazines affixed to the walls and pinned under glass on display tables. Later, I flew to San Francisco, meeting commemorators associated with the Lexington Archival Project at coffee shops and bars in the upscale neighborhood, which many Latinx households and LBQT+ individuals had once called home.

At first, I was curious. And perplexed. From what I could tell, those commemorating bars were, by and large, too young to have attended them; with the exception of those commemorating bars in San Francisco, most were college-educated professionals and artists in their late twenties and early thirties. They were also too young to have rubbed shoulders with many who identified as "dykes" and, on the whole, too highly educated to have spent much time in working-class dive bars. Thus, their fascination with "dykes" and their bars, located in gritty, ungentrified neighborhoods, stood out to me. While I was roughly five to ten years older than most commemorators, I was nonetheless young enough that my own time in bars was limited; until very recently, there were no official dyke bars in any of the cities where I have lived for the last fifteen years.[7] My fate, it turned out, was not to spend countless nights at Charlene's or at any other dyke bar. How would those who'd never had the opportunity to visit such bars remember them? Would they view them through rose-colored glasses? Or, alternately, might they be blindly critical? Might the answer depend on the backgrounds of those commemorating the bars? After all, much like literal gentrification itself, bars, when they flourished, provided an uneven set of opportunities for LBQT+ individuals; by most accounts, they provided the most favorable experience for White, cisgender women.[8]

From the start, these questions drove me to seek to learn as much about commemorators' backgrounds as I could, from where they went to school to where they lived, and how they identified (in terms of gender, sexuality, race, and class). Typically, I let commemorators select the places where I met them. A graduate of a women's college—a White, femme professional—suggested that I meet her for breakfast in a crowded coffee shop in northside Chicago's upscale Andersonville neighborhood, which has a long-standing reputation both as a Swedish enclave and as a commercial and residential locus for LBQ women.[9] We ordered vegan breakfast burritos and let the waitress refill our coffees several times. She told me about her work creating the *Lost and Found* exhibit, her Andersonville apartment, and her job in the tech industry. I also learned about her girlfriend (a bartender) and about her friendships with other commemorators, all of whom are femme-identified queer women in their thirties. In one newspaper report, they posed together, each sporting bright red lipstick and colorful manicures—a fierce commemorative trio.

A graduate of another highly selective Northeastern liberal arts college served me a whisky sour in the living room of their Mid-City New Orleans house, which they share with their girlfriend. Seated on a leather couch in a room full of books and art, including a framed map of the city's shuttered dyke bars, they told me about how, on evenings and weekends, they were drawn to collect oral histories of New Orleans dyke bars—after their day job as an accountant. As we talked, a loose hurricane shutter rattled harmlessly against the exterior of the bungalow in the warm, April breeze, and they spoke fondly of friendships they forged through their commemorative work.

Like the above two individuals, in Chicago, New York, and San Francisco, most—although not all—of the organizers I met are White, whereas in New Orleans the troupe is more racially diverse, including several African American individuals. Likewise, in most of the cities, most (although not all) commemorators are cisgender women, whereas in New Orleans commemorators include several nonbinary and transgender individuals. Most of the commemorators I met have stable professional positions at places such as a university, a drug company, nonprofits, and an advertising agency, or work in the arts, supporting themselves as educators or via a hodgepodge of day jobs so they can direct, dance, act, and create installations.

Thus, it was from this vantage point—as (mostly) highly educated LBQT+ people, many of whom (although not all) were White and in their late twenties or early thirties—that commemorators regarded dyke bars. To my surprise, despite their generational distance from dyke bars and the ungentrified urban neighborhoods in which they thrived, commemorators were neither wholly celebratory nor wholly critical of the bars they labored to remember.

Critical Nostalgia[10]

From the first days of my research into dyke bar commemoration, I was keenly aware that bars like Charlene's closed before most of the commemorators reached legal drinking age. As I have already hinted, I suspected this might mean that they had an overly romantic vision of dyke bars—a vision that might miss the security bars on the door at Charlene's and the fact that one had to ring the bell to gain entrance, or the basic fact that, because of their race or class or gender, some did not feel welcome ringing such bells. Conversely, I wondered if they'd considered how the insularity of the bar—the same faces, in the same space, night after night—might frustrate regulars, producing the involuntary instinct to scrutinize each new patron as they entered.

It did not take me long to realize that my concerns were misguided; dyke bar commemorators were not unwaveringly nostalgic. I launched my research over beer with two organizers of New Orleans's Last Call, an African American and a White individual, who are each nonbinary and in their early thirties, when they came to Boston to workshop their musical. In lieu of a lesbian bar (since, at the time, Boston did not have one), I suggested we meet at Casa Verde, a Mexican restaurant with an extensive beer list. The restaurant sits near the heart of the commercial center of the city's Jamaica Plain neighborhood, which has one of the highest proportion of same-sex female couples in the United States.[11] It seemed fitting that, since there wasn't an obvious bar at which to gather, I would meet dyke bar commemorators at a gay-friendly restaurant in a lesbian-friendly neighborhood. And, indeed, after we sat down, they told me this was the third time in a week that a Bostonian had invited them to meet at Casa Verde.

I left that initial conversation aware that at least some commemorators think carefully about problems associated with dyke bars. At Casa Verde, the New Orleans organizers told me, with great sincerity, that they recognize that dyke bars were highly imperfect places, in which inequalities and social problems reared their head and sometimes were exacerbated. Building on this, at a public talk in a Boston auditorium, a New York commemorator—a lesbian filmmaker in her early forties— told a room of undergraduates: "Bars aren't my thing." She explained to her young and entirely rapt audience, who had come to hear about dyke bars and other lost lesbian spaces, that they aren't her "thing" because they are exclusive. She told the young people before her, "Queer bars really don't function as social spaces for all people."[12]

A newspaper article reporting on Last Call's commemorative work in New Orleans echoes this semicritical take: "These lesbian spaces were not perfect, however. 'They were places of huge solidarity, but all of the oppressions of the external world were mirrored inside of the dyke bars,' says [an organizer]. This was more jarring in what was considered a safe space. Alcoholism and addiction surface in the oral histories, and 'domestic violence was something that people talked about as well as racist aggressions and issues around gender,' says [the organizer]."[13]

This is not to suggest that dyke bar commemorators only criticize bars. Their commemorative work includes moments of the unalloyed nostalgia for bars that we might expect those who labor to remember an institution to express. At Chicago's *Lost and Found* exhibit, the curator, a thirty-year-old White woman with a blonde bob wearing a 1950s retro dress, gathered an age-diverse crowd around a map of 1970s and 1980s lesbian bars. The audience exclaimed over the volume of spaces. A White woman in her sixties, recognizing a bar, said, "Marilyn's was a blast!" Her friend, of a similar age, added, "I walked in and I was the youngest one there. They were like *come in*! I had a great time." The crowd, which included several pairs of LBQT+ individuals in their twenties, responded to these memories of flirtatious intergenerational exchange with affirmative laughter.

Likewise, at the start of the 2019 New York Lost Dyke Bar Tour, a speaker painted a rosy picture of a lost world for those assembled at the Stonewall Inn. Having named numerous shuttered bars, she buoyantly insisted, "These were *lesbian* bars. There were more girls than boys in Greenwich Village. And lesbians!" Evoking ghosts of bars and those who peopled them, she implied that the scene before her—of LBQT+ individuals standing shoulder to shoulder in a barroom—was once commonplace. Offering a soft-hued representation of what such bars were like, the *To Know Herself* exhibit, located at the California Institute for Contemporary Art in San Francisco's Portrero Hill neighborhood, included a dance floor installation, marked by a disco ball and a sign, "You Can Dance If You Want To," and the song, "Save the Last Dance for Me," playing on a loop. Coasters, which the artist left on tables, read: "I came, I danced, I remembered." Text on a wall just outside of the exhibit read: "Exciting work and new commissions . . . direct our attention to the form of the lesbian bar, commenting on the importance of these convening spaces for building community, for bringing about social and political change."

Yet, as we have already started to see, these wistful and nostalgic scenes are balanced by critical representations of the bar.[14] Similar to the wistful memories detailed above, New Orleans' Last Call pays homage to the dykes who came before them when it tells its audience that "we are indebted to our elders." However, more frequently, Last Call, like other commemorators, uses the past to contemplate present-day issues. This is illustrated by a line from their musical, *Alleged Lesbian*

Activities, that asks viewers to consider, "How are we supposed to know where we are going if we don't know where we came from?" Crucially, they instruct that to "know where we are going," we must understand the past not only via a nostalgic lens that acknowledges debts to elders and the evocative power of a final dance, but by considering the problems of the bar.

I propose (borrowing the term from other scholars) that we think of this balancing of nostalgia for and sustained criticism of dyke bars (and associated lesbian identity politics) as commemorators' "critical nostalgia" or their "yearning for the past [that includes] a critical awareness of the negative aspects of that past" (McDermott 2002, 401). By criticizing and celebrating bars in equal measure, dyke bar commemoration sharply contrasts with more rose-colored ways of thinking about lesbian spaces.[15] Consider, for instance, responses to the closure of a San Francisco bar captured by a documentary released in 1989, more than three decades ago, *Last Call at Maud's*. The film begins with a woman saying she loved the bar because lesbians are "outlaws, and I hope we will always be outlaws." Likewise, the owner explains that lesbian bars are the "most open, honest, free place a woman could go." Those commemorating the loss of bars today are much less certain that bars were ever "open, honest, [and] free" for all. This is, in large part, because commemorators are more than thirty years removed from the heyday of lesbian-feminist identity politics that supported the notion that dyke bars are "open, honest, [and] free" spaces for women. Today, like many other LBTQ+ individuals, dyke bar commemorators worry about any institution organized narrowly around patrons of a single gender or sexual identity, and they are skeptical of claims that any space is truly "free" or "open" to all. Indeed, not all dyke bar commemorators identify as women; several engage in antiracism activism; and most, if not all, are mindful of how social differences, such as those related not only to race but also to class, shape access to and experiences of places and institutions.

In this spirit, commemorative events highlight problems inherent in dyke bars, primarily emphasizing their exclusivity. On a tour of the Chicago *Lost and Found* exhibit, the curator told the crowd, which was almost entirely composed of White middle-class individuals ranging from their twenties to sixties, that "there was a lot of racism" among lesbians in the 1970s and 1980s, the period featured in the exhibit. Gesturing to a poster, she told us that African American women began to organize their own parties when they realized they were asked for four or five IDs at a bar, while White women only had to show one. She also emphasized that a bisexual woman was ejected from an organization for not identifying as lesbian, and told us that, in 1975, Chicago's LBQT+ population was wrestling "with the problem of lesbian separatism" and that they "did not take nonbinary genders into account." Audience members listened attentively and nodded earnestly as she offered this sweeping criticism of 1970s lesbian identity politics and of the bars that helped to shape those politics.

Echoing this, at the 2019 Manhattan Lost Dyke Bar Tour, the guide—a petite White woman in her early thirties wearing a short dress and combat boots—instructed that, "like many bars at the time," the shuttered bar we stood in front of "was oriented around White butch/ femme couples." Her tone grew more somber as she added that "Black lesbians were not always welcome. . . . Audre Lorde would describe being always carded." Similarly, a Last Call oral history podcast informs the listener of how dyke bars reflected racial segregation in New Orleans. A narrator says, "As much as we sometimes don't want to talk about it, queer spaces are *not* colorblind. . . . New Orleans is deeply segregated, a landscape shaped by centuries of White supremacy." Another narrator adds, "And we want to be clear about this upfront, because we think it is an important thread in any story you can tell about the city and is going to be present in every episode of this podcast, whether or not it seems to be about race."

Emphasizing bars' gender exclusivity, in a short film documenting the *Eulogy for the Dyke Bar* installation, creator Macon Reed says that "people are still contending with what it means to have a space that's designated for women or for feminine-spectrumed people—and what does that mean for people who don't identify as that." As Reed speaks, they are framed by a poster, part of their Brooklyn *Eulogy* installation, that reads, "The Feminine Spectrum." Here, concern that dyke bars excluded transgender individuals is literally built into the commemorative object—flagged and framed for the audience.[16]

Last Call's musical, *Alleged Lesbian Activities*, encapsulates many of these concerns. In their 2018 production, a central character, played by a White actor, decides to participate in a drag performance. New to the bar, she nervously assembles a costume; as she selects items from a wardrobe rack, it becomes apparent that she intends to dress as African American. Enraged, other characters shout and stop her as she begins to don a wig—grabbing it away from her. At another moment, the same character tries to buy a drink for an African American woman. Grudgingly, the woman accepts the drink, ordering a gin and juice. The White character says, "I've heard you guys like that—but I've never actually seen someone order one." The African American bartender displays outrage (echoed by gasps from the audience) at the White patron's racism, asking her to step away. Another plotline pursues the tenuous inclusion of a trans female customer who, we learn, was barred from another bar because she is not cisgender. These scenes ensure that audiences cannot walk away without encountering the notion that bar legacies are fraught; that the dyke bar is worthy of commemoration but incompatible with a contemporary ethos that emphasizes fluid boundaries and inclusivity and that recognizes intersectional identities.

Across four cities and despite variation in the demographic and identity attributes of commemorators, these projects emphasize the problems of dyke bars. That is, instead of taking a purely nostalgic stance, commemorators present bars through a critical lens that signals their commitment to inclusivity and distance from traditional lesbian identity politics.

When Community Is Your "Thing"

If bars aren't commemorators' "thing," and if they recognize alcoholism, racism, and domestic violence that unfolded in bars, why do commemorators work to remember them? What *is* their thing? And what does all of this have to do with *gentrification*?

In simplest terms, commemorators work to remember dyke bars because they hope to establish new social ties. And, as we will soon see, talk of literal gentrification is a crucial tool they rely on to help foster connections, because *gentrification* also operates as a metonym for shared vulnerability and marginality.

One commemorator described her motivation for remembering bars: "I was feeling lonely . . . just really feeling this loneliness. . . . I was feeling so frustrated and was like, 'I need a space.'" A New York commemorator echoed this, saying she undertook dyke bar commemoration efforts because, "I had been feeling really, really sad about the lack of queer women in my life." A Lexington commemorator, a brunette femme in her early forties, expressed sympathy for younger LBQT+ individuals, whom, she said, can no longer move to San Francisco and become "entrenched into a community." She described how, a few years earlier, as bars, bookstores, and coffee shops—the places where she'd once reliably encountered other queer women—closed, and friends dispersed for more affordable places, she herself felt "like you're losing your city and your community." Thus, dyke bar commemorators remember bars not to revive them, but as a method for reconstituting community. That is, they hope their commemorative events will be a new means for gathering people together and for forging new, ongoing connections.[17]

This leaves dyke bar commemorators in a strange predicament. How do you call together a community of people with whom you hope you have some sense of common ground without relying on a singular, shared identity, or a brick-and-mortar institution? Moreover, how do you do it in a political and social moment when increased acceptance and rights have reduced the urgent sense of need for safety, mutual recognition, and social support that once drew some of us into bars like the one I visited in New Orleans? Strangely enough for this scholar of literal gentrification—who thought she was treading on new territory by studying dyke bar commemoration—the answer seems to be to pair critical nostalgia of a time and place of imagined community with talk of *gentrification*.[18]

In a sense, commemorators grapple with a question of our times, particularly for members of traditionally marginalized groups that have, over recent decades, achieved social, cultural, and legal victories. Specifically, they struggle with how to establish ties—how to meet people to date, to befriend, to hang out with, and to engage in activism with—outside of the context of the unmistakable shared vulnerability that earlier generations experienced. This dilemma is compounded by their criticisms of lesbian identity politics for producing insular, identity-oriented communities that left some out in the cold.[19] If you know you can't proceed as others have before you, but you nonetheless yearn for connection, where do you begin?

Despite their awareness of the pitfalls of earlier instantiations of community, commemorators' yearning for connection is unmistakable. In her documentary film, Alexis Clements—a forty-something New Yorker—describes herself as "looking for meaningful connection." Likewise, the artist Macon Reed explains that "something else that's been really important to me is that [*Eulogy for the Dyke Bar*] be a place of healing and reconciliation between people."[20] In the same spirit, New Orleans organizers have established friendships with several "elders" they interviewed as part of their commemorative research, providing resources—from housing to meals—when they are in need, and enjoying weekends at the rural home of an older couple who, in one commemorator's words, have become their "fairy gaymothers" (housing them, for instance, during hurricanes). When, at commemorators' urging, I interviewed one dyke bar elder, a retired social worker, in a subdivision just across the Mississippi from New Orleans, our conversation was interrupted by a commemorator coming through the door with groceries for her older friend.

My time at dyke bar commemorative events suggests that the commemorators I spoke with are not alone in yearning for connection. Take the middle-class, butch, forty-something African American woman who attended a sold-out Lost Dyke Bar Tour in July. We walked side by side on a steamy East Village sidewalk, and, slowly, began to share a bit about ourselves. As we passed shuttered bars that had become upscale coffee shops and condominiums, she communicated her ambivalence about dyke bars. She said: "I don't even really drink. But I'm lonely. I thought this might be a way to meet people. I am not even that worried about dating. I want friends." She shared a sidewalk with a White transgender woman from Westchester, cisgender queer female journalists, a White lesbian couple with a baby, a Latinx genderqueer individual who works in advertising, a woman in her seventies, and dozens of women in their twenties and thirties. While we might imagine that these crowds came in search of bars, the more time I spent at dyke bar commemorative events, the more convinced I became that they were there, more than anything else, simply to be with one another.

This was also evidenced by how, more than any other study I have ever conducted, the people I interviewed sought to stay in touch with me, introduced me to their friends, and offered to have a coffee or drink with me when I was back in town. Moreover, commemorative events are often at capacity. *Alleged Lesbian Activities* performances are nearly always full; elements of *Eulogy for the Dyke Bar* travel the world, and the Chicago *Lost and Found* exhibit left attendees clamoring for more. The *Last Call* cast described having to insist that audience members exit performance spaces, and organizers of *Lost and Found* extended open hours to meet demand.

Efforts to construct ties extend beyond commemorative events, including, for instance, monthly New York Dyke Bar Takeover events, and *Lost and Found*'s yoga-and-slow-jams sessions. In 2020, as Covid advanced across the United States, Last Call issued a "Better Together" newsletter. The newsletter suggested that "we will have to depend on each other even more and continue to lean into the rich history of resilience and community care of our Trancestors and Ancestors," and included a number of resources, from community funds for gig workers to a troupe member's "Social D-ist-ancing" YouTube channel, aimed at combating "any isolation." The channel promises that by watching videos of individuals dancing, "it will be like we are dancing together!" Crucially the "we" is left unspecified, implying that if you find your way to us, you will have a dance partner. Here, Last Call is not mobilizing protests or espousing cultural change; their goal, instead, is *social*: like so many other dyke bar commemorators, they wish, more than anything else, to reduce isolation.

Lost Dyke Bars and the Specter of Gentrification

What does this quest for community have to do with *gentrification*? *Gentrification*, or, more specifically, *talk* of *gentrification*, helps to solve the core dilemma that dyke bar commemorators face. As we've established, dyke bar commemorators want community and are somewhat nostalgic for institutions like dyke bars that once supported LBQT+ networks, but they worry greatly about the risks of exclusivity associated with such institutions. Moreover, they yearn for a greater sense of connection with other lesbian, bisexual, nonbinary, transgender, and queer individuals but are disenthralled with the idea of setting specific parameters around gender and sexual identity or of otherwise specifying how their identities might—or might not—constitute shared experience or social position.

They are also leery of forging community from a sense of common ground that is rooted in shared marginalization related to the notion of a shared gender or sexual identity. They recognize how, in the present day, LBQT+ individuals' vulnerability varies by group and place and even individual, and, how, for some, that marginality has significantly waned with recent legal and cultural victories. They are mindful, for instance, that the experience of a working-class lesbian might be wildly different from that of an affluent lesbian; that the experience of a bisexual woman in South Carolina might be quite different from the experience of a bisexual woman in Southern California, and that an African American transgender individual faces different barriers than their White counterpart.

Against this backdrop of reduced and variable marginalization and caution about institutions and communities narrowly associated with a specific identity group, commemorators turn to talk of *gentrification*. By *talk of gentrification* I refer to how dyke bar commemorators, like an increasing number of other individuals, rely on discussion of *gentrification* to achieve aims and convey meanings that do not directly or only pertain to literal gentrification. In most cases, underspecifying what *gentrification* "is" enables talk of *gentrification* to serve as a broad and flexible carrier of meaning, and therefore to work, however inadvertently, as a tool.

Dyke bar commemorators' events spotlight the toll that literal gentrification has taken on bars and on the broader LBTQ+ population. Why emphasize the consequences of literal gentrification, particularly when many commemorators privately acknowledge that other factors,

like the proliferation of online dating and increased access to heterosexual spaces, contribute to dyke bar closures? The specter of literal
gentrification gestures to a source of common ground that doesn't require specificity about what you have in common with someone—
beyond shared disdain for *gentrification*. Shared disdain for *gentrification*
does not require one to have a specific gender or sexual identity, race,
or even—as literal gentrification becomes more endemic in certain cities and housing becomes more unaffordable, even for highly educated
professionals—class. And talk of the threat of literal gentrification can
even sketch a sense of uniform, connective vulnerability among those
who take part in such conversations. Indeed, commemorators turn to
talk of *gentrification* again and again to cultivate a sense of shared vulnerability that unites disparate members of their audiences.

Thus, publicly, commemorators attribute bar closures to accelerating
(literal) gentrification associated with the movement of affluent individuals into historically working-class neighborhoods.[21] *Gentrification*
provides a catchall sense of vulnerability to which almost all audience
members can relate, whether they worry about losing their own housing or their friends (when they move away in search of affordable
housing), or, more often, urban institutions—from bookstores to co-
ops to bars—that lend meaning and pleasure to their lives and help
them spend time around others with whom they share an identity or
interests.

Commemorators are betting on the notion that for others, as for
them, literal gentrification is evocative of a weakened sense of community and of the displacement of social and cultural institutions and dispersion of long-standing neighborhood populations. As a result, in a
moment in which sexual and gender minorities experience increased
acceptance (however tentative and geographically uneven), commemorators rely on talk of *gentrification* to construct a new, shared vulnerability that creates a sense of "us" versus "them" without narrowly specifying in and out groups.[22] Their talk of *gentrification* as a looming threat
sets boundaries that allow for the sense that those on the inside—those
harmed by gentrification or aware of the harm that it might cause
others—share common ground, and perhaps even common injury. Of

course, this reliance on *gentrification* to provide an inclusive sense of shared threat only works in contexts in which what geographer Loretta Lees terms "super-gentrification" abounds; that is, in settings in which literal gentrification is so advanced and endemic and housing prices are so high that gentrification impacts even the middle and upper-middle classes.[23]

Commemorators use talk of *gentrification* to evoke a collective loss that includes the dyke bar but extends beyond it. By evoking mutually constitutive "ghosts of place," or social pasts that lend space meaning, commemorators evoke gentrification to create a new "us" who is under threat.[24] For instance, on a Lost Dyke Bar Tour of Lower Manhattan, guides reveal multiple specters that, together, grant significance to city streets: the ghosts of dyke bars, the ghosts of the dykes who once populated the bars, and the ghost of the neighborhood that bars and their clientele helped to define.[25]

Given that they grapple with this problem of trying to connect with others with whom they sense they have things in common (without specifying the source of that common ground) it is not an accident that commemorators rely on an increasingly widespread political-economic process—literal gentrification—as a basis for shared vulnerability. They present sexual and gender minorities, particularly LBQT+ individuals, as disproportionately economically marginal and therefore especially vulnerable to gentrification, but they do not regard literal gentrification as specifically targeted at them (in the manner of laws that criminalize sexual practices or facilitate discrimination). This allows them a great deal of flexibility and breadth as they seek to call together a community.

Disappearing Bars

On a Saturday evening in 2018, the cast and crew of New Orleans' Last Call prepared to showcase the latest production of their "dyke bar musical," *Alleged Lesbian Activities*. Inside the small theater space, in the Marigny neighborhood, with its proliferating bike repair shops, yoga studios, and music venues, audience members purchased drinks from the plywood bar at the center of the set. Already in character, an African

American genderqueer performer, "Franki," poured and bantered with the audience, composed of mostly LGBTQIA+ individuals and a smattering of heterosexuals, including the parents of one thirty-something androgynous lesbian. While the musical is ostensibly about bars, it charts sexual minorities' changing social position. It also centers how New Orleans is gentrifying and the consequences thereof for LBQT+ populations.

The musical grapples with issues that unfold in the bar that are also at the center of organizers' criticisms of dyke bars, including racism and transphobia. However, *Alleged Lesbian Activities* is also focused on external threats that dyke bars face. Two particularly somber moments anchor the performance, reminding the audience of how external dangers shape the life of all those within it. These moments reorient sensibilities about what makes bars vulnerable and, by extension, what constitutes the phenomenon sociologists describe as a community of "linked fate."[26]

The first is a recording that lists the names of women arrested in a 1960s bar raid. Quoting from the *Times-Picayune*, the list includes the age, address, and occupation of women arrested for engaging in "alleged lesbian activities" (a.k.a., dancing with another woman). After the recording, the cast—composed of LBQT+ individuals in their twenties and early thirties—breaks into a song and dance in which they wield barstools to protect themselves, spinning in circles, attentive to threats. The second deeply somber moment comes later in the production, when Franki, the bar owner, dashes from the bar at the sound of a police siren. A few moments later we learn that Franki owes $100,000 in property taxes and will have to close the bar. The news sends patrons into a panic. Here, the threat to the bar shifts from the police to price. As dialogue advances, it becomes clear that the new threat to the bar is the changing city itself: specifically, racialized "super-gentrification" (Lees 2003)—or literal gentrification that threatens to displace not only working-class but also middle-class people—and increasing dependence on tourism.[27] Here, the troupe suggests, the source of precarity and danger has shifted across generations, but precarity itself remains (somewhat) stable; the source of uncertainty has evolved, but the threat to a way of life endures. Instead of being on the lookout for police cars, they develop marketing strategies for attracting a broader clientele.

On breaking news of the impending closure, Franki says, "Today our bars fill up with White people in order to stay in business. Or they remake themselves to stay in business and then fill up with White people." After Franki's monologue, a recording lists the names of shuttered lesbian bars. Crucially, the same cast member who read the names of women arrested for alleged lesbian activities lists the names of lost bars. This time the cast does not arm themselves with barstools, but the characters frantically contemplate methods for staying in business. Seated on either side of the stage and sometimes made to banter with the cast, the audience has little separation from the alternatingly joyful, awkward, and tense interactions that unfold on set. Viewers are embedded in the shifting threats faced by the dyke bar and, consequently, are forced to grapple with the imperfect social world it depicts.

I recognize that in these pages I am taking you back and forth across the United States (much as I did when studying bar commemoration). I do so at the risk of dizzying the reader in order to reveal what was so striking to me: the remarkable synergies across projects, particularly in terms of their critical nostalgia and reliance on talk of *gentrification*, despite the independent nature of the commemorative projects and their geographic range. Over and again, commemorative events echo the plotline of *Alleged Lesbian Activities* by holding literal gentrification accountable for bar closure.[28] In the film documenting *Eulogy for the Dyke Bar*, Macon Reed tells viewers, "You'll see there's a common issue of money and gentrification" driving bar closings. Likewise, in the film *All We've Got*, a woman says, "[There's the] larger hurdle of real estate in New York. . . . That's real. The space is not a given." The film then cuts away to an image of an elevated train and a New York street as the filmmaker Alexis Clements instructs: "Gentrification and the financialization of real estate are among the top reasons why LGBTQ women's spaces have been closing in such high numbers."

Operating more subtly, "Lavender Menace" posters at the Chicago *Lost and Found* exhibit read, "We're here to infiltrate your daughter and reparate your real estate," and "We are coming for your real estate and the brides that came with it."[29] Organizers placed these contemporary territorial calls across from markers of lost space, including a map of numerous (now-shuttered) dyke bars, and an image from *On Our Backs* (a women's erotica magazine) of a "Psychosexual Subway Map of Urban Lesbian Life" (1984).[30]

Elaborating on this premise, in a film for *Vice*, JD Samson—a songwriter and vocalist best known for their work with the band Le Tigre—describes dyke bars "as casualties to [San Francisco's] economic boom." In an interview for the film, Lila Thirkield, the owner of the now-shuttered Lexington bar in the city's Mission District, said:

> It is a business model that tries to target like 5 percent of the population. It should not work. It is crazy. . . . A lot of things have changed. Rent pretty much doubled. You know, half of that 5 percent no longer lives in your neighborhood or even in your city, what are they going to do? Come over the Bay Bridge to have like one beer on your way home like you used to when you lived two blocks away? It is not going to happen.

Here, commemorators offer a causal argument for bar closures: (literal) gentrification-driven population dispersion combines with rising commercial rents to produce institutional loss.[31] Echoing this, a woman who spoke at a queer memoir night associated with *Eulogy for the Dyke Bar* said, "The reason there are no dyke bars left in Manhattan—except for Cubby Hole and Henrietta Hudson's—is because the rents. *There are no people left to go to them.*"[32] Her words were met by loud and enthusiastic applause.

In interviews, commemorators elaborate on this causal argument about how literal gentrification has shuttered bars. A New York commemorator said that the impact of gentrification on bars "goes without saying," and a San Francisco organizer said that the former owner of a bar was concerned its closure might be reduced to a story about literal gentrification: "She's like, 'I don't want it to just become that story.'" Her concern reveals the centrality of literal gentrification as an explanation that commemorators, and those in their orbit, rely on to explain bar closures. The San Francisco organizer said, "There's so many stories of gentrification in San Francisco."

Indeed, the commemorator suspects that for LBQT+ populations, literal gentrification's contribution to closures will not surprise:

> I think a lot of people—straight, whatever, across the spectrum—don't realize that San Francisco only had the one really. . . . You might think it's the gay capital of the world, but there was only one bar for girls and it's closing. I actually think that it's more surprising for straight people. . . . They're like, "What do you mean?" You're like, "Well, gay women don't have that much money. They're getting kicked out of that neighborhood," and etcetera, you know what I mean? It's like . . . it's not that surprising. It feels horrible, but . . .

Like others, she insisted we understand the bar's closure by turning to the changing economic landscape of the bar's neighborhood, the Mission, and the resultant dispersion of LBQT+ residents; after decades as a neighborhood in which working-class Latinx residents and LBQT+ individuals lived side by side, over the last decade and a half the Mission has seen an infusion of commercial and residential capital, driven, in large part, by the Bay Area's expanding tech sector. Today, affluent new-comers hold community meetings about rat abatement and shop in upscale independent boutiques and chain retail establishments. She said: "I think that's largely affected by the changing Mission, and the kind of money that people have. And that basically women, and queer women in particular, don't live in San Francisco anymore the same way. I mean, they either live in Oakland or not in the Bay Area, 'cause it's too expensive." In essence, she hears the same sirens deployed in *Alleged Lesbian Activities*; she can't imagine offering an account of the loss of dyke bars that is not also an account of literal gentrification.

Many commemorators extend this argument by elaborating on how LBQT+ institutions are especially vulnerable to gentrification-related displacement because they primarily serve LBQT+ individuals: "If you have two women who are not making as much money as their male peers or whatever you have less money in the queer community in general. . . . So things like gentrification really impact queer women's spaces more." This argument appears in their commemorative objects. In an interview featured in Samson's documentary, sociologist Arlene Stein echoes this: "Gay men have many more bars than lesbians do in part because they have access to more economic capital as a whole. Lesbians have been gentrified out of a lot of those neighborhoods." Here, gendered economic disparities and literal gentrification are wedded to explain the loss of bars.

Those LBQT+ residents who remain, a San Francisco organizer insists, engage in different cultural practices that are themselves "gentrified" (Schulman 2012). In short, she suggests that lesbians and those they socialize with have themselves "gentrified": "[The Lexington] was made in the late '90s. It was red walls, red and black. So maybe that scene, it's not like . . . the queer scene has cleaned itself up quite a bit. . . . In San Francisco specifically . . . because of the class changes. . . . [the Lexington] wasn't keeping up, it wasn't stylish enough for what the crowd here wants." In chapters 2 and 3, we will spend more time with the idea that some communities and individuals have, themselves, "gentrified," but for now, it's important to consider how contrasting this "cleaned-up" queer scene with the extant dyke bar, commemorators underline the fragility of the dyke bar—imagined to be a working-class dive bar (despite the heterogeneity, historically, of lesbian bars).

Relatedly, commemorators situate the heyday (or what Last Call refers to as the "hey-gays") of dyke bars in a period of nascent gentrification (in which these bars and their clientele played a part). That is, with the exception of work on San Francisco's Lexington, which opened in 1997 (in a neighborhood at an early stage of upscaling), commemorative work is situated in the pre- or early-gentrification of the city.[33] Nearly all feature dyke bars of the 1970s and 1980s, with particular emphasis on the 1970s. *Eulogy for the Dyke Bar* included several photographs and documents from the period. At the *Lost and Found* exhibit, a woman asked the tour guide why Stargaze, a long-standing Northside Chicago bar that closed in 2009, wasn't featured. "We chose to focus on the 1970s and 1980s," the curator responded.

Centering this period and spatial context means that organizers commemorate a time and place in which the lesbian bar was particularly likely to take the form of a dive (or *dyke*) bar—when the Mission, for instance, was still predominately Latinx and working-class or before the "super-gentrification" (Lees 2003) of Manhattan's Greenwich Village and Lower East Side.[34] Like the commemorators from New Orleans whom we met at the beginning of the chapter, they do not commemorate an Upper East Side lesbian bar that caters to professionals, nor do they celebrate spaces for LBQT+ individuals in contemporary, gentrified Brooklyn, such as Ginger's, or in Chicago's leafy upper-middle-class Andersonville; indeed, most omit mention of lesbian-owned bars in gentrified neighborhoods that cater to middle-class (i.e., non-"dyke") clientele, such as San Francisco's Wild Side West, not far from the Mission, which sports what *TimeOut* describes as a "lush patio."[35] As I mentioned at the outset of the chapter, this situating of the dyke bar in traditionally working-class locales forwards a memory of (dive) bars, clientele, and neighborhoods vulnerable to literal gentrification.

Disappearing Dykes

Commemorators do not merely reference literal gentrification to underline its costs for bars, but also to articulate for their audiences and themselves the view that LBQT+ populations have been disappeared via brick-and-mortar gentrification. In this sense, the lost dyke bar is indicative of a broader transformation that commemorators harness to call out a sense of shared vulnerability. In *All We've Got*, the filmmaker/narrator explicitly instructs:

> When I tell people one of the last lesbian bars has closed in San Francisco they are shocked. But very few young lesbian and queer women—the ones who are most likely to be in those bars—can afford to live in San Francisco. They're in Oakland or further out. And you see the same thing in countless other cities in the US. Not only is real estate impacting the businesses themselves it is also impacting queer women themselves who, like so many other groups, are getting pushed out and becoming more dispersed because of gentrification and financialization.

Likewise, in the final moments of another documentary, a woman, reflecting on gentrifying New York, says, "I do not wish to be an artifact."[36]

This dimension of their commemorative strategy calls audiences to experience the threat of price, and, in the context of advancing literal gentrification, to consider how it extends from the past to the present and from the dyke bar to the contemporary LBQT+ resident.

As part of constructing a lineage of threat, commemorators suggest that the working-class dyke has, indeed, become an artifact and that the dyke and her bar served as a canary in the coal mine of the gentrifying city.[37] To build this argument about how literal gentrification has harmed not just bars but also bar *dykes*, commemorators center a class of (less affluent) LBQT+ individuals whom they regard as typically invisible. One said: "[Back then] you had to be rough around the edges, and bash back, and this class of dykes doesn't normally get chronicled. . . . No one talks about the poor, working-class, punk, drug addict dykes, you know what I mean? That's not who gets put in the history books." For her, commemoration rights that omission. Crucially, she casts the ghost of this dyke in her "natural" habitat: a dive bar in a hardscrabble neighborhood that, crucially, has since gentrified.

A short film, *Never a Cover*, encapsulates this image of the dyke and her neighborhood as artifact. The film chronicles the closing of the Lexington, San Francisco's last dyke bar.[38] The individuals whom the filmmakers interview contextualize the closure in a history of economic struggle. As they present it, LBQT+ residents' economic marginality set the stage for the bar's shuttering, particularly once literal gentrification advanced. The bar's owner explains how and why the Lexington opened in the Mission, saying, "I'd always heard that the Castro was for gay men and you know the gay women couldn't afford to live there. So they lived next door in the Mission." A queer astrologist tells of moving to San Francisco in 1994 with "a couple hundred bucks and a bunch of astrology books. I fancied myself a baby butch and I had a couple pairs of men's slacks and T-shirts. And that's what I had." Indeed, those featured in the film offer a mythological portrait of San Francisco pregentrification; one says, "[W]hen I moved here in '86 there were so many dyke bars there was nothing special about it. There was one in every neighborhood." They nonetheless position the Mission as the heart of San Francisco for "dykes." One recalls, "We all used to live up and down Valencia. You couldn't walk down Valencia without some mohawked fuckin' pin-cushioned dyke walking out of their doorway with their $450-a-month apartment and saying, 'Hey Spike, Hey Spike, Hey Spike.' Everybody's named Spike." Here, they call us to see the person they describe, but also to see the neighborhood in which that person was embedded—and how, they believe, each depended on the other.[39] By merging ghosts of person and neighborhood, they lend the Mission meaning and significance, and establish a narrative about how literal gentrification displaced (working-class) dykes and their institutions, and altered their neighborhoods.[40]

Centering "Spike" presents the dyke as a vulnerable character—worthy of memory and care—by describing her as economically marginal, and makes a case for her "right to the city" by presenting her as resolutely urban.[41] Take, for instance, a quote by the scholar Jack Halberstam in Samson's documentary, in which he states that affluent lesbians do not frequent bars: "LGBT communities are very, very stratified by race and class. Affluent, middle-class, White lesbians are not spending their money going to bars." This frame underlines the vulnerability of the bar class, reminds audiences of linkages between the bar and lesbian identity politics (with its working-class roots), and provides a historical (and material) explanation for the disappearance of the dyke and her bar.

In addition, despite their presentation of the dyke as "hardscrabble," against the backdrop of "super-gentrification" commemorators present the plight of the disappeared dyke as prescient.[42] They link the loss of the dyke and her bar to the current economic struggles of LBQT+ urbanites, including those who, like most commemorators, are *not* working class.[43] They present the dyke to warn against the contemporary broad dispersion of LBQT+ populations within and across urban areas.[44]

However, a narrative that emphasizes Spike also decenters the struggles of long-standing poor and working-class Latinx populations. This partially reveals how their talk of *gentrification* is meant less to spur a broad antigentrification movement, and more to identify a sense of shared vulnerability among LBQT+ individuals. Commemorators evoke *gentrification* rhetorically to suggest that LBQT+ populations are vulnerable to literal gentrification, and, in so doing, they cultivate a sense of shared vulnerability—despite demographic and other differences among their audiences.

To call out a sense of shared fate despite their own privilege (nearly all commemorators have degrees from elite colleges or universities, and some occupy professions that ensure an upper-middle-class income), commemorators present literal gentrification as posing risks to an increasingly broad swath of contemporary LBQT+ residents—not just to the working-class clientele of shuttered dyke bars. One commemorator told her audience that *every* urbanite recognizes the "clear-cutting" gentrification induces, saying, "As anyone who lives in a city knows . . ." Speaking to college students, a commemorator—revealing her own cultural capital—said that "community" is increasingly "hard to maintain because gentrification and financialization push people out." She added, "Young dykes can't afford to live in San Francisco." She continued by saying that "dispersal and gentrification impacts not just people living in a [specific] place but a broader community and their institutions." Likewise, at the 2019 Manhattan Lost Dyke Bar Tour, a speaker said, "Of course, everything is in Brooklyn now because it is cheaper . . . not for long!" A moment later she listed the name of a closed bar and then remarked, "It was right where Starbucks is. Starbucks!" She continued, "The Sea Colony [was] . . . Joan Nestle's [the author and a cofounder of the Lesbian Herstory Archives] favorite place. Joan couldn't be here because they took away her rent-controlled apartment." Later, another speaker said, "We asked a diverse group of queer women and transgender individuals why dyke bars are closing, and they overwhelmingly said that the main reason is rent."[45]

A San Francisco organizer protected by rent control suggests that literal gentrification transformed the Mission by displacing others. This contributes to feelings of loneliness, and she contemplates relocating:

> I mean, mostly I think about leaving because a lot of my friends have left, and I miss them. . . . We have a rent-controlled apartment. . . . I mean that's one of the reasons we don't leave, 'cause if we left, we would never come back [because they would lose their rent-controlled apartment]. It's a very depressing way of living, actually.

Or it's a very stressful feeling. Not because I think we're gonna get kicked out, but it's just . . . you're like, "This is it." We could move to the East Bay, but we'd pay more for less than what we have.

She marveled that, because of rent control, "we live in a very fancy neighborhood"—but one devoid of networks she cultivated in her twenties and thirties, as well as of the institutions they relied on. Watching friend after friend leave for Oakland and other cities, she contemplates moving to a less gentrified city. Referencing Providence, Rhode Island, she noted that one could buy a house for "like a hundred thousand dollars. I'm like, 'That's crazy!' That's how much you have to have as down payment here!"

Organizers tell stories of their own encounters with brick-and-mortar gentrification to extend their frame of the vulnerable LBQT+ resident beyond working-class bar dykes, and to encourage awareness of transition from past threats to present and future risks; here, they work to establish a constant thread of threat and therefore an enduring sense of shared fate. A few present the closure of bars as a harbinger of their own future displacement. A White nonbinary New Orleans commemorator said, "New Orleans has been changing so rapidly. . . . If it continues to change in the way that it's changing, then, in ten years, maybe I'm not here. . . . The city is gentrifying so rapidly . . . I'm obviously not the first person who's going to be pushed out of a gentrifying city. . . . However, because of the work that I do [in theater], I think it's too expensive and we won't be able to afford it here." Another described a moment that made them feel as though they were already an artifact in San Francisco's "super-gentrified" Mission.[46] They reported that, strolling down Valencia arm and arm with two androgynous queer women, a straight woman eating brunch on the sidewalk exclaimed, "Well isn't that an adorable sight!"

Beyond their own residential experiences, commemorators present a portrait of how gentrification has altered public life for *most* LBQT+ individuals. A White Chicago organizer faults literal gentrification for the spatial dispersion of LBQT+ individuals, which acerbates loss and loneliness associated with bar closures. How, she asked rhetorically, can one cultivate community in the context of institutional loss *and* spatial dispersion? She said that areas with long-standing concentrations of LGBTQIA+ residents—like Boystown and Andersonville—are "not affordable" for LBQT+ populations.

Echoing this, the search for affordable housing in Brooklyn reminded one New York organizer of the dispersion of LBQT+ residents that they witnessed a decade ago in San Francisco. They recalled, "I lived in the Outer Mission. . . . [I]n 2008 a lot of the dykes would not want to go past 30th. They wouldn't want to go past 24th and Mission [the Inner Mission], and because of gentrification . . . more of them were moving to Oakland or [the Outer Mission]." This movement, they suggested, had dire consequences for the Lexington: "With the Lexington what happened was a lot of the queers moved to Oakland—so no one was gonna go to the Lex anymore." Like other commemorators, she presents gentrification's domino effect: first it came for the bar, its dykes, and the Inner Mission, then it extended to the Outer Mission and, eventually, pushed even some middle-class LBQT+ residents across the Bay, disappearing not only bars, but also dyke-density and territoriality.

Commemorators' work does not stop there; they extend this narrative further, proposing that density, territoriality, and institutional presence allow queer subcultures to thrive; they wish to live in cities where LBQT+ populations can afford to concentrate and live together in creative or "queer" ways.[47] Therefore, they present the loss of queer living configurations as among the potential casualties of literal gentrification. This narrative was especially vivid in New Orleans, as apparent in the words of an African American organizer: "I kinda moved in and took over and turned it into a Black queer, punk house. . . . We started a collective . . . we were all figuring out how do we hustle up money for the house together, cooking together, sharing food, sharing meals. *At the time, rent wasn't that expensive*" [emphasis added]. For this organizer, affordability not only supports institutions, such as bars, but, just as importantly, the formation of creative and experimental households. For them, what threatens their queer lifestyle is literal gentrification. For now, this organizer lives in the city's Mid-City neighborhood, not far from Bayou St. John, in a way that affirms their gender, sexual, racial, and artistic identities. Yet, even as they celebrate this, they worry about what the future will hold.

However, even this organizer—who reports that they live in an identity-affirming manner in their shotgun rental because of affordability—is mindful of their privilege, particularly of cultural capital associated with a degree from an elite college. They reflexively link that privilege to their own contributions to literal gentrification, and this shapes their residential choices:

> I lived in that house in the Ninth Ward for about four months or something like that . . . it was my house with me and my Black roommate. There was an older Black [veteran] who lived across the street and then a White couple that lived next to him. I could just see the White couple was really enthusiastic, waving to us and stuff. And no one else in the neighborhood would really wave to us. I was just like, "This is weird. We're making you [the White couple] feel more comfortable and welcome here." . . . And I was like: Oh! I am gentrifying this neighborhood. I should move.

As a result, they moved to the more gentrified Mid-City neighborhood to avoid operating as a pioneering gentrifier.[48] Their new residence, not far from a beer garden and independent coffee shops, "feels better" because they are not explicitly serving as a symbol of the nascent desirability of a neighborhood, but also because (thus far) affordability permits the kind of eclectic communal living they value.

Narratives about how commemorators contribute to literal gentrification are not limited to New Orleans, although they are particularly abundant in a city undergoing intensive gentrification post-Katrina that nonetheless still contains pockets of affordability (as an illustration, the median household income of New Orleans increased from $27,133 in 2000—about $48,088 in 2023 dollars—to just over $55,339 in 2023).[49]

A New York City commemorator, whose parents moved to San Francisco from South America and raised her there, said that the Lexington helped to gentrify the surrounding Mission. In turn, they concluded that as their friends were displaced from the Mission by rapidly escalating rents they helped to contribute to the gentrification of other areas:

"I mean, they're mostly moving to rapidly gentrifying areas." Written material accompanying the *To Know Herself* exhibit included reflections of an author on her role in literal gentrification: "When I moved to the Mission District in 2008, gentrification (particularly of Valencia Street) had long been underway. . . . Every year the fabric of the city turns over, and so much is lost in the debris." This sense of accountability for brick and mortar gentrification sketches a view of literal gentrification as insidious and systemic; as advanced even by those critical of the harm it causes the marginal—including commemorators themselves. This frame matters for those who fear being "tightly groupist" or, put differently, exclusive, because, by presenting gentrification as amorphous in its causes and of widespread impact, they avoid calling out an explicit "us" versus "them."[50]

Indeed, while commemorators acknowledge their role in literal gentrification, they do not present the loss of bars or dispersion of dykes as "a penalty we impose[d] on ourselves" (Orne 2020, 41)—a frame that some use to explain the transformation of "gayborhoods" and their institutions as they become more and more upscale. Rather, their talk of *gentrification* gestures to how dyke bars and their past and prospective clientele are caught up in the upscaling of the city. For instance, a Chicago organizer who works as a party promoter reflected:

You can't open a bar [today]. . . . This is actually a really important part: the way they were able to do shit in the '70s and '80s or even '90s is so different than now. The fucking hoops you have to jump through! The money you have to have! The political ties you must have! . . . And if you're wealthy what are you? . . . If you're wealthy, statistically speaking, you are probably also White. And probably male and straight. . . . People ask me a lot, are you going to open a venue? When we did the dyke bar project, everyone was like, "Okay, when are you opening a bar?" I'm like . . . like I was saying before, a really important point about why don't we have these spaces: it's because it's too expensive, too daunting . . . the system isn't manageable. They make it so hard. You've got to have a broker for this, a lawyer for that, the paperwork is fucking crazy. . . . To get a tavern license here, it's near impossible, and then the people who get priori- tized are grandfathered in or it's because they've had success with like big business . . . then there are all these restaurant groups, why they're so popular in Chicago, it's because how easy it is for them to get [a tavern license] because they've got the capital and the connection.

The organizer describes a city economy increasingly oriented around consumption and tourism to a degree that prohibits the reestablishment of bars.[51] Of course, she presumes that LBQT+ individuals are econom- ically marginal—that one has to be White and heterosexual to have wealth and connections to establish a bar in the contemporary city. She calls audiences to wrestle with how contemporary urban (material) conditions and gendered economic inequalities alter urban life. In so doing, via this story of loss and dispersion she gestures to a common, urban, material experience that unites LBQT+ urbanites, calling out a community of linked fate.[52]

Talk of *gentrification* calls out a sense of shared fate, in part, by some- times explicitly suggesting that audiences are together on one side of a battle against (literal) gentrification. In an essay accompanying the San Francisco *To Know Herself* exhibit, Yomna Osman writes of a film, *In the Last Days of the City*. The essay reads, in part, "The character Bassem . . . had this thought while talking about how much more Lebanese citizens enjoyed Beirut during the war. I thought about the relationship urban citizens have with their city: Do they enjoy their cities more during times of war? Do they become nostalgic for that intensity? Does it have to be a war that brings people together?" Osman's essay does not specify which "war" she imagines LBQT+ populations currently fight, but the rest of her exhibit suggests that while they once fought sexual margin- alization, they now confront literal gentrification. This language of "war" was echoed at a Boston performance of Last Call's *Alleged Lesbian Ac- tivities*. There, a voiceover from an oral history interview recounted vio- lence that LBQT+ individuals faced, detailing how dyke bars were safe havens, as well as sometimes sites of targeted violence. Yet, the voice concludes, "there are still battles to do." Of course, as the plot develops they instruct that the new battle is literal gentrification.

Reconstituting Community Against
and Through *Gentrification*

The plaque outside of the Lexington Club hints at the degree to which commemorators wed the mourning of dyke bars and of the neighborhoods that housed them. It reads, in part, "Here marks the site of the Lexington Club, 'your friendly neighborhood dyke bar.'" Here, bar and neighborhood entangle. A music video by Sapphic Lasers echoes this. The song emphasizes that dyke bars often have short lives ("I remember when that bar up and closed because of money or problems, nobody knows") and that what makes the Lexington's closure distinctive is how the Mission also changed, dispersing residents. Sapphic Lasers sings, "The Lexington just closed for good and none of my friends live in my neighborhood anymore. I turn to you and say, 'Where do you want to go?' Oh and you say, 'Hey, boy I just don't know.' . . . We say, 'Dyke bars never last . . .'"

If "dyke bars never last," why do organizers in four cities find their closures to be remarkable and, indeed, worthy of commemoration? Despite all of their talk of *gentrification*, they do not commemorate urban dyke bars because they are antigentrification activists or especially concerned about the future of American cities. Rather, dyke bars and the gentrifying neighborhoods in which they are located serve as what the sociologist Jeffrey Olick (1999) terms a "technology of memory" that commemorators leverage to construct ties with other LBQT+ individuals. That is, dyke bars, situated in stories of literal gentrification, are a tool that commemorators rely on to reconstitute community; remarkably, in this context, literal gentrification—despite being something that so many people debate—is a neutral source of common ground. Indeed, it is neutral in part because it is so frequently debated; this renders *gentrification* simultaneously highly recognizable and somewhat opaque, allowing commemorators and their audiences to bring their own, individual conceptualizations of gentrification to the table. Just as they don't have to specify exactly what *queer* means, *gentrification* remains loosely defined and therefore a highly accessible symbol. It is the ambiguity of *gentrification* as a concept that allows commemorators to use it so effectively to call out a sense of shared marginality. After all, if they were abundantly clear about who or what causes literal gentrification and who or what literal gentrification harms, they might actually redraw the very boundaries around the inside and outside of their community that their talk of *gentrification* is poised to loosen. We might even consider that talk of *gentrification* works particularly well for bar commemorators because the ambiguity of *gentrification* pairs so well with the ambiguity (and inclusivity) of *queer* (something I'll say more about in the book's conclusion).

Does telling a story about how literal gentrification came for the dyke bar and is coming for remaining residential and commercial concentrations of LBQT+ individuals accomplish commemorators' goal of reconstituting community? In other words, how well does talk of *gentrification* work as a tool for forging social connection?

Commemorators report some success with reducing isolation in their own lives via their commemorative work. Some have established romantic, sexual, and friendship ties via commemorative organizing and events and have observed the same occur for audience members, too. I interviewed one commemorator on a quiet, residential street in the small New Orleans bungalow they lived in with their partner— another member of their commemorative collective. The two met through Last Call, and for several years they built a life together. As I previously mentioned, others have established enduring friendships with some of the "elders" they interviewed for their dyke bar research.

Above all else, commemorators suggest that their events have produced an enhanced sense of connection to other LBQT+ individuals and therefore helped them reestablish an amorphous feeling of community. A New York commemorator recalled "looking at the Facebook invite [for their first event] and being like, 'Oh my God, a thousand people have said they're coming. I don't even know a thousand people in New York.'" They said that this response, "Made me feel so much less alone." Moreover, it mattered to them that their commemorative effort called together a diverse set of LBQT+ individuals: "There were a lot of different genders in the room that night [at the event], so it felt like I'd done something right, because they all felt like it was . . . their conversation."

For her part, a New Orleans commemorator said that feelings of isolation declined even before commemorative events began, "Honestly my best memory of this project is fundraising parties." The fundraisers, she said, "felt to me like an idealized version of what being at a dyke bar was like. . . . Some were at my old house, which had a long double parlor. We'd get a DJ and someone to bartend. Our signature drink was the Lavender Menace. . . . Sometimes we'd have eighty people in a living room." She described an age-diverse crowd of LBQT+ individuals and how the crowd that filled her living room reduced the loneliness that called her to commemorate dyke bars in the first place.

These accounts suggest that, yes, talk of *gentrification*, when combined with critical nostalgia for a lost institution, can help a disparate group of people find common ground, and, in so doing, establish meaningful connections. We will find in chapter 2 that dyke bar commemorators are not alone in using *gentrification* to make claims about community. This is, in part, because *gentrification*—even when used metaphorically—is so evocative of place, and it seems that many people think of community as situated in place, whether a brick-and-mortar bar, a block, a neighborhood, or a city. Of course, this is also because so many people of all walks of life yearn for deeper, more "authentic" community and look for ways to mark and explain experiences of community dissolution and disruption.[53]

Gentrification and the Unifying Ghosts of Place[54]

Although dyke bar commemorators remember bars both critically and nostalgically, they create a sense of shared lineage for their audiences and for themselves by gathering people together to remember the ghosts of bars, of the lesbian identity politics they nurtured, and, crucially, of the neighborhoods that once housed dyke bars and their clientele. By presenting those ghosts as casualties of literal gentrification, they aim, implicitly, to unify those who gather at commemorative events without specifying a source of shared vulnerability or a specific unifying identity—beyond shared disdain for and concern about *gentrification* and its consequences for LBQT+ institutions and population centers.[55] In place of a shared sexual identity that operates as a primary orienting identity or a "master status," they position the shared lineage of the bar (remembered critically and nostalgically) and common vulnerability as cities become more and more expensive as new bases for ties. Thus, with *gentrification* constituting a new sense of shared threat—one that does not neatly define "us" and "them"—they work to provide a new sense of common ground for themselves and their audiences.

Gentrification answers a parallel question about why commemorators remember bars rather than other lost institutions.[56] These include lesbian bookstores, coffeehouses, bathhouses, and performances spaces, all of which played crucial roles in shaping LBQT+ identities, politics, and communities for decades. Yet many such spaces closed before the last bars, and their shuttering is more frequently attributed to factors other than literal gentrification, such as the rise of chain bookstores and coffeeshops.[57] In other words, what makes the dyke bar resonant is its association with the urban and the working class and, by extension, its utility as a symbol of not only lesbian identity politics, but also of how brick-and-mortar gentrification alters cities.[58]

Relatedly, the "ghost" of the working-class "dyke"—imagined to more commonly frequent the bar than the bookstore—is particularly evocative, because she is imagined to have been instrumental in forging public lesbian identities and communities in the last three decades of the twentieth century and as having been particularly vulnerable to literal gentrification.[59] Thus, this "ghost" (think of "Spike") reminds those at a generational remove of shared lineage and vulnerability, and it is her special claim to the (dive) bar that partially empowers that bar, and its neighborhood, as an evocative symbol of shared roots and collective loss.[60] Evoking Spike and her displacement via literal gentrification also allows dyke bar commemorators to evoke class without having to identify class as a possible source of identity or a basis for social organization. Much like *gentrification* and *queer*, *class* is communicated via specific representations, such as through commemorators' use of *dyke* and stories of Spike.

When I set out to study dyke bar commemoration, I never imagined that the project would take me back to the questions about gentrification that I had spent the first decade or more of my career grappling with. If anything, I thought that the research might evoke my own "critical nostalgia" for bars I had once visited.[61] Yet, without the happy accident of realizing how dyke bar commemorators leverage talk of *gentrification* to forge community, I might not have embarked on the research for this book. Witnessing, again and again, how talk of *gentrification* served as a new grounds for bringing people together—not to fight literal gentrification or even to rebuild bars but to establish ties with one another—made me begin to recognize how people use *gentrification* for myriad purposes. And I began to see how underspecifying what *gentrification* "is" partially enables the concept to be leveraged by so many people in so many different ways.

Dyke bar commemorators use *gentrification* to refer to literal gentrification, but, in so doing, they evoke more than that. In the realm of dyke bar commemoration, *gentrification* is also a metonym for vulnerability and marginalization; for being embedded in a system in which the decks are stacked against everyone other than the most privileged.[62] *Gentrification* makes most LBQT+ residents vulnerable, they suggest, just as police raids once rendered dyke bar patrons—to varying degrees, depending on their status, connections, and demographic traits—vulnerable. From commemorators, we learn how *gentrification* can be multivocal, gesturing both to literal gentrification (however loosely defined) and to metaphorical "gentrification" that calls out feelings of exploitation, marginality, and of the loss of shared (figurative) space.

For dyke bar commemorators, the goal they seek to reach by talking about *gentrification* is that most personal and essential of yearnings: to find connection and companionship among sympathetic individuals. While their challenges are somewhat specific—the desire to forge community without naming the "glue" that connects those who attend their events to one another—commemorators are nonetheless far from alone in turning to *gentrification* to answer that yearning. In the next chapter, we will see how others use *gentrification* for similar aims as they grapple with nostalgia for long-since-passed White ethnic urban enclaves and the communities they fostered, as well as for spatially rooted communities composed of Latinx and Black residents. As with dyke bar commemorators, this nostalgia is more for communities and identities that long ago transformed than for truly ungentrified space. We will see again how talk of *gentrification* allows cultural producers to mark change and loss associated with how we, as individuals and groups, transform and grow—both together and apart.

2

A Funeral Mass
for the Triple Decker

How *Gentrification* Marks the Loss
and Transformation of Community

Moving away from the organizers who drive dyke bar commemoration but remaining attentive to the imbrication of *gentrification* and *community*, this chapter explores how cultural producers evoke *gentrification* in art that captures the transformation of the communities of people presumed to share a common defining trait, whether related to shared ethnicity, race, or class—or some combination of the above.[1] Whereas dyke bar commemorators use talk of *gentrification* to forge community without having to specify what those they assemble together have in common, other cultural producers rely on talk of *gentrification* to mourn the transformation of ties forged among those whom they presume have much in common, including shared space. Think here of the dissolution of an urban ethnic enclave such as a Chinatown or of the dispersion of African Americans in the wake of urban renewal or a natural disaster. For cultural producers representing such losses, *gentrification* operates as a metonym for the structurally induced transformation of identity-community and place-based ties.

In this chapter, I rely on four examples of artistic representations of community decline that rely on *gentrification*. I highlight these examples because I find them to be particularly interesting and because they are distinctive from one another. The four works that I feature are part of a much broader constellation of artistic creations that evoke *gentrification* to tell stories about how communities change and to express feelings of loss and grief associated with such transformations. Each, in their own way, relies on *gentrification* to mark and mourn forms of social change, some of which, from afar, some might regard as positive changes, such as those associated with upward mobility or increased access to opportunities from which a group was once excluded.

Collectively, the works that I discuss capture four different locations in three different cities, and feature members of different social groups, from Italian American Bostonians to Black San Franciscans. The works also span different artistic forms, from documentary to sculpture to television and film.

By no means do these four examples capture the full heterogeneity of art that relies on *gentrification* to tell stories about how place-based social ties change. However, together, they tell us something about the differences and similarities in how *gentrification* appears in art as a metonym for structurally produced community transformation.

There are some striking commonalities across these four distinct artistic creations. Each presents a community of people who share a set of core traits, from race to class to ethnicity, as well as a common location. Each piece, implicitly, defines community in some way and represents the tensions of community change, including some of the conflicts that emerge from heterogeneity within a community. Finally, they all rely on the premise that place-based community upholds identity and provides social support.[2] This, of course, stands in contrast to how dyke bar commemorators use talk of *gentrification* to generate community without having to name a specific, unifying identity trait or common geographic location that connects members to one another. Instead, the works that this chapter features rely on *gentrification* to mourn or to express nostalgia for community predicated on shared identity and shared space.

Yet there are differences among the four pieces, too—both in terms of how they represent *gentrification* and how they represent community. Two works situated in Boston present urban neighborhoods as falling neatly into two distinct camps: B.G. and A.G. (before literal gentrification and after literal gentrification), while two works situated in California present literal gentrification as evolving over time and space, with distinct dynamics in distinct contexts.[3] Two of the works confront the role of individuals in community change, and they ask hard-hitting questions about individual moral responsibility for community evolution. In so doing, they acknowledge, more than the other two pieces, how experiences of community vary from individual to individual. In contrast, by relying on *gentrification*, some dodge sustained engagement with how some individuals and groups have accrued increasing privilege. Or, by relying on *gentrification*, they avoid direct acknowledgment of how the social and economic position of a social group—or at least of some members thereof—has changed. While each piece presents community as an essential resource, some are more nostalgic than others; they vary widely in whether they present community as entirely positive or as a site of conflict and tension.[4] Indeed, while the two pieces on Boston are overtly nostalgic, the two pieces on California grapple with more recent and enduring changes, and, partially as a result, are more mournful than nostalgic.

As I've already started to unpack by thinking through the example of dyke bar commemoration, there are a few reasons why *gentrification* appears front and center in such accounts of community change.

First, by default, communities are bounded; a community feels like a community in part because there are boundaries between "us" and "them" or between members and nonmembers.[5] To feel that one is a part of a community is to feel that one is inside of something. I will take up the broader significance of community in the book's conclusion, but for now, it's important to note that, of course, the boundaries that delineate whether one is inside are, in some circumstances, rigid, and, in others, porous.

For instance, my youngest children attend a large urban elementary school of about a thousand children. I feel that I am a part of their school community, but my connections to other members are mostly casual and require modest obligation and generate minimal expectation. I greet parents and teachers and assist with fundraisers and events when

I can. I trust that other parents will look out for my children on the playground after school, and I frequently do the same for others. In contrast, my responsibility to and expectations of my more intimate community of friends is much deeper; we offer one another assistance when ill, provide support in times of sorrow, and attend one another's milestone events. I have a much more explicit sense of who belongs in that community and of who does not. This is all to say that while there is variation in the rigidity of their boundaries, *all* communities have an inside and an outside. After all, part of why so many of us value community is because of the sense of belonging that community membership provides; a belonging that depends implicitly, whether we like this idea or not, on knowing that not all belong with us on the inside of that particular community.[6]

What does this have to do with *gentrification*? As dyke bar commemoration reveals, literal gentrification—especially advanced gentrification—presents a neat case of us versus them or of inside versus outside. Some people are old-timers and others are newcomers; some are yuppies or hipsters, others are not; some are rich, others are poor. Some are White, some are Black. Using advanced (literal) gentrification as their model, dyke bar commemorators present an "us" who is displaced or at risk of displacement and a "them" who displaces. The *gentrification* that is evoked is not one driven by individual urban pioneers moving in, but of a unified, intentional effort by economic and political elites to transform cities. Presented thusly, *gentrification* provides a sense of membership in a very open and general "we"—a membership that many yearn for.

This chapter reveals that talk of *gentrification* is purposed to express the fragility and value of community not only by bar commemorators, but by a broad and heterogenous group of cultural producers. *Gentrification* is increasingly apparent in narratives of community change, including, in contrast to dyke bar commemoration, in narratives that feature communities composed of those who share specific identity traits and common urban locales—whether a triple-decker house, an ethnic enclave, a multigenerational home, or a family-owned restaurant. These are potent symbols of community, of that which literal gentrification transforms and threatens, and of how structural forces alter intimate facets of our social lives.

Another reason why *gentrification* works to explore community change is because, as the art work, documentary, TV series, and film that this chapter explores illustrate, gentrification externalizes the source of community change. Across three of the four works that this chapter documents, change is largely something that happened *to* a community rather than something a community engaged in. This is especially the case in narratives of how White working-class ethnic communities evolved. *Gentrification* helps cultural producers tell stories of community evolution that place the onus on something other than the group itself. These works use *gentrification* to communicate that *they* made us change.

Third, talk of *gentrification* works to encapsulate a set of complex forces that have, in some cases, reshaped community. In the narratives this chapter charts, *gentrification* serves as a shorthand for a broad set of political-economic changes that began in the mid-twentieth century. In one sense, those who evoke *gentrification* in this way are quite right to do so. The lineage of disinvestment and reinvestment, starting with suburbanization and urban renewal (when the US government sought to remove urban "blight" and concentrated poverty by bulldozing certain urban neighborhoods—typically neighborhoods that housed poor and working-class ethnic and racial minorities) that this usage evokes, set the stage for the dominance of literal gentrification in contemporary cities.[7] After all, there is no reinvestment without disinvestment, and therefore no literal gentrification without the devastation of urban renewal, White flight, and suburbanization.[8] In this spirit, *gentrification* is a neat metonym for how structural forces influence social ties, or community.

On the other hand, using *gentrification* as a broad hand for more than a half-century of structural transformations oversimplifies, creating a too-neat visage of what produces community change. Some cultural producers also use *gentrification* to stand in for social changes concomitant with but not always directly related to how cities have themselves changed; these include changes in the social mobility of specific ethnic and racial groups, changing dynamics of racial and economic inequalities, and transforming gender and sexual politics.

Finally, *gentrification* works especially well to narrativize the transformation of ties forged among place-based identity groups. This is because *gentrification* is itself a place-based process. The four works that this chapter explores each rely on *gentrification* to present an account of how community, and the identities that nurture and are nurtured by our ties to one another, emerges from place, and especially from a tradition of sharing space with others with whom one shares a core identity. Think of informal, lifelong friendships between neighbors, and of the bonds that emerge from engagement with formal neighborhood organizations, such as a block club or a community church.[9] Indeed, to varying degrees, the pieces I write about hit us over the head with the idea of place-based community by zeroing in on very specific locales: a type of building; a tiny urban neighborhood; a house; a family-owned taco shop.[10] We might anticipate that *gentrification* will be evoked in narratives of how place-based community changes more often than in narratives of other types of community that are less rooted in place, such as a dispersed group of college friends or a network of gamers who interact online.

Each work that I highlight below emphasizes the built environment and the role of speculative real estate in driving broad changes that include, but also extend well beyond, *gentrification*. Yet, at heart, these are stories of identities and communities that might have transformed regardless of literal gentrification. In this sense, we see again how *gentrification* serves as device for marking community change and for pursuing the regeneration of community even if literal gentrification is not the only or actual root cause of community loss or change. Indeed, we see how *gentrification* both encapsulates and, alternately, turns attention away from a host of other historical and contemporary dynamics that have shaped cities and the communities that call them home. These include, but are not limited to, redlining, financialization, segregation, suburbanization, and White flight.

Boston, Massachusetts: A Wake
for Twentieth-Century Immigrant Enclaves

An Italian American Story

In 2018, filmmakers John Balcom and Maureen McNamara, in conjunction with producers associated with the North End Historical Society, released a documentary about Boston's Little Italy, *Boston's North End: An Italian American Story*.[11] The film commemorates the North End— which sits on a peninsula that extends into Boston Harbor, and is a short walk from the city's governmental and financial centers—in the decades when it was a predominately working-class Italian American neighborhood.

Drawing on footage of everyday street life and of crowds gathered for Catholic festivals, and interviews with residents and natives of the North End, the film captures rosy memories of the bustling, densely populated neighborhood at midcentury. It also offers an account of how and why the North End has transformed into an expensive and performatively Italian neighborhood.[12] At the center of the film's explanation for this change, and the loss of community it has wrought, is literal gentrification.[13]

The film paints an unambiguously nostalgic portrait of neighborhood life in the mid-1900s.[14] The filmmakers, with the aid of the legions of Italian American residents whom they interviewed, present family, shared ethnic identity, and community as almost inseparable and as deeply embedded in place—both in the "old country" (Italy) and in the North End. The film mourns this intimate connection between family, community, and neighborhood, presenting it as a casualty of literal gentrification.

This story of how the North End, as a community, has changed, and of how it has "gentrified," is, like most we will encounter in this book, on its face accurate. To be sure, the North End is unambiguously gentrified. While there surely still are Italian American residents, on any given day in the contemporary North End, one is more likely to encounter a young man in a suit walking home from his finance job, a flock of law students leaving their rental, City Hall workers picking up lunch, and well-heeled women walking their dogs, than they are to see an Italian grandmother exiting a bakery. Today, listings in the North End include three-bedroom apartments for two million dollars and one-bedroom condos for half a million dollars.[15] Recently, I could not take my children to our favorite, family-owned North End bakery because Matt Damon and Ben Affleck had rented it to film a movie scene.[16] Crowds of tourists stopped to watch them film.

As these anecdotes suggest, demographic and commercial changes indicative of literal gentrification are abundant in the North End. In recent years, median household income in the North End has reached $118,749 (versus a city median household income of just over $94,755),[17] and unemployment is extremely low.[18] Nearly 35 percent of the population that is twenty-five or older has a graduate or professional degree, and less than 8 percent of residents aged twenty-five and older have only a high school degree.[19] Between 2000 and 2015 the share of people over the age of twenty-five with a bachelor's degree increased from 62 percent of the population to 79 percent.[20] The neighborhood is predominately White, as it was for much of the twentieth century (some readers might be interested in scholarship on the changing racial classification of Italian Americans in the twentieth century—or in how they came to be considered White).[21] Yet residential density has increased in recent decades, after a rapid decline in neighborhood population in the latter part of the twentieth century: "Between 2000 and 2015, the population of the North End grew by 13 percent,"[22] and the share of foreign-born residents has steadily declined.[23] Despite its many Italian restaurants and bakeries, the North End is no longer a predominately Italian American residential enclave.[24]

However, emphasizing how literal gentrification transformed community in the North End tells a slice of the story of how and why family, community, and neighborhood have changed for North Enders. Spotlighting literal gentrification redirects attention from upward mobility, reduced immigration from Italy, suburbanization, White flight, and urban renewal, all of which contributed to the slow dissolution of the North End as an Italian American ethnic enclave.[25] Indeed, the North

End very nearly met the fate of the neighboring West End neighborhood, which was bulldozed to make way for gleaming new residential
towers and the expansion of Massachusetts General Hospital (Gans
1962). Some middle-class North Enders followed the example of friends
and family from the West End who, after urban renewal flattened their
neighborhood, made new homes for themselves in surrounding
suburbs.[26]

Gentrification also distracts from the role that the upward mobility
of some members of a once maligned ethnic group played in the dispersion of that group across metro Boston and far beyond. For instance,
Boston's North End: An Italian American Story does not dwell on the
transformed social position of Italian Americans over the last fifty or
sixty years; specifically, their increasing access to resources, changed
racialization, and decreasing stigmatization.[27] Instead, the filmmakers
imply that the source of change was literal gentrification, which, to be
sure, was swiftly accelerating in 2018, when the film was released.[28]

To underline the points just made, while the neighborhood's recent
literal gentrification is significant, it would be a mistake to regard that
change as totally distinct from the broader transformation that
Boston—and Italian Americans—underwent in the decades following
World War II. In other words, the transformation of the North End and
of the broader city was in motion before literal gentrification reached
Boston's Little Italy, beginning in the late 1970s and greatly accelerating
in the early-twenty-first century (Smajda & Gerteis 2012).[29]

Indeed, Boston went through a major demographic transformation
in the 1900s, losing 238,450 residents between 1950 and 1980; whereas
in 1950 Boston contained more than 800,000 residents, "by 1980, Boston's population fell to under 563,000 residents."[30] In this period, the
North End lost 47.1 percent of its residents.[31] Despite literal gentrification, today's North End has a lower number of inhabitants than it did
in 1950. This is partially attributable to smaller family sizes and the high
cost of living in today's North End. However, the dramatic population
decline of earlier decades set the stage for current population dynamics
and the dramatic in-movement of capital that the neighborhood has
experienced over the last several decades.

Why did Boston, and its North End, lose so many residents between 1950 and the onset of the neighborhood's gentrification? Many previously flourishing industrial US cities lost population in the decades after World War II.[32] This population loss emerged, in large part, from a series of coordinated federal, state, and local policy choices that sought to remake cities and their surrounding metro areas.

Among these policies was *urban renewal*: governments, typically relying on eminent domain, seized privately owned property and cleared it, repurposing the area, which they designated "blighted" or a "slum," for more high-end residences.[33] Leading up to this, federally subsidized suburbanization, which created new housing opportunities for White households, rapidly expanded. This government-supported suburban housing development was aided and abetted by concomitant federal highway expansion, which increased the ease with which residents could travel from a home in a suburb to work in the city.[34] These processes were racialized, with the targeting of lower-income and working-class racial and ethnic minority neighborhoods for "slum" clearance, and the flight of middle-class Whites away from cities to surrounding suburban areas.[35]

At the same time, changing opportunity structures for White ethnic populations, and, in Boston, the court-mandated desegregation of Boston public schools in 1974, coincided with suburbanization to encourage more resourced White urbanites to move out of Boston.[36] Indeed, it is crucial to keep in mind that Boston's population decline was not random; it was largely driven by the departure of Whites from the city.[37] As the Boston Planning Agency writes in a report, "In 1950, Boston was only 5.3 percent non-White," whereas by 2015 it was a majority-minority city and remains so today.[38]

Where did residents of the North End go? While thoroughly answering that question is beyond our scope, the presence of high populations of Italian Americans in Boston suburbs, particularly north of the city, provides a preliminary answer. Consider, for instance, that 17.9 percent of residents of the suburb of Medford report that they are of Italian heritage, whereas today only a little over 7 percent of Boston residents identify as Italian American.[39] While Medford has a particularly high number of residents of Italian heritage, other suburbs have even higher proportions; for instance, nearly 30 percent of Saugus residents report Italian heritage.[40]

As I have mentioned, a large portion of Boston's West End, which also housed high numbers of Italian Americans, was bulldozed as part of Boston's urban renewal plan.[41] As a result, between 1950 and 1980, the West End lost almost 67 percent of its population. To be sure, residents of the nearby North End watched closely as this unfolded.[42] Indeed, partially as a result, they successfully resisted the demolition of their own neighborhood.[43] Undoubtedly, with the demolition of the West End, some North Enders witnessed friends and relatives leave Boston, and this may have set the stage for their own eventual movement from the North End.

By tracing this history my goal is not to debunk the film's argument about literal gentrification, but, instead, to illustrate how documentaries such as *Boston's North End: An Italian American Story* let *gentrification* mark and mourn a broader set of changes. The changes relate to cities, and to how they have transformed, but those changes encompass more than just literal gentrification, including suburbanization, White flight, urban renewal efforts, and even the influx of chains moving into urban commercial districts. Of course, the changes also extend beyond cities, involving the changing social status of an ethnic group throughout the United States.[44] These changes are evident in my own family. While my Italian American grandfather had to leave school after eighth grade to sweep the floor and wash dishes in a bakery, and later spent his career as a welder in a factory, I have had access to elite universities, the opportunity to secure a PhD and, ultimately, the type of job of which my grandfather dreamed.

Below, I aim to get at what North Enders, as presented by the film, believe they lost as a result of this bundle of transitions (which they package together and call *gentrification*). Namely, they suggest they have lost spatially rooted community predicated on family connections and shared ethnic and religious identity. They present the North End as having been home to a rare and incredibly valuable social world. In the pages that follow, I explain why I think the film turns to talk of literal gentrification to denote those changes.

The film relies heavily on interviews with North End natives and residents, all of whom articulate heartfelt nostalgia for a specific type of dense, urban, familial, and community connection that they associate with the North End in the middle decades of the 1900s.[45] They capture apartments brimming with large families, with, in one instance, seven sisters sharing one bed. They describe those busy apartments as themselves packed into densely populated buildings; one resident recalls "150 people in a building." They describe schools in similar terms, with students chockablock in classrooms of up to fifty children.

Those whom the film features smile as they recount these details, and look wistfully off to the side, as if this other time of abundant place-based family and community remains almost within reach. In other words, their depictions communicate a sense of residential intimacy and warmth. Despite being only a generation removed from similar configurations (both of my parents grew up in large, Catholic families) and my own experiences as a small child in rooms overflowing with siblings and cousins, this viewer found herself yearning for that crowded, boisterous apartment as if it belonged to another world entirely.

The documentary presents this community as not only deeply rooted in Boston's North End, but also, sometimes, in parallel, specific places in Italy. One resident recalled, "When they moved to the North End, Italians tried to recreate the village that they came from. So they lived together in an apartment complex or across the street from Paesani." Another echoes this, "When you came over you tried to recreate where you came from."

According to the film, these intimate ties, rooted in place, were shored up by shared institutions, common culture, and shared language. Each distinct part of the neighborhood, populated by people from distinct parts of Italy, sported their own grocery store, bakery, and residents who spoke the same dialect. Thus, the documentary implies that the North End was made up of a set of tightly interlocking social groups, each of which remained connected to the villages in Italy that residents left behind when they came to Boston (Whyte 1943). Together, though, the film suggests that those groups constituted a single, supportive neighborhood entity.

As part of this, they highlight the blurring of family and broader community. They imply that each constituted the other. One resident explains, "Growing up here as a kid, everyone was family." A woman says, "We were very protected here. We did everything together . . . Knowing everybody's parents, everybody's grandparents." Indeed, they describe a neighborhood marked by mutual aid and independence. A man describes how his family would bring food to another family if the breadwinner had lost their job. He added, "And they would return it if we were in need."

Often, the film suggests, this mutual aid was experienced merely as routine and even as a pleasure. The same man who spoke of mutual aid describes "ten to fifteen people" at Sunday dinner. He also described how, as a child, after 9 a.m. Sunday mass he would "stop by for a meatball in one [apartment], dunk a piece of hard, crusty Italian bread in a bubbling pot of Italian gravy in another. Have a piece of ravioli in another, have a piece of lamb in a neighbor's house. It was just a wonderful, wonderful day, spending time with food and with family."

This community, interwoven by shared place, family, food, and mutual obligation had firm boundaries that shored up the intimacy that those on the inside of the North End community enjoyed. The film captures one longtime resident who recalls, "Outsider was a pretty generic term North Enders used for anyone they didn't know. Because all they knew was their friends and their families."

Despite these firm boundaries, the community that they depict was nurtured not just in the private sphere of families and apartments but also in the neighborhood's public spaces. Indeed, the film turns again and again to the notion of porous boundaries between the public and private spheres, with particular emphasis on the neighborhood's vivid street life. Interviewee after interviewee describes children in the streets playing sports, and offering to serve as guides for tourists. Periodically, the documentary features an acapella group that winds its way along the streets, and feasts—Catholic festivals—that bring streams of revelers into Hanover Street. One resident tells the camera, "We were street people. Everybody knew everybody. We'd hang out on the streets."

Of course, the film offers this nostalgic portrait only because this version of the North End no longer exists. While there is some acknowledgment of movement to the suburbs in the 1960s (one man says he's not sure why he moved to the suburb of Medford, except that "parking was an issue" in the North End), the film emphasizes the role of literal gentrification in the neighborhood's transformation. Alternate explanations, such as White flight, suburbanization, and increased opportunity for Italian Americans, largely go unmentioned. Instead, literal gentrification is provided as both a marker for how the North End has transformed and as an implicit explanation for that change.

Providing a timeline for the viewer, one interviewee tells the camera that "rents were still reasonable in the '80s." Another recalls that in 1961 he paid $30 for an apartment. In 2016, he tells the camera, the same apartment rented for $1,500 (if inflation were the only factor, 2016 rent would have been closer to $300).

The film informs us that, beginning in the 1980s, "outsiders trickled in. Students. People who were working in the city." Another says, "People came in. They just loved the neighborhood. They loved that you could walk down the street and be safe." However, the film suggests that newcomers eventually became less embracing of existing neighborhood culture, which they characterize by depicting rooftop grape arbors and basement wine casks. One resident recalls, "It was a neighborhood culture that was still very much alive when I arrived. I didn't realize that it was going to change very, very quickly."

What one person featured in the film describes as "housing problems," or what we might today call *affordable housing shortages*, began to arise. These shortages were exacerbated by the end of the redlining of the neighborhood.[46] Now that the neighborhood was no longer deemed a "slum" and redlining was outlawed, newcomers could more easily secure mortgages for North End properties. One resident muses, "It was bound to happen, don't you think? We are close to downtown, close to train stations, they can walk to work."

The film suggests that what a resident describes as "tremendous gentrification" has "dramatically" altered the North End. Literal gentrification, the film proposes, has led to the out-movement of many Italian American residents: "I saw a lot of my friends leave and a lot of the people I'd see every day go."

As this quote implies, the film does not just suggest that literal gentrification has progressed, but, also, that literal gentrification has dramatically altered (read: disrupted) the neighborhood's community. The film presents the loss of community as the ultimate casualty of literal gentrification.[47]

Specifically, they articulate the loss of a neighborhood community constituted by a vivid public life that included recognizing and warmly greeting most people one passed on the street, as well as the loss of interwoven familial and community place-based ties that, they suggest, characterized the North End at midcentury.

One says mournfully, "I've lived here fifty-four years, but if I stand in front of the door, I'm a stranger." Another says, "Now it is like I'm an anomaly. It is like, 'What, you've lived here your whole life?' Say good morning and nobody answers." Still another suggests that the community's "values are gone." And a neighborhood priest says the North End has lost its distinction—which rested on the interlocking sense of familial and neighborhood community—and is now like other upscale Boston neighborhoods. He says, "I see the North End becoming more like Beacon Hill. In other words, people mind their business, they walk their dogs . . . not like the old North End where everybody got involved in everybody's life."

Instead of residents who are engaged in one another's life, there are "million-dollar condos." Now, it costs "$700 a square foot to buy a condo," and, as a result, "you can't have that neighborhood store anymore. It just doesn't make sense. You're being priced out. You sense resentment." Building on these themes, the final chapter of the documentary is titled, "Is the North End still an Italian neighborhood?"

The answer to this question, the film proposes, is that literal gentrification threatens the North End; some of those who appear on film even suggest that as a result of literal gentrification, the North End is no longer "Italian."

That literal gentrification has remade the North End is indisputably true, but, irrespective of literal gentrification, both immigration trends and what it means to be Italian American have changed tremendously since the mid-twentieth century.[48] Thus, the answer to the question of whether the North End is "Italian" might revolve less around literal gentrification and more around the changing social status and geographic range of White ethnic groups in the contemporary United States, reduced immigration from Italy, and the increased economic and social mobility of the baby boom generation.[49]

Why does *gentrification* work to tell this story of an ethnic group's mobility and of the broader ways in which urbanites responded to the government-driven revisioning of cities in the twentieth century? Like other cultural objects we will encounter in this chapter, it is easier to tell a story of external threat to a closely bounded social group than to tell a story of internal or within-group change.[50] Again, those whom the filmmakers interview are entirely correct to suggest that literal gentrification is part of how and why the North End looks, sounds, and even smells distinct from how it did several decades ago, but fully explaining why Little Italy might not be "Italian" anymore requires attending to additional factors. This might even include examining whether *anyone* in Boston or anywhere else is "Italian" anymore, and explaining why the kind of community the film nostalgically recalls is harder and harder to find in any little Italy today.[51]

What are the consequences of elevating the role of literal gentrification in an account of how a place like the North End has changed?

On the one hand, one could consider this story of gentrification-induced transformation to be harmless. After all, it is a narrative vehicle that animates a wonderful history of the North End of Boston, made vivid by oral history interviews. The perceived threat of literal gentrification to neighborhood culture and community may have even encouraged efforts to mark that history via a documentary, and it is even possible that the sense of marked change that literal gentrification presents could have increased participation in the interviews that are the film's cornerstone. There is also the possibility that the film served as a vehicle for exposing new residents to the neighborhood's history, and, even more likely, it may have retimbered ties among neighborhood old-timers at screenings. Indeed, I attended an early screening at Emerson College in downtown Boston that reminded me at once of a family reunion and of the after-mass socials my own grandparents once took me to. Audience members, dressed formally for the occasion, warmly embraced one another and exclaimed happily when they saw former neighbors. Here, talk of *gentrification* operates to reinforce existing ties, just as it works to foster new ones at dyke bar commemorative events.

On the other hand, attributing neighborhood change narrowly to literal gentrification dances around questions that might call residents to grapple with their increasing (White) privilege, and related economic resources. What would such a film look like if the final chapters did not point to the threat of change out there (literal gentrification), but, instead, to an examination of what it means for familial and place-based neighborhood ties for some members of a once maligned social group to achieve new opportunities? Might this film, and others like it, examine to what degree longtime North End residents are victims or beneficiaries of these broad social, cultural, and economic changes?[52] Might it also dodge direct engagement with the grief that some might feel about how their own family and the broader social group of which it is a part has changed?

Moreover, by emphasizing literal gentrification, the film largely avoids discussion of some very troubled decades in Boston's history, as the city battled over urban renewal efforts that threatened neighborhoods like the North End, White flight, and suburbanization, and significant division emerged over court-ordered busing to integrate racially segregated Boston public schools.[53] In actuality, those fraught years, as well as the rise of crime and drug use in the North End itself, contributed to why some moved to suburbs like Medford, as did desire for worry-free parking and abundant backyards.[54] And, as in so many cities, that movement itself helped to open up certain North End properties for speculation, thus contributing to the neighborhood's broader literal gentrification.

Gentrification is a vehicle for grappling with a whole host of changes—including, as we have seen here, the transformation of neighborhood-based communities interlaced with deep family ties. However, by relying on literal gentrification as a vehicle, cultural producers may also detour past direct examination of the complex, intersecting reasons why communities evolve, change, and even dissipate.

In this instance, focusing on literal gentrification keeps us from really—or perhaps better put, *fully*—looking at how a neighborhood, and the community it fostered, changed. By "really" or "fully" I mean taking a long view of history; to "really" or "fully" look at how place-based immigrant communities like that depicted in the North End changed would be to examine a complex intersection of factors that drove the urban transformation that *Boston's North End: An Italian American Story* ably documents. We would need to start our clock long before literal gentrification reached the North End, and to grapple with questions of what it means for community when some members of a social group achieve opportunities from which they were historically excluded.

Mourning the Triple Decker

In the fall of 2019, Boston artist Pat Falco placed an exhibit, titled *Mock*, in the city's rapidly developing and increasingly upscale Seaport District, which is not far from the North End. However, the North End and the Seaport have long experienced different fates, and even the way in which they have each gentrified diverges.

For its part, the Seaport has recently transformed from a working port to an upscale corporate and residential neighborhood. The exhibit—consisting of two walls clad in white siding and sporting a single window anchored by black shutters—was shadowed by recently constructed high rises draped in reflective glass.

Indeed, wharves and warehouses no longer characterize the Seaport. Upscale residential towers, Boston's Museum of Contemporary Art, corporate offices, and tourist-oriented commercial establishments now dominate the neighborhood. Whereas the Seaport (then called the South Boston Waterfront) was among the Boston neighborhoods that lost the highest share of residents between 1950 and 1980 (67.3 percent of a population of 2,183), rapid planned redevelopment has reversed that fate.[55] Between 1980 and 2015, the neighborhood's housing units increased by 42.1 percent, with most of that growth occurring in recent decades.[56] The working port has now become a highly desirable residential and office location—for those who can afford to live or work there.

Today, the Seaport is highly affluent and predominately White (over 77 percent), with Asians constituting 8.6 percent of the neighborhood's population.[57] Median household income is among the highest of Boston neighborhoods at $165,842—nearly triple the city's per capita median income and close to double the city's median household income.[58] More than half of residents aged twenty-five or older have graduate or professional degrees.[59] Less than 2 percent of residents have a high school degree, and the unemployment rate is less than 1 percent.[60]

In self-conscious contrast to its upscale and contemporary surroundings, Falco's exhibit pays homage to the humble and utilitarian triple decker: a three-story, affordable, working-class housing form that once was home to White immigrant populations and was especially abundant in Boston neighborhoods. Today, in neighborhoods like Jamaica Plain and Roslindale, triple deckers increasingly house affluent gentrifiers, and they sell for huge sums as rental buildings or as individual condo units.[61] In Boston's neighborhoods with higher shares of people of color and higher poverty rates, such as Dorchester, Mattapan, and Roxbury, triple deckers are more likely to house working-class immigrants of color.[62] However, even in such neighborhoods, literal gentrification pressures have led to recent rent hikes and condoization.[63] Unlike the outer neighborhoods of Boston in which triple deckers remain a feature of the built environment, new developments closer to downtown in neighborhoods like the Seaport tend to eschew the form of the triple decker, favoring steel and glass and other contemporary signals of opulence.

Displayed on a street in the Seaport, *Mock* offers critical commentary on, among other things, speculative real estate and financialization.[64] However, this is not all that *Mock* imparts when viewed through the lens of an interest in *gentrification*'s communicative power. The exhibit models how talk of *gentrification* sometimes marks the loss of communities associated with specific groups—in this case, the Irish, Italian, German, and Portuguese working-class Bostonians who once built homes in the city's triple deckers. This is notable given the degree to which the dispersal of Boston's working-class White households occurred *before* literal gentrification became ascendant in the city, as suburbanization, urban renewal, economic mobility, and White flight led the White working class outside of the city center.[65] In this sense, *Mock* engages nostalgia for communities that were in large part lost before literal gentrification became rooted in Boston; works like *Mock* evoke *gentrification* to hearken a sense of loss, even if literal gentrification (alone) didn't actually produce the changes to local communities that they bemoan.

Falco adorned the interior walls of *Mock* with red and orange wallpaper sprouting stems abundant with leaves and fruit—in the shape of a triple decker—as well as text that calls the viewer to critical contemplation. Phrases, imprinted on a white background in the shape of street signs, read, "A Nod to Our Colonial Future," "The Illusion of a Single-Family Home," "We Still Will Not Move! To Hell with Urban Renewal," "Here Lies the Body of Democratic Architecture," and "Romantic Capitalism, Nostalgic Nationalism." Frames also adorn the walls: photographs of triple deckers; laundry hanging on a line in the shadow of a triple decker; a triple decker with a "release for demolition" sign; and a map of Boston neighborhoods.

When I visited *Mock* I had the feeling of being transported to a bustling Boston neighborhood circa 1940. I could imagine children playing in the street, and I could almost hear a grandmother, seated on her back deck, making small talk with a mother hanging laundry from her own deck one door down. In short, *Mock* readily brought to mind the type of vibrant early-to-mid-twentieth-century (White) working-class community often depicted in fiction and film as marked by familial ties and mutual dependence that were born, in part, from shared economic struggle and social marginalization.

By placing an installation festooned with antique photographs and frames in the city's busy Seaport, amid upscale construction projects erected on what was once the city's working port, *Mock* cannot help but evoke nostalgia for precisely the slice of lost Boston that came to mind as I stood inside the exhibit. This, a warm and casual early-twentieth-century apartment, is what we have lost, *Mock* insists. Yet Falco intends to render this loss general rather than specific; that is, *Mock* does not explicitly communicate nostalgia for a *specific* family or a particular triple decker, or a specific social group, but, rather, for the working-class immigrant populations whom triple deckers housed in the period that the installation evokes and for the communities they forged.

Mock drew not only audiences, but also media attention, with coverage in local print and radio. The coverage reveals that the exhibit encouraged precisely the type of conversation about development that Falco, in an interview with me, disclosed he hoped the exhibit would generate.[66] He told me, "There was a bunch of empty land. We have a housing crisis. We need to house people instead of being like, 'Let's build bigger, better homes.'" He hoped media coverage would zero in on the sculpture's political message rather than its aesthetic qualities, and that, he found, was just what occurred. Over coffee, he told me, "Sometimes with art, the best thing I guess you could do is get attention, good or bad, because then at least it's talking about [the issues]. . . . It felt like an accomplishment [that] nothing was about the formal or the aesthetic qualities of it. It was actually about housing, which is great."

Falco is quite right in this regard. For instance, an article by WBUR, a Boston NPR station, emphasized the juxtaposition between the skyscrapers that surround *Mock* and the form of the triple decker: "The sight of construction in progress is pretty common in the neighborhood as it rapidly developed over the past decade. What's *not* common is the style of this full-scale mock-up: a classic New England triple decker."[67] The article adds that "Falco's installation gives us the opportunity to consider how the Seaport could have developed differently."[68] Of course, by differently, they do not mean to reference simply a different architectural form, but, also, how the Seaport might have come to house a more heterogeneous confluence of Bostonians.

For its part, *The Scope*, a digital journal run by Northeastern University's School of Journalism, is specific about the social groups whom the Seaport does *not* house: "In his study of the three-decker and workforce housing, [Falco] highlights the contrast in the Seaport area, which has seen the development of more high-end housing instead of more necessary workforce housing. . . . In the highly-concentrated developments of the Seaport district, mock-ups are common for large-scale developments that represent the wealth and power that only a small percentage of the population are included in. However, this small mock-up of a three-decker seeks to remind people of a more diverse, inclusive and affordable Boston."[69]

On Falco's website he echoes this, specifying that Mock is meant to remind us of a time when housing was built "from the ground up"—meaning that it was built, first, to serve working people.[70] It is also meant to remind us of how and why the triple decker ceased to be a ubiquitous housing form in Boston. He writes, "Anti-immigration and racist backlash grew at the turn of the 1900s, and wealthy housing reformers worked to ban the construction of three-deckers. . . . The consequences of these actions helped build the framework of Boston's current housing crisis."[71]

Thus Falco positions Mock as protesting the current housing crisis. With the work, he aimed to draw linkages between hypergentrification (or the advanced, endemic quality of literal gentrification in places like the Seaport) and a long history of housing policies and trends that have shunned the poor and working class, immigrants, and people of color, prioritizing the city as a space for White, affluent populations.[72] The Seaport is a fitting place in which to make this point. In brief, this is the political position on Boston's housing crisis and on the complicity of planners, politicians, and architects therein, that Falco intends for Mock to call the viewer to consider.

However, as I have alluded, I argue that Mock communicates more than criticisms of hypergentrification (as embodied by the Seaport). The snapshots of early-twentieth-century triple deckers—and of associated lifestyles in the neighborhoods where they are concentrated—can't help but communicate an unmistakable nostalgia for Boston's working-class communities—a past well represented by the triple decker but not limited thereto. Because the exhibit pairs a housing form that, traditionally, housed White immigrant working-class people, with photographs and memorabilia from a time when those populations populated most such homes, Mock gestures to a more specific nostalgia for the city's White, working-class, ethnic communities that have long been dispersed by suburbanization, economic mobility, and mid-twentieth-century urban renewal.[73]

To a degree, this reliance on signals of the early twentieth century conflicts with Falco's wish to use *Mock* to tell a very broad and inclusive story about social and economic inequalities and contemporary (literal) gentrification; a story that points to broad problems of economic injustice and a developer-state. After all, as Falco is well aware and quick to communicate in media interviews, on his website, and in conversation with me, today those who inhabit triple deckers in places like Boston's Mattapan, Dorchester, and Roxbury tend not to be White and looming literal gentrification threatens their ability to stay in those units. However, he relies on a symbol that is so coded as White ethnic (at least in Boston, and in the period that *Mock* gestures to) that, whether or not he intended to do so, *Mock* communicates nostalgia for a particular group and community; a community who dispersed in significant numbers before literal gentrification became ascendant in Boston.[74]

It is plausible that Falco's piece could leverage that nostalgia to garner support for those most at risk of displacement by literal gentrification today, who, as he is well aware, tend to be poor and working-class people of color. But by situating *Mock* in the past, with decor reminiscent of the first half of the twentieth century, *Mock* nonetheless gestures to a time when Boston was more White than not, and therefore calls out nostalgia for that past.[75]

Consider, for instance, that affixed to an interior wall of *Mock* is a black and white photograph of laundry lines extending from a triple decker; crisp white undershirts extend to the end of the photograph's frame. Consider also the vibrant wallpaper that frames the inside of *Mock*, which gives one the feeling of having stepped inside a modest but carefully presented living room; a room that is surely full of the lively sounds of a big, bustling family. The nostalgia *Mock* communicates— intentionally or not—is not just for a specific housing form, but, more generally, for the social groups with which that form is associated and the communities that they constituted. A conversation with Falco revealed that, in this case, nostalgia is not just leveraged for political purposes, but is also quite personal.

For Falco, triple deckers represent the casualties of literal gentrification, but they also remind him of his own family and of his family's evolving—and sometimes tenuous—position in the city. While Falco set out to feature the triple decker because it was a powerful method for speaking out against hypergentrification of the kind that has transformed the Seaport, mid-endeavor he realized he was delving into his own family's legacy of "getting displaced and moving around."

He told me that, "randomly" while he was working on his first exhibit related to housing policy—called *Luxury Waters*—he found "this article from the '80s or '70s." To his complete surprise, he discovered that his uncle was quoted in the article: "[He was] talking about housing gentrification and displacement in the North End in the '70s. . . . And he was just saying the same stuff [that I was saying in my art]." This was a piece of his (working-class, Italian American) family's history that Falco had not thought much about, but, by the time he began preparing *Mock* he was mindful that he was marking a process—of displacement and devaluation—that his own family members had experienced in Boston.

He said of his uncle's quote in the article: "He was just talking about how they were worried. The North End was this really tight community and they were worried that they were making the neighborhood safe and clean in a way that was actually hurting them because it made it more attractive to outside. He was trying to find the balance of how to make your neighborhood good, but not *too* good for your own good. I think [that] was the quote. So then I was like, oh, there is this connection that I didn't even really know about to people I'm related to, thinking about this?"

This familial connection, not just to displacement and neighborhood transformation, but, specifically, to triple deckers, seems to inform Falco's work. One can imagine that it might also shape Falco's nostalgia for a specific architectural form, the triple decker, which he acknowledges that he questions intellectually, despite his nostalgia. After all, triple deckers have been criticized for reasons from fire safety to the fact that they are vertically limited, and Falco is aware of such concerns about the form he celebrates.[76]

As a child, Falco's father worked as a delivery driver and his mother as a cafeteria worker and house cleaner. Falco recalls, "They've all kind of maintained different jobs at different points." Falco and his family lived in several different parts of Boston, as well as on Cape Cod. Some-times they lived in the very housing form, the triple decker, that *Mock* features. He recalls, "Yeah, I think I've lived in three or four."

Thus, it was quite meaningful for Falco to take his father to see *Mock*. "I actually took my dad to *Mock*," he says, "and we actually went to Brighton and we were looking at . . . it was kind of a cool . . . we just went to see this old house. And I was trying to put it in a context of, here's a sculpture I did. This is what it's referencing. That was cool for me . . . it just kind of unlocked something and [my dad] was talking about his life in the city. That was kind of cool."

For Falco, *gentrification* is a device that allows him to critique housing policy, architectural trends, and even planning. However, it is also a ve-hicle that allows him to communicate with his family and perhaps even to connect to his own individual past. It is a method for letting his family know that he sees how they have struggled, and, more generally, for connecting over their shared history; a history he sees as under threat in a changing Boston—but also one that he is increasingly separate from, as he has earned a degree, secured arts fellowships, and achieved accolades for his work. In this context, recognizing how a changing city can produce shared harm is a means for forging familial connection, which is its own form of community.

This harm is not limited to Falco and his family, and I don't mean to suggest that Falco's concern is only—or even principally—for his family members. Falco doesn't think of the harm that *Mock* identifies as limited to his family. Rather, he sees it as extending well beyond them to count-less other families and the communities they constitute. For instance, when he thinks of the significance of triple deckers he says, "Working people lived in them, and people who were sometimes shunned by White, affluent populations." However, his understanding of his own family as among the "working people" who have lived in triple deckers underlines the significance of such housing for the artist.

Having insights from his own and his family's experience undoubt-edly lends Falco insights that give *Mock* some of the significance I felt as I stood inside the sculpture. Of course, using literal gentrification as a narrative device did not hurt either; indeed, this made the contemporary relevance of the work readily apparent to the reporters and others who viewed it.

Like *Boston's North End*, *Mock* evokes what was lost with some of the major changes that occurred in cities in the twentieth century: White flight, suburbanization, urban renewal, and subsequent literal gentrification. To a degree, these are processes of change that some of those depicted in the North End documentary and certainly some of those who once resided in Boston triple deckers knowingly participated in. Imagine, for instance, a young Italian American couple searching for a house with a yard and a driveway in the Boston suburb of Medford. To a degree, they are following their dreams for themselves and their family to the suburbs; they may have also sought distance from certain (typically non-White and poor) urban populations. Keep in mind, though, how their choices were informed by a major urban transition that planners, politicians, and business elites put into place—with the express interest of upscaling and transforming the city; of ridding it of so-called tenement neighborhoods that poor and working-class racial and ethnic minorities had long called home.[77]

While the loss of place and community experienced by working-class White ethnic populations—many of whom achieved not only geographic but also social and economic mobility in the proceeding decades—pales in comparison to the multigenerational agony of concomitant "Negro Removal," they nonetheless experienced and express pain associated with their separation from natal urban communities.[78] We see that pain—and how gesturing to *gentrification* is used to express it—in works such as *Mock* and *Boston's North End*.

Mindy Fullilove, in her book *Root Shock*, diagnoses and contemplates this pain.[79] She writes of what White, working-class urban dwellers discovered they had lost after moving out of the city in the mid-twentieth century, as planners and politicians sought to reinvent the places they had called home, both by bulldozing poor and working-class urban housing and by building alluring highways to the suburbs. In essence, Fullilove suggests they lost community and the vibrant institutional density that sustained it: "The pubs of the Irish, the street festivals of the Italians, the minyan of the Jews, the monumental buildings of the

English: these were artifacts of the city that flourished amid tenements and, let me dare say it, diversity. This dismemberment of our cities was sponsored by an elite that reorganized the metropolitan regions to maximize their wealth and power" (2016, 225).[80] This displacement scattered people and severed connections and support structures on which they had once deeply depended (2016, 16).

Of course, racism fed White working- and middle-class urbanites' departures from the city at midcentury; specifically, aversion to sharing neighborhoods with people of color encouraged movement away from cities in which poor and working-class people of different walks of life were increasingly called to share space as cities engaged in the planned shrinkage of traditional tenement neighborhoods. Fullilove proposes that this class of people nonetheless faced a terrible dilemma. She writes, "But what a bitter set of choices is presented in this fight-or-flight scenario, and the suffering imposed by the forced choice is enduring. White people, too, loved their neighborhoods and to this day mourn their lost homes" (2016, 225).[81]

Thus, the nostalgia for White immigrant working-class urban communities that some, like Falco and the filmmakers of *Boston's North End*, turn to *gentrification* to express is not unproblematic or simple. But to call that nostalgia a response to literal gentrification is to take a snapshot rather than a landscape view of history. It is to start the clock in the wrong decade and to overlook the earlier "root shocks" (Fullilove 2016) that partially opened the city to present-day hypergentrification and that shape nostalgia for earlier urban decades and the communities that we imagine flourished then.[82]

Some mourn and mark such community by building monuments to neighborhoods and a specific architectural form, and, as we will see in the next section, to a family-owned restaurant, and to a multigenerational home. Some seek to empower that mourning by attributing the loss of such things to literal gentrification, but we lose something too when they do so.

Specifically, we lose a more complex, detailed rendering of the broad set of changes that shape who each of is and how we connect to those around us. Some, like Falco, set out to tell a broader story that spans from the losses experienced by White ethnic working-class residents of early-twentieth-century triple deckers to those that Black, Asian, and Latinx residents of some of the same buildings face today. But *gentrification* is a faulty metonym, not only because, more often than not, it represents more recent history, but also because it is often paired with specific frames for the past; in this case, a frame that hearkens more to a pre–World War II Boston than to the present-day and thus evokes some groups and their struggles more than others—despite the artist's intention to gesture to a much broader set of working-class Bostonians.

Mourning California Community

This is not just a Boston story, and not just a story of the loss of identity-based communities associated with White ethnic groups. Popular culture is rife with stories of community and collective identity evolution and of the feelings of loss some experience when the communities in which they are embedded change. And, increasingly, these stories are situated in contexts grappling with literal gentrification.

As we have started to discover, these stories are of a type; they emphasize alterations to the built environment and the role of speculative real estate and financialization in driving broad changes that include, but also extend well beyond, literal gentrification. More than anything else, they are stories of how identity communities rooted in place change, irrespective of literal gentrification. In this sense, *gentrification* sometimes operates as a metonym for the structurally induced loss of place- and identity-based ties.

In the next pages I highlight two new examples of this account of community change. Each unfolds in a California neighborhood, and in contrast to the works on Boston that I profiled in the previous section, they grapple with recent change (in the form of literal gentrification). As a result, they articulate grief that this recent community change evokes, more than nostalgia for long-altered communities like those in Boston. The Netflix series *Gentefied* depicts the literal gentrification of

Los Angeles's predominately Latinx Boyle Heights neighborhood, while the film *Last Black Man in San Francisco* depicts the loss of territory for African Americans across the eponymous hypergentrified city, but especially in its Fillmore neighborhood.

Relying on a taqueria (*Gentefied*) and a house (*Last Black Man*), the series and film reveal how literal gentrification threatens centers for and symbols of community. However, they each also gesture to the loss of a broader, spatially rooted cultural identity and the sense of community that emerges from and helps sustain such identities. For instance, *Last Black Man in San Francisco* documents a broad set of changes in San Francisco, from urban renewal to gentrification to environmental racism and drug dependency, and their consequences for African American residents, before zeroing in on the loss of a particular house. Each relies on *gentrification* to present an account of how identity emerges from place, and especially from a tradition of sharing space with others with whom one shares a racial and/or ethnic identity that is at the core of one's self understanding. One (*Last Black Man*) principally wrestles with what happens to community when there are external threats to a social group, and the other (*Gentefied*) pays greater attention to internal threats to a sense of shared "groupness." They focus on the loss of built, tangible spaces because the places where members of a community come together are crucial mechanisms for forging and maintaining ties, but also because such spaces are powerful symbols of community and family.[83]

In subtle contrast to *Boston's North End* and *Mock*, we will discover how engagement with literal gentrification does not always distract from internal sources of community change, such as increased within-group economic heterogeneity. Instead, sometimes depictions of literal gentrification spotlight or serve as a mirror for such internal changes and the problems that characterize any community, and gesture to the structural roots of within-group change. Still, as we saw in the film and sculpture about Boston, here *gentrification* also works to communicate how forces larger than any individual change and ultimately weaken social connections.

Saving Mama Fina's

The Netflix series *Gentefied* takes place, in large part, in the Morales family's Boyle Heights taqueria, Mama Fina's. Mama Fina's, with its barebones decor, original menu (still written in the penmanship of the now-deceased family matriarch), and working-class Latinx regulars, clashes with the neighborhood's new upscale residents—depicted, universally, as White hipsters—and the galleries, coffee shops, and upscale restaurants that serve them.

The series introduces and reintroduces not only the possibility that Mama Fina's will be a casualty of literal gentrification, but, even more centrally, the recurring question of whether characters—members of the extended Morales family and their intimates—are themselves complicit in literal gentrification or, put differently, engaged in *gente-fication*, the gentrification of Latinx neighborhoods by more affluent Latinx individuals.[84] This is how we know that the series leverages *gentrification* to tell a story about community and about the forces (beyond literal gentrification) that threaten the ties that bind community members to one another.

Some characters insist that the Morales cousin, Chris, is a gentrifier because he has an MBA and an affluent father. Others argue that Chris's cousin, Ana, advances literal gentrification because she paints murals featuring queer Latinx residents for White property owners.

These claims and questions, about who bears responsibility for literal gentrification, and whether participation in brick-and-mortar gentrification is ultimately forgivable, are not presented lightly. They tear at relationships, animating not only the series' plotline but nearly all of the conflict that occurs between characters. Tears are shed, relationships end, and family members drift outside of the family's primary orbit.

However, the reader will not be surprised that I believe these are not really questions about literal gentrification, but, instead, about what happens as communities become more culturally and economically heterogeneous as a result of changing opportunity structures, or the "gentrification" of some community members.[85] The two-season series, which was created by Marvin Lemus and Linda Yvette Chávez and first appeared on Netflix in 2020 and 2021, grapples with what happens as a Mexican American family's grandchildren—the second generation to grow up in the United States—experience newfound opportunity and privilege, from economic opportunities to new cultural outlooks (e.g., calling out "toxic masculinity" and proudly owning one's queerness).

There is, of course, a question of whether the Morales family, and others like it, are, in fact, *becoming* more heterogenous or, rather, whether, in the current political and cultural moment, they are increasingly mindful of the differences that nearly always characterize any family, and especially families that have experienced recent mobility associated with immigration and related generational differences in the accrual of resources.[86] Regardless of whether there have been objective changes, the question of what differences within a family or neighborhood mean for human connections drives every episode of *Gentefied*, and pursuing questions about individuals' roles in literal gentrification shines a spotlight on broader questions about what it means to be a family or a community, despite members' differences, and against the backdrop of the new opportunities that some members of the family have access to.

Over and again, the plotline raises questions about the durability of family and neighborhood connections. For instance, the series asks whether two cousins, Erik and Chris, can get along, despite differences between their bank accounts, educational backgrounds, and childhoods, as they tussle in their grandfather's kitchen. Erik's father suffers from drug addiction and is unhoused in Los Angeles, and Chris's father is affluent and resides far from the rest of the family in lily-White Idaho.

When they break up over political differences related to literal gentrification, the series suggests that two lovers—Ana and Yessica—cannot stay together because one is an affordable housing advocate and the other paints murals on a developer's buildings and makes art for Nike. It also predicts doom for Chris and his new girlfriend, who break up when the girlfriend follows her dream of being head chef at a brick-and-mortar upscale restaurant, coming to work in a new restaurant located in the space that housed Mama Fina's, Chris's family's restaurant. By spotlighting Erik, who has long worked as a cook at Mama Fina's, bumbling through life as a new stay-at-home-dad in Palo Alto, where his girlfriend, Lidia, is an assistant dean at Stanford, *Gentefied* casts doubt on the possibility that two people of different economic and educational backgrounds can have a successful relationship. In yet another scene, a Morales friend who works as a mariachi musician must choose whether to honor his passion for music or sacrifice his calling and support his family by working on a Central Valley farm with his brother.

These are the dilemmas, about how we all navigate difference and connection, that motivate episode after episode. Can a family accept a cousin's love interest if that love interest—in this case, Yessica—has a darker skin tone than the rest of the family? Are you lovable even if you move away and achieve financial success? Can a family remain connected, even if the government deports their *abuelo*? Can a grandfather be the grandfather he wishes to be if his daughter and granddaughter move away in search of career opportunities?

These stories of the differences that threaten to separate family members from one another, and therefore threaten communities, are embedded in narratives of literal gentrification. Indeed, the series is set in a neighborhood that, in actuality, has undergone recent rapid literal gentrification.[87] Historically, Boyle Heights has been predominately Latinx, with most residents of Chicano heritage.[88] The neighborhood has also long had higher poverty rates and lower education levels than most of the rest of Los Angeles.[89] However, between 2010 and 2023, median household income nearly doubled in Boyle Heights, and the median value of owner-occupied homes in Boyle Heights more than doubled between 2013 and 2023.[90]

Given this, a casual viewer might believe that it is literal gentrification itself that threatens to break the Morales family apart, as well as the broader place-based Boyle Heights community in which it is embedded. After all, the characters fight about how to save Mama Fina's when the landlord dramatically raises rent and, later, when the building is sold to a developer intent on replacing the shop with an expensive restaurant. They fight about whether they ought to change their menu to appeal to gentrifiers' tastes. They fight about whether their patriarch, Pop, should sell his home (for a handsome sum) and move to Mexico.[91] They fight, often, about whether members of the family are unintentionally aiding and abetting literal gentrification.

These themes are readily apparent in nearly every episode of the series. Take the episode "Protest Tacos," which pits the cousins and their grandfather against their cousin Ana's longtime girlfriend, Yessica, who works as an affordable housing advocate. Yessica is gravely concerned when she learns that Chris has had Mama Fina's listed on a neighborhood food tour that is notorious for bringing "outsiders" (a.k.a. affluent White hipsters) into Boyle Heights. Chris has hatched this plan as a last-ditch effort to support Mama Fina's, which, without a sudden infusion of cash, will be evicted from its storefront because they owe back-rent.

Yessica marches into Mama Fina's and confronts Chris, who stands behind the counter. She calls on him to recognize that "welcoming outsiders en masse with open arms like this is pushing people out of their homes and into the tents around every corner." Chris does not disagree. He tells her, "I get it. I've been listening to [the podcast] *There Goes the Neighborhood*. But Yessica, I need the money."[92]

In response, Yessica evokes "the community" of Boyle Heights. She tells Chris, "You think that there's only one way to save the shop? That your only option is selling out your community? *My* community?" Here it becomes clear that preserving "the community" is the ultimate concern driving the conflict between Chris and Yessica. For Yessica, preventing literal gentrification is crucial for saving community. From Chris's vantage point, preserving Mama Fina's and therefore his family's ability to stay in Boyle Heights is essential for preserving "community."

In a sense, the characters grapple with enduring questions that anyone, whether in Boyle Heights or the Seaport or the North End, will inevitably ask about what exactly constitutes community. Is it family? Neighborhood? Shared identity? Shared circumstance?

This conflict ultimately pits the lovers Ana and Yessica against one another. Chris runs to his cousin Ana to tell her about his argument with Yessica. He says, "Apparently Yessica is planning some food tour guerrilla warfare type shit. And, apparently, I am responsible for LA's staggering rate of homelessness. And you, you've got to do something about your girl."

Despite Chris's admonitions, Ana is unable to stop Yessica from organizing a protest that takes place during the food tour. Mid-protest, Pop, who owns the store and has known Yessica since she was young, confronts her, asking her what she is doing. Yessica says, "I care about this community, Pop." Pop says, "I do, too. I am part of this community." Yessica suggests that Pop's concern with staying in business is clouding his judgment. She says, "Maybe you don't see it now, but in the short or long term, our community will suffer."

Ultimately, Yessica and Ana fight, as most lovers sometimes do. Yessica tells Ana that Ana's family treated her "like an angry Black girl," and she accuses Ana of letting herself be pimped out as an artist by the White developer who employs her to paint murals on his properties. Presumably, they are fighting about how they position themselves relative to literal gentrification, but their conflict engages much broader themes about strategies for navigating capitalism and how intimates plot a course (or courses, as the case may be) related to upward mobility, occupation, and finding a path that one feels is morally acceptable. It also engages the even more general theme of how we stay connected, as lovers, family members, or the broader communities of which those units are a part, even when we disagree. Here, to blame literal gentrification for conflict is to rely on it as a metonym for the differences that many of us must navigate in our relationships, romantic or otherwise, particularly when a social group encounters expanding opportunity structures.

Why does *gentrification* work to explore these broader themes? In part, it is because neighborhoods diversify (initially) as they gentrify; people of different walks of life find themselves living side by side and navigating how to live with one another. Often, gentrifiers and longtime residents alike grapple with whether it is possible to forge a community, despite their differences.[93] Thus, spotlighting literal gentrification—and especially *gente-fication*—allows the series to explore similar issues as they relate to family heterogeneity: the most intimate of community forms.[94]

Ultimately, *Gentefied* uses *gentrification* to grapple with age-old questions about whether community emerges from our differences or our commonalities. It also uses *gentrification* to explore the perception that, as the structural position of some Latinx individuals changes, there is increasing heterogeneity among Latinx residents of neighborhoods like Boyle Heights. By looking at this heterogeneity, the series individualizes community-transformation more than works like *Boston's North End* and *Mock*, recognizing that some community members choose to stay while others choose to go. Ultimately, the anxiety that drives the series, coloring nearly every conflict in every episode, is less about literal gentrification than it is about the consequences for community ties of uneven access to opportunities for mobility among Latinx residents of neighborhoods like Boyle Heights.

The Last Black Man in San Francisco

On its surface, *The Last Black Man in San Francisco* appears to be a part of a new genre of what the scholar Rebecca Wanzo calls "gentrification films."[95] I do not dispute the film's inclusion in this genre, for literal gentrification is, without a doubt, at the center of the film's plot, which charts the loss, repossession, and loss again of a family home in San Francisco's increasingly gentrified Fillmore neighborhood. Moreover, a film like *The Last Black Man in San Francisco* will indisputably sustain *gentrification*'s symbolic power, and its utility as a storytelling device. Given its critical success, it may even beget more gentrification films.[96]

Why might some consider *The Last Black Man* to be a gentrification film? The film opens with a Black street preacher, in a dark suit and a pink tie, standing on a milkcrate in Bayview-Hunters Point, the San Francisco neighborhood that has the highest proportion—albeit a steadily declining number—of Black residents.[97] His voice carries across a neighborhood currently being cleaned by men in hazmat suits, while Black residents move through the neighborhood unprotected. By offering visuals of neighborhoods beyond the one in which he stands, most viewers will recognize that the preacher's worry is not just for his neighborhood; he sounds a clarion call that San Francisco itself is being cleaned and readied for something new.

Bible in hand, the preacher booms: "*This* is the San Francisco that they never knew existed." Here the film cuts, briefly, to images of Black residents throughout the city; they interact, happily, with other Black San Franciscans on city sidewalks as they go about the business of daily life. The preacher continues, his tone incredulous, "And *now* they come to build something new? . . . Whole blocks half in the past, half in the future . . . look at them look at you. Look down at you. But *we* built them." He continues, "We *are* these homes. Their eyes, their pointed brims. We move if they move . . . this is *our* home!"

The preacher speaks as though a whole congregation is gathered in front of him, but his audience is, in fact, very small. A young Black girl stops to listen but is soon called away by her mother. As she leaves, the camera turns to find the film's two main characters, Mont and Jimmie, sitting, waiting for a bus, listening intently to the preacher. Mont and Jimmie, who are Black and appear to be in their late twenties or early thirties, are in no particular rush as they sit in the afternoon sun waiting for a bus to arrive. Jimmie wears a knit winter hat and a red plaid shirt while Mont wears a suit (these are their uniforms throughout the film, clothing them in almost every scene). Mont has his notebook open, pen in hand; he looks up from the page as Jimmie muses about whether the sermon is rehearsed.

"They got plans for us," the preacher warns his small audience. In saying this, he implies that a land grab is behind the cleanup and that Black residents will soon be displaced. The area has been contaminated for half of a century, he says, and sudden interest in the community's well-being strikes him as suspicious. "I urge you! Fight for your land! Fight for your home!"

That is precisely what Jimmie, a nursing home attendant, does, with the ardent support of Mont, a fishmonger and novice playwright. *The Last Black Man* follows Jimmie's quest to reclaim his family's home in the increasingly White and gentrified Fillmore District, which was, until it was destroyed by urban renewal, the cultural and commercial heart of Black San Francisco and home to a renowned jazz scene.[98] Jimmie speaks with reverence for the home, which, at the film's start, houses a middle-aged White couple. When the couple is out, Jimmie is in the habit of trespassing to paint trim and tend gardens, lovingly caring for a home, which, he tells everyone he knows, was built by his grandfather after World War II; we learn that three generations of Jimmie's family have called the house home.

When Jimmie appears, uninvited, to care for the house, the bespectacled White couple who reside there throw croissants and vegetables at Jimmie, imploring him to leave. In one scene, the wife threatens to call the police if Jimmie does not descend from the ladder on which he is busily painting, but the husband admonishes her, reassuring Jimmie that "of course" they will not do so.

Of course, the Fillmore was not always home to croissant-carrying White gentrifiers. Indeed, while Jimmie works on his birthright, a guide brings a crew of White tourists to stand in front of the house. He tells them about the neighborhood's history as a Japanese enclave, disrupted by the US government's forced internment of the Japanese during World War II. He also mentions how Black residents migrated to the neighborhood in significant numbers during World War II, and the tour guide applauds the audience for being "hep cats" who want to see "the *real* San Francisco," by visiting "the Harlem of the West." He does not mention that urban renewal decimated the Black population of the Fillmore, disrupting its recently established reputation as a center for jazz and as a broader cultural hub for Black San Franciscans.[99]

The viewer learns that Jimmie's family lost their Fillmore home—an ornate Victorian—in the 1990s, but that Jimmie spent part of his childhood within its wood-paneled walls—before spending time in a group home for children, living in a car as a young adult, and, ultimately, coming to sleep on the floor of Mont's bedroom in Mont's grandfather's house—close to the bay where the environmental cleanup is taking place.

Over the course of the film, Mont and Jimmie come to briefly reinhabit the Fillmore house when the White residents unexpectedly leave; Mont and Jimmie encounter the couple, distraught, as they load a moving truck (moving as a result of a family conflict over an inheritance). After the couple drives away, Mont and Jimmie move Jimmie's grandfather's formal Victorian furniture, which was long stored at an aunt's house far outside of San Francisco, back into the home. Once reinstated in the house, the two men painstakingly care for the home, making repairs and arranging furnishings.

This homecoming is short-lived, however; ultimately, literal gentrifi-cation prevails. Jimmie's family home is put back on the market for $4 million and the White listing agent tosses Jimmie's family's furniture to the curb and threatens to call the police if Mont and Jimmie do not depart. Jimmie begs a banker to offer him a loan, volunteering to be saddled with a high interest and flexible mortgage rate. But his dream goes unrealized.

Despite the obvious threat that literal gentrification poses to Jimmie's desired homecoming, *The Last Black Man* is about homelessness more than it is about literal gentrification. And literal gentrification is just one of several factors that renders a person homeless in *The Last Black Man*.

By *homeless*, I do not just mean the loss of housing, which, admittedly (like literal gentrification), is itself one of the film's central themes. As with *gentrification*, direct and indirect references to literal homelessness appear throughout the film. As a man drives a battered older-model sedan past them, Mont asks Jimmie, "Isn't that the car that you used to live in?" The man driving Jimmie's former residence offers to give Mont and Jimmie a ride (the bus is late again). While they ride in the car that Jimmie used to live in, they pass a building that is under construction. The driver says, "It was a hundred motherfuckers in there, rent-controlled. The landlord burned those people outta there. They thought they owned that shit." Jimmie responds: "You never own shit."

In still other scenes, homelessness looms. A Black man's face appears in the window of a large single-resident-occupancy building (often the most affordable temporary housing a city has to offer); the window out of which he peers is situated in the midst of a mural advertising a new upscale hotel called "Stay." Here, as in so many scenes, the present tips into the future, and the future is a San Francisco that does not have rooms—let alone grand Victorians in the Fillmore—where (Black) men like Mont and Jimmie can stay.

Despite this exploration of the loss of housing across the film, I do not mean to argue that the film is about *literal* homelessness; instead, I mean something more abstract. By *homelessness*, I gesture to the sever-ing or loss of authentic, empathic connection to those with whom one shares a community, whether that community is constituted by family;

a neighborhood; a network of those with whom one shares a racial identity or another master identity; or composed of those who share residence in a city. *The Last Black Man* is a film made poignant by the loss,
at different turns, of each of these types of community, and by how that
loss leaves one unmoored, adrift, and, ultimately, alone.

In *The Last Black Man*, literal gentrification is a mechanism that leads
to "homelessness" or the degradation of ties that root one to people and
place, but it is not the only such mechanism. The film provides a vivid
sketch of factors that send one out to sea (the final image with which
the film ends—when Jimmie rows, alone, into the ocean and away from
San Francisco), including drug addiction; class heterogeneity within
families, neighborhoods, and cities; gun violence; child abandonment;
poverty; wealth and the contests for money that sometimes come with
it; and even environmental disaster. Urban renewal, which I explored
above in conversation with the North End of Boston, goes unmentioned. However, by situating Jimmie's house in the Fillmore, the mass
eviction of Black residents that urban renewal entailed in San Francisco,
and particularly in the Fillmore, which, preurban renewal was a social
and cultural hub for Black residents, looms large for those in the
know.[100] In other words, *The Last Black Man* explores systemic factors
that weaken the ties that are meant to buoy us. To be sure, literal gentrification is among the forces it evokes, but literal gentrification is not as
central to the story as it may seem.

Principally, the film explores the loss of community among African
American San Franciscans, with literal gentrification as one of the
mechanisms that drives this disaggregation. Take, for instance, an interaction between Jimmie, Mont, and the older Black man who now drives
the car that Jimmie once lived in. The driver tells Jimmie, "I saw your
dad the other day. He was good and lonely. By hisself. . . . I told him you
need to get you a cat or a dog or a woman or something. . . . He's home
alone. Well, he ain't home, but he's alone. He's alone with no home." He
asks Jimmie when he last saw his father. Jimmie winces, and the pain of
family dissolution pervades the scene. This pain is underlined by the
knowledge that the two men have, at different times, each called the car
in which they ride home.

Last Black Man makes it clear that most of the characters do not have anyone or anywhere to catch them. In one scene, Jimmy says, "Where am I going to go? My dad is in the SRO. My aunt is out in bum-fuck. My mom. I don't even know where my mom is." That dispersal is not just about literal gentrification, but about the challenges that Jimmie's family has faced, from drug addiction to child abandonment, foreclosure, and racialized poverty.

We are not meant to be indifferent to this suffering. We are meant to feel the disappointment that Jimmie himself feels and to let *gentrification* convey suffering and loss; to make the viewer feel the pain of homelessness, both literal and metaphorical. Take Mont, listening attentively, to a Black sidewalk singer, who sings the 1970s anthem, "If you come to San Francisco, there will be gentle people there. Gentle people will be a lovin' there . . . Summertime will be a love-in there." The canyon between that image of San Francisco and the city that Jimmie has always experienced looms painfully across the film.

Hypergentrified San Francisco circa 2019 (when the film was released) does not allow even the gentlest among us to live gently. Mont, a soft-spoken artist, bludgeons fish in a market for a living, and Jimmie cares for elderly people who do not know who he is or where they are; in other words, they do not truly *see* Jimmie. Black men of Mont and Jimmie's age in their neighborhood stand on the street and argue, taking one another on, day and night. They taunt Mont and Jimmie, and, in their absence, turn on one another. Ultimately, one member of this neighborhood chorus is shot, a casualty of their everyday conflict. Jimmie's father openly criticizes his son; berating him, for instance, for dressing "like a White boy." The White couple who inhabited Jimmie's ancestral home fight with one another and weep about the impending loss of their property, and Jimmie's father speaks to his son in biting, derisive tones. On the bus one day, Jimmie unexpectedly encounters his mother, unaware she had returned to San Francisco. She promises to call him, and Jimmie reminds her he does not have a phone. She promises to visit, but she never appears.

This San Francisco is not gentle, and nearly everyone is not only unhoused or on the brink of being so, but also permanently unmoored.

However, there are two exceptions to this disaggregation, and both involve Jimmie's intimate, Mont.

One of the most tender relationships in the film exists between Mont and his grandfather, who is blind. They share a small home in the neighborhood by the bay where the preacher warns of coming doom and displacement. Mont's grandfather urges Mont to read drafts of his plays to him, and lets Jimmie share Mont's bedroom. Mont patiently, sweetly, and even enthusiastically describes scenes that unfold in a film to his grandfather, while Mont, Jimmie, and the grandfather sit together in a small living room. Other than Mont's relationship to Jimmie, this is by far the most intimate, empathic, and supportive relationship that unfolds in the film. It is thus not a coincidence that the single stable home that Mont and Jimmie have is under Mont's grandfather's roof.

The other crucial exception, which is at the film's heart, is the love and respect that Mont and Jimmie share. Mont and Jimmie curate one another's lives and are nearly inseparable. They are immensely supportive of one another, and consistently gentle—almost always speaking in thoughtful, quiet tones. Jimmie invariably encourages Mont's art, and Mont is always by Jimmie's side as he cares for his home. The men share their most intimate thoughts and feelings with one another, and when one of them shares a feeling, experience, or idea, the other listens attentively and finds ways to support his friend. Rebecca Wanzo (2021) writes of their relationship, "The profound intimacy between Jimmie and Mont (Jonathan Majors) in *The Last Black Man* is the emotional core of the film. Their sexuality is undefined, but 'bromance' is too light a term for two men who hold each other's dreams as close as if they were their own."[101]

As Wanzo notes, the film leaves Mont and Jimmie's relationship ambiguous; as a result, it models in general terms the empathic community that is absent from most of the characters' lives. This allows the relationship to stand in for the kinds of connections many of the characters live without and might benefit from; from deep friendship, to romantic love, to supportive family. By leaving the precise nature of Mont and Jimmie's intimacy veiled, the viewer can regard it as a model that might work for most of us. This is an everyman's intimacy; it stands in as a model for deep friendship, the intimacy of lovers, and even for surrogate family.

Yet the relationship is not perfect; Mont breaks Jimmie's heart when he produces a play he penned—*The Last Black Man in San Francisco*—in the attic of Jimmie's family's house. Specifically, he breaks his heart by revealing that, despite family lore, Jimmie's grandfather did not, in fact, build the house. This not only means that he did not craft it with his own hands, but that the grandfather likely took advantage (as many others did) of the US government's interment of the Japanese during World War II to purchase a home belonging to a family whom the government displaced. Thus, Jimmie's lineage is one of both repossession (of another family's home) and dispossession (when his family ultimately lost the home in the 1990s). Jimmie's grandfather was the "first Black man in San Francisco," as characters routinely refer to him, because of the displacement of those who came before him in the Fillmore. This truth-telling leads Jimmie and Mont to separate for a time.

As this suggests, communities are heartbreakingly broken in *The Last Black Man in San Francisco*. The community that is San Francisco writ large; the Japanese American community who once populated the Fillmore; the African American community who followed; and the smaller communities that most of us call family. Trust is broken, such as when Jimmie's mother fails to call or visit; intimacy is broken, such as when friends and family deride one another. Mont studies all of this, taking notes (literally) and mimicking the conflicts he overhears, sometimes acting them out as if they are a play in front of the characters themselves.

For instance, Mont takes in, seemingly impassively, men from the neighborhood verbally attacking Jimmie saying, "You're not better than us." Talking about lace curtains and "feminine stuff up in that house." They end by saying, "Jimmie, go home!!!!" The attack stings all the more, for it is led, and fueled by information from, a friend among the group whom Mont invited to the Fillmore house. There, the friend and Jimmie reminisced about times in the group home in which they both lived as children. The three men took a sauna together, rendering this exchange all the more intimate. Later, it is this same friend who dies of gun violence; a victim of conflict on an even more severe scale.

Arguably, literal gentrification does not produce these conflicts. It is one mechanism that drives fractures, but really it is a metonym for all that separates us, even as we live side by side.

In *The Last Black Man*, *gentrification* serves to reveal fractures that damage community, rendering them obvious. Perhaps because under literal gentrification, before complete displacement—before, say, the last Black man leaves San Francisco—neighbors are side by side yet nonetheless incredibly separate from one another.[102]

Drug addiction is not produced (independently) by literal gentrification, nor is family dysfunction. Racism, historical injustices such as the internment of the Japanese and forced displacement of racial and ethnic minorities under urban renewal—all of the things that have pulled apart those who people *The Last Black Man*—are not direct products of literal gentrification. This is not to suggest, for even a moment, that literal gentrification is irrelevant to the film (or unrelated to racism and related injustices or that it does not contribute to family destabilization). Rather, it is to suggest that in *The Last Black Man*, *gentrification* is a metonym that allows the filmmakers to trace the much bigger problem of how deeply entrenched structural forces and processes produce broken, fractured community. It allows them to package the forces that conspire to render Jimmie the last Black man in San Francisco and that, ultimately, send him out to sea—rowing away from his beloved city and his beloved Mont.

Counterintuitively, *gentrification* allows the filmmakers to shine a light on this broader set of forces that cast Jimmie away from San Francisco. That is, by setting up the dilemma that Jimmie faces as related to literal gentrification, they provide a doorway into a broader set of historical and structural/economic forces that have shaped Jimmie's life and that strained his ties to his community of origin. Indeed, this is precisely what *gentrification* is a metonym for in the *Last Black Man*: structural forces that break people apart, especially the most vulnerable among us.

By the end of the film, Jimmie has been dispossessed not only of his ancestral home, but also of many of the features that make one feel at home in a place, such as family and a community of those with whom one shares interests, tastes, or outlook. Save for Mont, Jimmie is alone, and the film lets *gentrification* pull back the covers for the viewer so we can see the broad set of forces—so much bigger than any individual and so much bigger than any singular process of brick-and-mortar change—that can call one away from home, family, and community.

Conclusion

In Courtney Barnett's song "Depreston," she sings about a realtor encouraging her to look at a home in Preston, a subdivision outside of her home, Melbourne; the implication being that literal gentrification has priced Barnett out of the city. Barnett sings, "You said we should look out further/I guess it wouldn't hurt us/We don't have to be around all these coffee shops/Now we got that percolator/never made a latte greater/I'm saving $23 a week." Literal gentrification makes Barnett consider a life apart from the coffee shops she's accustomed to—a life, her song implies, of suburban isolation; indeed, it makes it seem worthy of her, albeit depressing, consideration. Who needs coffee shops and the warm, informal community popularly associated with them if you can percolate your own cup at home?[103]

As Barnett's musings illustrate, *gentrification* can be found almost anywhere in contemporary popular culture, including in art, such as in the works that this chapter features. Often, as the song and the works we've encountered in these pages reveal, cultural producers rely on *gentrification* to tell stories about community transformation, and especially community dissolution. This is a common theme in art that engages literal gentrification, but as "Depreston" suggests, it is not the only one. The next chapter, for instance, will explore how songs like Barnett's are as much about the transformation of the self—*how does one come to live in a suburban cul de sac*, Barnett essentially asks—as they are about changing places and the connections forged therein.

Still, the theme that this chapter traces is prevalent. Indeed, we have seen how *gentrification* is used in a range of art forms as a metonym for how and why communities, particularly those that emerge among people who share a defining trait and reside together in urban space, are at the mercy of structural forces. By situating stories of community change in specific physical locales that are under threat, such as an Italian enclave; a triple decker; a taqueria in a Latinx neighborhood; a family home in a historically Black neighborhood, these works underline the fragility of place-based community and attribute that fragility to political-economic forces. In the cases I've highlighted here, they use *gentrification* as a metonym or a shorthand for those political-economic forces that threaten to alter or obliterate community.

This chapter reveals some of the promise and some of the peril of turning to *gentrification* in accounts of community change. *Gentrification* allows cultural producers to powerfully gesture to structural explanations for within-group changes, including those that extend well beyond brick-and-mortar gentrification. *Gentrification* is also highly evocative of place and thus underlines how community emerges from and gives meaning to the places in which it grows. Given how *gentrification* signals disruption, its usage reminds us of the fragility of any community. Finally, given how evocative and politicized literal gentrification is, deploying the term in this manner has the potential to engender mobilization on behalf of communities.

On the other hand, in some cases, relying on *gentrification* in this way could allow audiences to miss the complex ways in which structure gets into all of us. We have seen this in the works featuring Boston that I have highlighted. The works are right to suggest that, for the most part, things "out there," even if they are not reducible to literal gentrification, produce change and that powerful forces beyond an ordinary individual's personal control drive them, such as government policies and racialized processes of capital accumulation.

But using *gentrification* as a stand-in for a broader set of changes complicates cultural producers' ability to pinpoint the precise policies and structural conditions that threaten community, as well as to acknowledge how the individuals who comprise a community are intermediaries between structural forces and changed social ties. While ordinary urban dwellers did not create suburbanization, urban renewal, and changed opportunity structures for White ethnic urbanites, many *did* respond to them. And that response, however incrementally, contributed to the transformation of the communities that these works mourn.

It is likely not an accident that the two works that prominently feature racial minorities go one step further toward acknowledging how the individuals who compose a community sometimes respond to structural conditions in a manner that has implications for their social ties. One takes a deeper dive into how *gentrification* is a metonym for changes in opportunity structures within a social group that influence ties and weaken a sense of connection (*Gentefied*). The other considers how structural forces (including but not limited to literal gentrification) and enduring inequalities shape the units that compose a broader, place-based community, from the individual to the family to the neighborhood (*Last Black Man*). Here, an abiding awareness of how social structures and inequalities shape both the self and the group influence how cultural producers deploy *gentrification* in narratives of community.

In the end, though, these four works are more similar than different. They rely on *gentrification* to tell stories about community transformation, but they are not *really* or *only* about literal gentrification. In some instances, they call us away from a more robust interrogation of how decades of urban transformations, such as suburbanization, urban renewal, White flight, and ghettoization shaped ties. In others, they evoke that long litany of structural transformations, encapsulating them with the term *gentrification*.

Thus, this chapter serves, in a sense, as a cautionary tale of its own kind. Given its visibility and resonance, cultural producers may evoke literal gentrification when, in actuality, they mean to conjure the broader idea that financial and political forces and the social inequalities that they produce influence the lives of individuals and of the groups that they compose. *Gentrification* is a powerful shorthand for communicating how structure impacts our most intimate and meaningful connections.

Yet I caution that we do not want to let *gentrification* stand in for structurally driven change writ large, especially when, after all, literal gentrification would not exist without some of the earlier changes that I have called our attention to in this chapter (e.g., suburbanization, urban renewal, and White flight).

I also caution that, in some instances, using *gentrification* in this manner risks losing the opportunity to acknowledge the role that any of us plays in community change. This is particularly the case when one's racial and economic privilege gives one the mobility to walk away from community in search of new opportunities—even a community that one might highly value.

And, of course, we ought to be cautious about the nostalgia for communities of the past that we see in the Boston cases, as this often covers over the ways in which any community can be constraining, a site of conflict, or exclusionary. For instance, it would be unreasonable to expect that a gay man or a transgender woman who grew up in the mid-century North End would have the same experience of community as their heterosexual and cisgender peers. Likewise, not every triple-decker living room or Fillmore Victorian sheltered warm, welcoming, and supportive family connections. Looked at uncritically, it is easy to let community communicate only positive associations and to present itself as safely outside the bounds of capitalism; a point made, fifty years ago, by the esteemed cultural analyst Raymond Williams.[104] Clearly, these positive associations and the notion of community as something harmed by capitalist forces (read: *gentrification*) endure.

More than anything, this chapter suggests that we ought to read art and academic texts alike with an eye for how some use *gentrification* as a catchall for structurally produced change and related inequalities. I have relied on works that feature community change to highlight this point, but we need not stop there. There are numerous instances in which *gentrification* evokes a broader set of structural forces and associated problems; this chapter has provided a window into how some rely on *gentrification* to explore and explain the transformation of communities rooted in place and united by shared identity.

3

The "Gentrification" of the Self

THIS CHAPTER engages with parables of the "gentrification" of the self; it analyzes books, including fiction and memoir, a television series, and a film that set stories of transforming individuals against the backdrop of literal gentrification. Despite differences in medium and genre and in the characters they feature, from a Black Harlem playwright to a queer Latinx executive in Los Angeles and a bisexual woman in Portland, Oregon, each cultural object provides a cautionary tale about what is lost when an individual "gentrifies" or becomes more upscale, rarified, or mainstream.

I propose that we think of these stories as parables of the "gentrification" of the self. Across a diverse set of cultural objects, I find a common moral arc that spotlights problems associated with personal upward mobility and of becoming more aligned with the elite or with those with outsized economic and cultural influence. In these parables, individuals grapple with how their personal "gentrification" separates them from natal ties, supportive communities, and a more "authentic" self. It is the persistent presence of a moral arc that moves in a repeating direction that prompts me to categorize these metaphors of *gentrification* as parables.

While their creators may not have explicitly intended them to be so, I propose that we think of these parables as expansions of Sarah Schulman's notion of the "gentrification of the mind," which she describes as "an internal replacement that alienated people from the concrete process of social and artistic change" (2012,14). Schulman offers a powerful argument about how the tragedy of the AIDS pandemic (the disease itself and the homophobia that stalled governmental response, leading to mass death) and literal gentrification produced a "gentrified" mentality that replaced creative, experimental, and activist frames of mind among queer artists in New York.[1] In Schulman's powerful rendering, marginalized individuals increasingly seek security, and, as a result, experience a kind of spiritual and philosophical "gentrification," becoming mainstream, dumbed-down, and self-interested versions of what they otherwise would have been.

The works in this chapter tell stories that are in line with Schulman's argument in two ways. First, some, especially those that explore "gentrifying" sexual personhood, are, like Schulman, attentive to how the manner in which their subjects regard the world and perceive of their place in it has changed. Second, this chapter features cultural objects that, like the rest of my archive, follow Schulman by relying on *gentrification* as a metaphor to capture change. Indeed, Schulman (2012) relies on the metaphor of *gentrification* abundantly; she suggests that literature has "gentrified" as has the "art world" (104), gay politics (111), specific publications (117), and even "happiness" (161). Indeed, Schulman's brilliant 2012 book may have helped to open the door not only for the representations of "gentrified" selves that this chapter attends to, but for the broader reliance on *gentrification* as a metaphor to which this book attends.

However, by attending less specifically to a "gentrified" mentality and more broadly to their subjects' "gentrified" social position, whether that positionality relates to class, racial, or sexual identity, these works can be read as extending Schulman's thesis, presenting not just "gentrified" minds or ways of perceiving of the world, but "gentrified" people. As an assemblage, the works consider how facets of personhood, from economic position to modes of sexuality and to racial identification and affiliation, transform, changing where their subjects live, how they dress, how they relate to those around them, and how they locate themselves in the broader social order. Crucially, they all depict characters who at least contemplate transforming their lives to achieve access to resources that have, traditionally, been sequestered by others. In short, the works offer fully formed portraits of "gentrified" personhood; personhoods that, in many cases, are at least partially characterized by what Schulman terms the "gentrification of the mind" (2012).

While the cultural objects this chapter features rely on literal gentrification to drive plotlines, the parables they offer are, like so much that I explore in this book, not *really* about *urban* upscaling (although they do reveal insights about how cultural producers frame literal gentrification). Rather, they engage literal gentrification because it mirrors their true message, which spotlights the risks of the "gentrification" of the self or of seeking status, resources, and security traditionally possessed by members of a different social group. Within these parables, this chapter argues, *gentrification* operates as both a metaphor and a metonym for personal "upscaling." More often than not, cultural producers position such personal upscaling as either morally problematic or as producing feelings of loss akin to those we encountered in chapters 1 and 2, often by isolating an individual from community.

The stories that these TV series, films, and books present of how individuals change are related, of course, to age-old narratives about how people change as we age. However, the themes of individual "gentrification" that this chapter highlights are nonetheless distinct from the dominant narrative of that change.

Many readers will be familiar with the idea that one becomes more mainstream at midlife. Some (at least those my age or older) might recall 1980s television shows and films on this theme, such as *Thirtysomething* and *The Big Chill*. They grappled with the surprise and sorrow that some White, upper-middle-class boomers felt as they settled into parenthood, marriage, and professional careers, leaving them wistful for their carefree youth characterized, so the story goes, by drugs, alcohol, artistic expression, sexual freedom, and progressive politics.

I remember feeling relieved for my parents as I watched these shows in our back-to-the-land passive-solar house in western Massachusetts. I imagined that, somehow, they had made it to the 1980s with their 1970s values intact—evidenced by the slew of bumper stickers on their cars, a kitchen stocked with co-op fare, the protests that my sisters and I attended with our mother, and my father's frustration when Reagan-era War on Drugs helicopters scoured neighboring acreage for pot groves.

The television shows and films that I watched as a child told me that my parents had achieved a rare accomplishment; most of us, they instructed, change as we age, and we tend to age in the same direction (toward status and conservativism). Put differently, we might say that the expectation of those classic 1980s films and television series is that most of "us" eventually "suburbanize." Here, I self-consciously deploy "suburbanization" as a metaphor for personal change, borrowing from the playbook of the cultural producers whom this chapter features who rely on "gentrification" in a similar manner.

Yet the parable that the books, TV series, and film that I capture in this chapter present is not the same that we find in *Thirtysomething*. While it is about how individuals transform, it is not the story of a White, suburban, upper-middle class man who inevitably settles down and becomes more conservative, finding himself either wistful for or embarrassed by his wilder youth. Instead, this chapter charts a cousin of that narrative; one that sees personal transformation not as inevitable, but, as with literal gentrification, either as a gamble that some, *especially those who have traditionally had limited resources*, make to acquire opportunity and security, or as a transformation that they are compelled to make alongside others like them as the social position of their group changes, such as when sexual minorities acquire new rights or as barriers to education and employment recede (at least some) for members of a racial or ethnic minority group.

Several of the works this chapter highlights imply that some individuals speculate on the self, taking a chance that, with sweat equity, their personal value, like a house in an as-yet-ungentrified neighborhood, will appreciate with time. In this sense, the characters they present are model neoliberal subjects who, in the context of a political and economic system that calls on the individual to establish their own security and mobility, labor to "gentrify" themselves. By telling these stories, I argue that such works (often quite unintentionally, I suspect) can be read as holding upwardly mobile individuals morally liable for their "gentrification," rather than the systems that render such transformation a personal responsibility and that sequester opportunity and privilege in specific places (e.g., in Manhattan but not in Brownsville) and among specific social groups (e.g., with heterosexuals and not among LGBTQIA+ people).[2]

Borrowing a page from the cultural producers this chapter features, we can think of the middle-class White man who morphs, at middle age, into someone who golfs and whose politics edge rightward as a story of the "suburbanization" of the self. Such accounts present an image of how some settle into or become at home in their privilege. In subtle contrast, stories of the "gentrification" of the self point to how, with age, some labor to become more resourced, mainstream, and "respectable," and, as a result, become less creative and free, separating them from their community of origin, whether that community was forged around shared race, class, or sexuality.[3] If, in our dominant cultural scripts, "suburbanization" is something that just "happens" to some (privileged) people, or something that some eventually cede to, cultural producers present the "gentrification" of the self as, instead, something that certain people or groups *work* for, only to find they've gambled away meaningful ways of being and of connecting with others.

In my archive, stories of the "gentrification" of the self feature those who, historically, have had far fewer resources and opportunities than the White, cisgender, heterosexual dad I conjure above. These include LGBTQIA+ individuals, racial minorities, and women. Indeed, nearly all of the accounts that comprise the archive of parables of the "gentrification" of the self that I have compiled, and all of those that this chapter features, highlight queer individuals and/or women of color.

This is not a coincidence. For such individuals, enduring structural inequalities mean that settling into privilege in the manner of a White, middle-aged man who joins a country club is rarely an option. Parables of the "gentrification" of the self do not present personal upscaling as inevitable in the manner of the once-progressive dad who, despite the best of intentions, now golfs and keeps a watchful eye on his investment portfolio. Rather, they position the "gentrification" of the self as an accomplishment, one that requires labor and intentionality, either on the part of the individual or of the social group to which they belong (e.g., queer women who lobbied for marriage equality).

Why present the accrual of resources as voluntary when the person accruing them is a woman and a racial and sexual minority, and not simply as the inevitable path one takes in a capitalist society (cue the regretful upper-middle-class adults in *Thirtysomething* and *The Big Chill*)? What message do such parables convey by presenting personal "gentrification" as a choice, and personal "suburbanization" as inevitable? Above all, to varying degrees these parables present personal "gentrification" as intentional and thus as a process of transformation that one may opt in or out of or that a group, such as sexual minorities, might have opted in or out of. Building from this starting assumption, parables of the "gentrification" of the self may call subjects who have traditionally had fewer resources or reduced access to the mainstream to consider the moral implications and unintended consequences of opting to pursue personal upscaling.

Underlying parables of the "gentrification" of the self are anxieties about group belonging and membership that some experience—not only as the result of individual change but also, as we have seen in chapter 2, as historically marginalized groups (e.g., certain immigrant groups and some sexual minorities) achieve new access and opportunities. They engage weighty questions that circulate in contemporary culture, such as what is lost and what is gained as members of a group that once depended on one another for survival achieve new privileges and freedoms, including greater access to the mainstream. Am I still *me* if I achieve new opportunities? Can I still come home to my family and neighborhood of origin if I "gentrify"? How do I seek status and security without "gentrifying" core facets of myself?

Parables of the "gentrification" of the self also risk feeding an alternate anxiety, one that some in society hold about marginalized individuals' upward mobility. Specifically, parables of personal "gentrification" risk feeding cultural ambivalence about what it means for those who were once marginal to acquire newfound status, capital, and security. While some celebrate such achievements, others take a darker view. Essentially, they ask: What does it mean for "us" (those in power) when "they" (those who have traditionally had little power) enter the gentry?[4]

According to Ruth Glass's original definition, two core attributes of literal gentrification are the displacement of working-class residents and the in-movement of affluent newcomers. Parables of the "gentrification" of the self similarly present the changed self as having displaced an earlier and more "authentic" version of a person; a version of the self that was deeply embedded in communities composed of those with whom one shared a core identity trait, whether working-class Latinx neighbors or a lesbian social group. The parables also caution that when one "gentrifies," a spiffier, more mainstream, and, often, a more self-focused alternative comes to replace an original and more "authentic" and "ungentrified" version of the self.

Novels, TV series, and films do not explore the "gentrification" of the self in a singular manner. Some present stories of the "gentrification" of the sexual self, while others focus on economic "gentrification" or how a person changes as they acquire economic resources and the cultural capital that often facilitates economic mobility.[5] Still others aim to capture what we might think of as racial "gentrification," or efforts by racial minorities to secure resources traditionally sequestered by White individuals and to gain entrée into spheres of life that are typically White-dominated, whether certain professions or neighborhoods.[6] Thus, cultural producers rely on "gentrification" as a metonym to grapple with how specific dimensions of the self—whether sexual, economic, or racial—become more upscale or more aligned with the elite. The stories they tell rely on this metonym to offer parables of personal transformation that highlight the consequences of those changes not only for the changed, but for those around them, too.

Of course, as humans we are each multifaceted and our experiences as members of racial, economic, sexual, or other groups interact and intersect to shape how the world views and approaches us and how we view and approach the world.[7] However, as we will see, each of the cultural objects that this chapter features, whether a book, TV series, or a film, highlight a *specific* facet of the changing self, spotlighting how one's economic position, cultural capital, or racial or sexual identity changes. This singular lens surely oversimplifies reality, turning away, in most cases, from a more intersectional approach to thinking about identity that recognizes how a personal identity *and* one's social position emerge from intersecting personal attributes whose meaning and significance vary with context.[8] Nonetheless, at least in my archive, this is how cultural producers present parables of the "gentrification" of the self: they spotlight how one part of the self acquires access to resources and privileges that are usually found elsewhere or sequestered by others, and, in essence, upscales and becomes more mainstream.

There is one other source of heterogeneity in the narratives that I engage below, and that pertains to the degree to which cultural producers emphasize structure versus agency in their accounts of personal "gentrification." More explicitly than other works, those that present the "gentrification" of the sexual self tend to contextualize that "gentrification" in an evolving social, legal, and political context that impacts more than just the individuals at the center of each author's parable. They suggest that other sexual minorities and broader sexual cultures are changing in parallel with the "gentrifying" primary character (in response to how the world around them has changed, too). Still, perhaps quite unintentionally, by centering a primary subject's "gentrification," rather than narratives of group transformation, they join the other cultural objects that the chapter engages in presenting "gentrification" as a personal responsibility.

By writing this chapter, am I exacerbating the tendency to use *gentrification* as a metaphor to describe the upscaling of that which is not brick-and-mortar gentrification? Might I even, quite unintentionally, risk mimicking some of the cultural producers whom this book engages, who use *gentrification* as a metaphor, even when they aim to make a point that has little to do with literal gentrification? On one level, one could read this chapter in that manner; after all, by offering a reading of these cultural objects as relying on *gentrification* to comment on the upscaling of traditionally marginalized actors, I am myself, in a sense, using *gentrification* to call for critical reflection on such representations of personal transformation. However, I offer this reading because I believe that the objects I engage here call for cultural receivers (Griswold 1986) to interpret them in this manner. Why do I find this to be true? The cultural producers whom this chapter engages leave a multitude of signposts that signal the availability of *gentrification* as a lens through which to regard their primary characters. These signposts can be found in dialogue, conflict between characters, and, above all, in the prominence of literal gentrification as the backdrop against which dialogue, interaction, and plot unfold. My close reading suggests that these works emphasize parallels between the gentrifying settings in which they locate their plots and the "gentrifying" subjects embedded in their landscapes. Based on these signals, I offer readers an argument about how some cultural producers rely on *gentrification* to present moral lessons about the risks of personal upscaling.

I begin the chapter with the novels and memoirs that called me to recognize the abundance of parables of the "gentrification" of the self, before turning to television and film. The books with which the chapter opens feature LBQ+ individuals whose *sexual* selves gentrify over time; the books depict them as distancing themselves from sexual freedom and experimentation, becoming more conventional. We might say that, like city neighborhoods that have undergone literal gentrification, these characters become more "refined" or "respectable" in their sexual deportment. Later, I explore economic "gentrification" as presented in the TV series *Vida*, followed by the "gentrification" of the racial identity of a Black woman artist as it unfolds in the film, the *Forty-Year-Old Version*.

We will see, again and again, that parables of the "gentrification" of the self rest on the dubious notion that one possesses a singular and unambiguously "authentic" self and that upscaling threatens that "authenticity" (or the notion of a "true" or entirely sincere self).[9] Personally, I am just as skeptical of the notion of individual "authenticity" as I am of the idea that any neighborhood has a singular "authenticity" rooted in a specific decade or social group (that can be spoiled by literal gentrification). People, like neighborhoods, are constantly evolving, and their evolution occurs in relationship to broad forces that extend beyond any individual. This is not a normative claim. I do not mean to argue that, by definition, all change (whether personal or urban) is good or even neutral. Nor do I aim to deny how neoliberalism, racism, sexism, classism, and homophobia put pressure on individuals to change.

Instead, I zero in on narratives of the "gentrification" of the self to reveal how certain cultural objects individualize what it means to adapt to structural conditions, and present some adaptations as morally dubious.

More often than not, people change together as the world around them changes, too. Yet parables of the "gentrification" of the self vary in the degree to which they acknowledge this. Some acknowledge how personal "gentrification" arises in relationship to changing social context but nonetheless mourn the loss of "authenticity" associated with individual transformation. Still, by representing how people adapt to changing social context by centering an individual's evolution, they risk presenting that transformation as an individual choice. Others more explicitly present personal "gentrification" in this manner—that is, as an individual choice—and therefore as avoidable. In so doing, they imply that literal gentrification is itself a discrete, individual-driven process that could be stopped rather than one that is embedded in broad systems of corporate capitalism and neoliberal governance. Often, we blame the couple who renovate a nineteenth-century rowhouse and not the historic preservation tax credits that encourage such endeavors.[10] Or we place the onus for literal gentrification on the highly educated individual who purchases a derelict house in a working-class neighborhood, without situating that choice in the context of federal interest rates that make purchasing in an already gentrified neighborhood prohibitive. Thus, in the pages to come we will encounter insights about how cultural producers frame not only personal evolution, but also literal gentrification, as an individually-driven endeavor.

The "Gentrification" of Sexuality

I began to take note of parables of the "gentrification" of the self in a small class of memoirs and novels that capture the lives of LBQ+ individuals in specific times (typically the 1970s and the 1990s) and places, such as New York's East Village, San Francisco's Mission District, Portland, Oregon, and Provincetown, Massachusetts. Written across a span of three decades, these books conjure a time when such places were less gentrified than they are today, and they present moral tales that empha-size what is lost when members of a social group encounter opportuni-ties they were once denied and, in pursuing them, come to "gentrify."

They first caught my attention because of the prominent role of literal gentrification in the texts; they are rife with nostalgia for un- or less-gentrified cities. However, the more I read, the more I recognized that the books weren't really or truly centering nostalgia for (ungentri-fied) *cities*. Instead, ungentrified cities mirror and elevate portraits of "ungentrified" people—all of whom, in my archive, are gender or sexual minorities, and most of whom, like many of the commemora-tors whom we met in chapter 1, are queer women. By presenting these portraits, they mark how people have transformed, underlining the moral consequences, for individuals and communities, of such transformation.

Consider a novel by Andrea Lawlor, *Paul Takes the Form of a Mortal Girl*, which offers an ambitious tour of lost people and places of the 1990s. Published in 2017, the book features Paul—or Polly, as they are sometimes known—as they traverse a set of queer-friendly US cities and towns, including Iowa City, San Francisco, New York, and Provinc-etown. Paul, who is in their early twenties, is a shapeshifter who can change their anatomical sex and gender presentation at will. They are Polly in Provincetown and at the Michigan Womyn's Music Festival; Paul in New York; and both Paul and Polly at different moments in Iowa City. In different forms, Paul/Polly pursues romantic and sexual en-tanglements, all against the backdrop of rough-around-the-edges cities and tumbledown towns—each of which has become far more gentrified in the decades since the 1990s. While the book highlights the character of such places in the 1990s, when, Lawlor implies, they were more humble and more fun, it also provides a tour of a mode of sexuality that Lawlor suggests thrived in those places in that period: one that is pro-miscuous, edgy, and pleasure-seeking.[11] Polly has sex with a new acquaintance in a tent in Michigan; Paul has sex with men in San Fran-cisco bars; Polly has sex with a girlfriend in the Provincetown apartment that she shares with a gaggle of other lesbians, and with another woman in a Provincetown coffee shop bathroom.

Published in 2017, *Paul* provides the contemporary reader with a portrait of how people and places have changed in sync with one another. Indeed, Lawlor writes of Paul/Polly's experience at Michigan: "*Paul felt like a time traveler, a tourist at a gay reenactment—Hidden-from-History Town*" (2017, 84; my emphasis). Having Paul time travel to ungentrified cities and events of the 1990s presents how refreshingly "ungentrified" Paul/Polly is.

As with other texts of its kind, in *Paul* ungentrified cities and "ungentrified" characters reflect and reinforce one another. Lawlor writes, "He thought about the smell of piss baking on the August streets of the East Village. He imagined drinking Patti Smith's piss, then Robert Mapplethorpe's. Then Jean Genet's. Then River Phoenix's." To remind us that both Paul and the city are ungentrified, at the book's very close Lawlor writes: "[Paul] saw the city, as good-smelling and various as himself" (2017, 354).

Books like Lawlor's call out nostalgia for cities that were demographically, culturally, economically, and aesthetically heterogeneous, and even for places that smelled of piss. As we will soon see, Lawlor enters a venerable tradition. Take the poet and memoirist Eileen Myles, writing nostalgically of New York's Chelsea in the 1970s: "Urban nothing—I liked it so much. . . . The summer of three dyke bars in the West Village. We were rich. This one looked like a Chinese restaurant. Several stars were twinkling outside. The bartender waved. I owed her money. We went downstairs" (1994, 259). Here, the city is a vessel of memory, and by revisiting it we encounter lost cities but also lost ways of being, or earlier and more "authentic" sexual selves (versions of the self that, the text implies, we ought to mourn). Lest we doubt that Myles is writing as much about lost ways of being as a person as they are writing about a foregone Chelsea, consider that they write: "I thought 'it is so artificial/so dark and so beautiful' referred to New York. Now it strikes me that I was talking about my life" (1994, 123).

Such texts call out nostalgia for those like Paul/Polly and the pleasure-seeking queer lifestyle they embody. Most readers will recognize that the San Francisco abundant with cheap apartments with a rotating cast of queer roommates, the Provincetown full of penniless, lesbian co-ops, and a Lower Manhattan "rich" with dyke bars no longer exist; not only have those places (literally) gentrified, gender and sexual minorities navigate a transformed identity landscape marked by new opportunities, such as legally recognized marriage.[12] By suggesting that we were once rich, they imply that we are now poor.

Paul Takes the Form of a Mortal Girl is part of a (small) genre of books from my archive that entangle nostalgia for ungentrified cities and for what, on my read, the authors present as "ungentrified" sexual selves. They mark and mourn a turn toward homonormativity—the idea that sexual minorities increasingly adopt mainstream, normative approaches to sexuality.[13] Homonormativity changed what it is to be LGBTQIA+, centering monogamy, marriage, child rearing, and a kind of all-around middle-class respectability.[14] They present this turn to homonormativity as a kind of "gentrification" of sexual personhood that has consequences for cities and people alike (see Schulman 2012).

Such texts recognize that individual LGBTQIA+ subjects changed alongside others like them and in concert with a changed social, cultural, and legal landscape for many gender and sexual minorities. That is, the characters that they present changed as same-sex marriage became legal; as new avenues for same-sex adoption and parenting arose; and as some sexual and gender minorities gained newfound access to economic, professional, and social opportunities.

Despite recognition of the systemic origins of personal sexual "gentrification," such texts are so wistful for "ungentrified" sexual subjects that they imply the virtue of resisting such personal transformation. Regardless of whether they present personal "gentrification" as compulsory, they present it as extremely costly.

If it seems like there is a tension between accounts of structural change and personal agency in these works, it is because I believe there is. Parables of the "gentrification" of the sexual self at once gesture to the historical and structural roots of this "gentrification" and imply that it is an individual's moral or ethical responsibility to resist upscaling and mainstreaming. I suspect that the cultural producers whom this chapter features do not intend to cast blame at their protagonists. However, they face a dilemma common to many works that articulate nostalgia for how things used to be: how to express yearning for the way things were, without casting stones at emblems of change, in this case at the "gentrified" characters their works present?[15]

Paul Takes the Form of a Mortal Girl introduced me to a world of texts that mourns the Paul/Pollys of earlier decades, in part by portraying them as synonymous with the rough-around-the-edges ungentrified places where they lived. Their stories of how places have changed—how they have literally gentrified—convey how what it means to be a gender or sexual minority has "gentrified" too (Schulman 2012). "Gentrification" here operates as a metonym for the transformation of a person, group, or object to a more elite or mainstream version. If cities are becoming like suburbs, then people who "gentrify" have more and more in common with a White, cisgender, heterosexual suburbanite.

Situating Sexual "Gentrification"

Many such books feature the 1990s. This is not a coincidence. Scholars present the 1990s as the beginning of the end of an era that began in the 1960s, which was marked by sexual liberation, expanding LGBTQIA+ identities, and increasingly visible gayborhoods.[16] In the latter half of the twentieth century, the city was thought to constitute a queer refuge from suburban norms.[17] For as long as sociologists have written of cities, they have noted the artist bohemias and the sexual freedoms that they fostered for same-sex and opposite-sex couples alike.[18] However, this association became increasingly evident after the Stonewall riots, and the broader sexual revolution of the 1960s and 1970s, and as gay neighborhoods and their lesbian equivalents became increasingly visible and, in some cases, formally demarcated.[19]

For the latter half of the twentieth century, queer individuals flourished in urban settings, fueled by the hallmarks of urbanity: density, anonymity, and heterogeneity (Wirth 1938), as well as by affordability that allowed queer writers and artists to concentrate in cities (Schulman 2012). The 1990s were the last moment before many cities tipped unambiguously into the hands of literal gentrification, rendering many cities less affordable. Rudy Giuliani was revamping Times Square into a sanitized tourist destination, and San Francisco was on the cusp of a tech invasion.[20]

However, literal gentrification is not the only reason why the authors I engage below present the 1990s as the end of an era. For much of the 1990s, gay marriage and other LGBTQ rights movement victories had not yet fully arrived.[21] The 1990s were situated just before a rapid expansion of LGBTQIA+ rights and opportunities, which facilitated the concomitant rise of gay marriage and increased emphasis on monogamy, child rearing, and respectability politics.[22] In the span of my own early adulthood, I would go from a 1990s world in which Lesbian Avengers offered fire-eating demonstrations on my college campus (Smith, in Northampton, Massachusetts), clad in combat boots and dark jeans, to one in which, as we approached thirty, most of the LBQT+ people with whom I attended college were weighing whether to have children, buying starter homes with partners, and attending weddings in states in which same-sex marriage was legal. Thus these books take us back to the last moment before cities and mainstream LGBTQIA+ politics fundamentally altered.

Authors such as Jay Orne (2020) and Sarah Schulman (2012) argue that in the twenty-first century, hubs of queer life "suburbanized." Schulman depicts an urban world in which more and more individuals are compelled to distance themselves from the arts, radical queer politics, and sexual freedoms, embracing stability in the form of degrees, professionalization, and marriage.[23]

To understand why some draw parallels between literal gentrification and what some cultural producers present as sexual "gentrification," we have to consider how *gentrification* is, in some individuals' viewpoints, tantamount to "suburbanization." Paradoxically, literal gentrification, a process that many believe originated in a rejection of suburban aspirations (Glass 1964)—when the children of midcentury suburbia eschewed their parents' white-picket dreams—led to what some regard as a "suburbanization" of the city, as baby boomers flocked to the city and remade it in their own image (Schulman 2012). Specifically, urban neighborhoods that were once working class and, often, populated by racial and ethnic minorities, came to host increasing numbers of White, upper-middle-class households (many of which were constituted by heterosexual couples and, sometimes, their children). With these de-mographic changes, institutions, from schools to businesses, trans-formed to meet upper-middle-class tastes and expectations.[24]

As a sign of the resonance of 1990s nostalgia, in June 2022 many flocked to a San Francisco exhibit, *We Were Renegades*, of photographs by Chloe Sherman featuring LBQT+ residents of San Francisco's Mis-sion neighborhood in the 1990s. Journalistic accounts of the exhibit crackle with nostalgia for an earlier sexual personhood situated in un-gentrified San Francisco before the city underwent intensive gentrifica-tion and before a broadscale shift in sexual identities and communities occurred.[25] In contrast to the works this chapter features, journalistic accounts of the exhibit offer an explicit causal argument about why "un-gentrified" sexuality flourished in certain 1990s urban neighborhoods. One article, by Kristina Feliciano (based on a conversation with the photographer), casts a portrait of the neighborhood in the 1990s.[26] Sherman suggests that cheap housing allowed for experimentation and institutional density (e.g., dyke-oriented bars, cafes, and bookstores), which, in turn, helped LBQT+ residents establish a rich set of ties. Sher-man recalls of the 1990s: "Housing was cheap, and the low rent allowed for youth, outcasts, risk takers, artists, and free spirits to move to the city from across the country and the world. They had time to be creative and experimental, and it was a vibrant and dynamic era. . . . The queer scene arose from this energy."[27]

This queer scene is depicted in portraits; they capture butch/femme couples canoodling at bars and on a picnic blanket at Dolores Park; dykes with their bikes or motorcycles; a crowd in tank tops and leather pants headed to Folsom Street Fair. Universally, those depicted are young— easily under thirty—and appear in their finest thrift store apparel. The exhibit and the crowds it drew indicate the perception that a tidal shift has occurred since the 1990s. The 1990s serve as an anchor point for nos-talgia for LBQT+ individuals, for it was, definitively, a time when cities and the sexual and gender minorities that they housed were different than they are today; the 1990s were the last moment before cities and the sexual minority communities they housed were poised to change.

In other words, the title of Sherman's exhibit, *When We Were Renegades*, doesn't just gesture to youth writ large, but to a period when sexual identity and difference meant something different for many LBQT+ individuals than it does today; and when sexual identity and difference were more salient. Talking about how places like the Mission were different in the 1990s than they are today is a way of talking about how *what it means to be a gender or sexual minority is different today than it was then*. Specifically, it is a way of talking about the belief that LBQT+ individuals have experienced a "gentrification" of the sexual self. This is largely why, as we will see below, so many accounts of sexual "gentrification" feature 1990s cities.

Sexual "Gentrification" in Fiction and Memoir

Chelsea Johnson's novel *Stray City*, set in 1990s Portland, Oregon, provides ample opportunity for the reader to recognize how the gentrified city and the "gentrified" self mirror one another.

The book features Andrea Morales, a transplant from Nebraska, who settles in Portland after dropping out of college. The reader learns that Andrea left college after her devout Catholic parents cut her off financially when they discovered she had a girlfriend. Affordable and LGBTQIA+-friendly Portland becomes Andrea's refuge.

Andrea makes ends meet by sharing a rundown apartment with a friend and holding part-time jobs at a vintage furniture shop and a record store. In her spare time, she makes art, spends time with a group of lesbian friends that refers to itself as "the family," adopts a cat and dog, and engages in activism with a collective of artist-activists that she characterizes as the "Lesbian Mafia."

Andrea's visage is featured in her ex-girlfriend's lesbian photography exhibit, and on weekends she sees friends' bands play. Her life centers not around money or work or school, but, instead, around art, friendship, community, and, sometimes, sex and romance.

Johnson writes, in Andrea's voice, of how Portland (in the 1990s) and the protagonist (in her twenties) matched one another:

> Portland in the nineties was a lot like me: Broke, struggling with un-employment, mostly white, mostly hopeful even though there was no real change in sight. For all the drive-through espresso stands and downtown restoration, the new paint on aged bungalows and vintage glasses on young women, it was still an old industrial river town in a remote corner of the country. Hard to get to. Hard to leave (Johnson 2018, 1).

In case the reader has missed the parallels between Andrea Morales and the city where she lives, Johnson writes, "The town matched something in me. . . . I loved the slightly ruined quality of everything—the rusted joints, the mossy edges" (2018, 1). This is a world in which little has been oiled, buffed, or rehabbed to suit San Francisco tastes. The reader is meant to see Andrea as akin to the old bungalow in an ungentrified neighborhood in which she lives; she hasn't been cleaned up or carefully maintained or curated for an upper-middle-class audience. The book does not present Andrea as in need of any kind of renovation; instead, Johnson writes of 1990s Morales and her 1990s city with considerable nostalgia.

The book follows Andrea over more than a decade, as she slowly sheds her own rusted joints and mossy edges, eventually acquiring a degree and a professional position as well as a child and, later, a wife. Although the book provides a detailed portrait of the city pre-gentrification, Johnson's nostalgia is not principally for rough-around-the-edges Portland at the close of the twentieth century. Instead, it is for the rough-around-the-edges person whom Andrea constituted in that period, and, more specifi-cally, for the sexual identity, and the community of others who shared it, that she possessed. In this narrative, anxiety is not that Andrea or her city will decline, but, instead, that they will upscale and lose some of the char-acter and originality that made both Portland and Andrea distinctive in the 1990s. It is that rehabbing that is the moral problem at the center of this parable of the "gentrification" of the self.

Andrea's way of thinking about her sexuality throughout most of *Stray City* is characteristic of the lesbian identity politics that was relatively dominant in the 1970s, extending into the 1980s and early 1990s and exemplified by fierce gender and sexual boundaries (i.e., strong stigmas against cavorting with men and therefore against bisexuality, and, in some instances, against transgender individuals), as well as by adherence to feminist politics.[28] The period is marked, perhaps most iconically, by the aforementioned activist group the Lesbian Avengers, who made their presence unmistakable at rallies, protests, marches, and celebratory events by chanting, before eating fire, "The fire will not consume us. We take it and make it our own" (Cogswell 2014: 2014).[29]

Stray City is peppered by nods to a way of thinking about and doing sexual identity that the Lesbian Avengers embodied. Johnson writes, "It was Queer Night, I'd made the posters, my friends' band the Gold Stars [a term, popular in the 1990s, for a lesbian who had never had sex with a man] was playing" (5), and several pages later, "It was hard for me to abide a drink bought by a man" (12). As the plot develops and Andrea falls for a man, we see her grow, slowly and painfully, away from the neat gender and sexual boundaries of the Gold Stars and of a time when she thought it only right to reject drinks purchased by a man. Johnson captures a time that was, at once, more restrictive and freer; the rules of the lesbian-feminist world Andrea belongs to are constraining, but by following them (when she did) Andrea remained at a distance from the strictures of heterosexual society, including dominant expectations about how she ought to dress, what her home should look like, and the kind of professional and financial goals she ought to pursue. Andrea is unmarried and has one-night stands; she doesn't have a college degree and she holds part-time jobs that allow time for art and impromptu afternoon swims.

When Andrea confesses to friends that she has become pregnant after secretly dating a man, a friend implies that she's a sell-out and says, in the midst of a fight, "I can't even *believe* you would do that" (178) and, later, "At least I didn't secretly fuck a man" (184). Andrea's development as a person might, for some, reveal the fragility of a community predicated on a single shared trait that members regard as immutable, but

Johnson doesn't present this strict boundary-keeping as a damning critique of lesbian identity politics.

Instead, Andrea's evolution only amplifies nostalgia for an earlier sexual-personhood. Her individual loss of an unambiguous "lesbian" identity presages changes ahead for LGBTQIA+ identity politics. Specifically, Andrea slowly loses what Johnson presents as the privilege of recognition—certainty of a shared trait—that was a cornerstone of the identity politics of the period.[30] Johnson writes, again in Andrea's voice, "I was an organizer in the Lesbian Mafia and printed art and commerce and went to shows full of girls who looked like boys and made my heart stop, and when I walked into any of these places someone knew me. Someone *knew* me. We knew each other. I've never known anything like it and won't again. To recognize someone anywhere you go. To recognize each other everywhere: the coffee shop, the sidewalk, the bicycle commute, the bookstore, the bar" (114). This recognition, which rests on the presumption of a shared, knowable trait or sameness, is what Andrea is wistful for as she becomes entangled with a man, and, later, as she and everyone around her moves away from lesbian identity politics. We are made to think that she lost this comfort of recognition, first by becoming involved with a man, and, later, as the identity politics that she and her friend group adhered to, evolved, and, finally, to the literal gentrification of Portland and the resultant scattering of queer community. Andrea eventually transforms into a married professional with a child, and, in so doing, comes to take a shape reflective of the increasingly gentrified city in which she lives.

Lest the reader doubt that nostalgia is at the center of the book, Johnson pines for "that smell of old decades. I even missed the ones I hadn't been alive for" (79). Of course, the author is nostalgic because in the 1990s change was on the horizon, both for cities like Portland and for queer people like Andrea. This is why 1990s Portland serves as a crucial touchstone for representing what has changed. Johnson writes, "In a few years vegans would become butchers, but at this point everyone was still vegetarian, and I craved the forbidden despite myself" (117). In other words, not only were places like Portland about to rapidly gentrify, but the lesbian identity politics that Andrea delighted in—until she found them too constraining as she began dating a man and, in so doing, risked community and friendship and identity—were on their way out, too.[31]

Soon, queer politics, emphasizing the fluidity of identity, hyphenated identities, as well as increasing attention to intersectionality, the rise of transgender awareness and politics, and, eventually, for some, a "post-identity politics" borne of increasing acceptance and what some might call assimilation, would take root.[32] All of these things would make existing in a bubble of (mostly) White, female-identified lesbians passé, and, as the dyke bar commemorators from chapter 1 opine, recognizably problematic.

And yet, via Andrea, Johnson communicates nostalgia for precisely that bubble and the rough-around-the-edges city that contained it. She writes of Portland's lesbian bar:

> Portland had only one lesbian bar, the Egyptian Club, which every-one called the E-Room. A scowly woman called Mom took your five bucks at the door, which I think was half to filter out the curious or unserious straights and half to keep the place alive since it was empty much of the time. It wanted to be a lesbian pleasureplex but usually felt more like a tomb. The first room had pool tables and a bar slumped with haggard old dykes (134).

Again, this nostalgia is partially rooted in the sense, encapsulated by Andrea's dalliance with a man and a resulting pregnancy, of new things on the horizon and of being situated, in time and space, on the cusp of that change. Indeed, Andrea's vantage point is that of someone who is both part of a community and the "scene" it constitutes and partially outside of it; this aids Johnson in presenting a portrait of a world that is about to change—a world that *everyone* will be outside of soon. She writes, again in Andrea's voice, of the E-Room: "We always went with equal measures of irony and hope, every six months or so—just long enough to forget that after the last time we'd sworn never to return" (Johnson 2018, 134).

Of course, the E-Room no longer exists. To explain this, literal gentrification reenters the story, as it often does in *Stray City*.

Only now that we can never return, now that the E-Room is razed and gone, a LEED-certified new Portland condo built over its ruins, do I know that those lesbians I had always mocked or turned away from, those bulldaggers and diesel dykes, those denim vests and feathered bangs, those mullets and dated glasses, eyes roaming the room, were not worst-case scenarios—they were me in another life (Johnson 2018, 135).

Here, via Andrea's voice, we catch glimpses of what her life might have been at midlife if Portland had not (literally) gentrified, if *she* had not "gentrified," and if her community of other queer women and nonbinary individuals had not "gentrified." Were it not for gay marriage and pressures to acquire degrees and health insurance, and the lesbian baby-boom, Andrea and her friends would today resemble something closer to pre-gentrification Portland, with its "cheap burritos, karaoke seven nights a week at Chopsticks III How Can Be Lounge, video rental stores with the business-sustaining porn corner behind a curtain in the back, strip clubs, dive bars that were not yet Dive Bars™, disheveled houses and cars from the 1970s and 1980s" (357).

Instead, Johnson describes Andrea at midlife gathering with her queer family for a restaurant meal; a far cry from their vegan potlucks of yesteryear:

That weekend, no one felt like cooking family dinner, so they all biked over to the new gentrified pizza place in Woodlawn where Lawrence's girlfriend, Carson, worked. She'd offered up her employee discount, which was a good thing: 'Twenty-three dollars for a pizza?' Andrea said, scanning the menu. 'North of Alberta, no less.' Her stomach turned. . . . All over town, new earth-toned paint sleeked over old wooden siding—conspicuously and deceptively neutral. Bright cedar privacy fences sprang up where chain-link and open space had left the view clear. Unruly front yards and tangled rose-bushes were shamed out by tidy mulched beds, every plant mapped and spaced. Black neighborhoods were becoming white neighborhoods and white neighborhoods were becoming rich neighborhoods. . . . Hatchbacks and hoopties gave way to strollers and

Outbacks. One corner of the Pearl warehouse where they'd mounted their queer art show now housed a coffee shop with a $10,000 espresso machine, and the rest contained a store that sold hand-tanned leather couches that cost five figures and décor gathered—no, 'curated'—from around the globe (357).

While Andrea's queer family is not among those buying curated couches, they have also developed in a manner that, as Sarah Schulman (2012) lays out, wasn't always possible (or necessary) for many LBQT+ people. By marrying, having children, acquiring higher degrees, and buying property in search of security, they have come much closer to resembling the Outback-driving, stroller-pushing gentrifiers whom Johnson describes.[33] Andrea and her friends might be appalled by $23 pizzas, and they may even have to stretch to pay for them, and yet there they are, accepting a seat at a table in the type of restaurant where they might not have been welcomed before.

Like so much else, *Stray City* is ultimately nostalgic for a time when those like Andrea did not have such a seat. And, like other books of its kind, it communicates that nostalgia by encasing a portrait of earlier identities in the context of an ungentrified (1990s) city that, like people akin to Andrea, has since transformed. This urban context helps the reader encounter and gaze at the "gentrification" of the sexual self.

Johnson is not alone in her nostalgia; neither in general nor specific terms. She joins a small chorus of others who express nostalgia for the 1990s sexual identities of LBQT+ individuals, remembered against the backdrop of ungentrified (or less gentrified) cities.

Consider Kelly Cogswell's 2014 memoir, *Eating Fire*, which at once documents her life in Manhattan in the 1990s and her activism as a founding member of the aforementioned Lesbian Avengers. In the course of capturing actions and group dynamics for the reader, Cogswell also depicts the city. Manhattan, in her rendering, is unpolished—and, in so being, sexy. She writes, for instance:

It was still broiling when we [Cogswell and her girlfriend] left, walking west to the Hudson piers where it smelled of salt and fish and rotting wood. From a distance, Lady Liberty watched over the

cruising men like a kind of saint, and blessed them as they looked for
lovers or, having found them, locked hands or mouths or hand jobs
beneath a brutal sun. There was something comforting about it. All
that faggy sexual energy, none of it directed toward us. We walked
toward the end of the water, admired the pier, and began to kiss.
Kissed some more. Sat weak-kneed down on the soft splintering
planks as the gulls screamed (59).

Here, the city, which, in the 1990s, is still a place that smells of "fish and
salt and rotting wood," is a site in which those on the sexual margins find
one another, connect, and in so doing, become their "authentic" selves.

As the book progresses, Cogswell finds the city increasingly and dis-
tressingly upscale. At the same time, she bemoans waning engagement
from within the LBQT+ population with the Lesbian Avengers'
visibility-oriented activism and declining support from outside that
population for the same. The fate of the city parallels the fate of the
brand of in-your-face visibility activism in which the Avengers engaged.
She writes, "Somebody had to remember who the streets belonged to.
Especially when they were being tidied up. All the squeegee men gone.
The homeless not housed, but shoved out of sight. The parks closed.
And the music dimmed" (Cogswell 2014, 91).

Cogswell suggests that the way people express rage, like the city itself,
was changing in the early 2000s. For instance, New York lost the spaces
of sexual freedom that Cogswell associates with her youth: "In the East
Village, the scraggly weedy lots down the block had been pimped up to
look like suburban office buildings but were actually luxury apartments
for the horribly rich. Access to the river was blocked. Pissed-off people
didn't take to the streets; they went online and shrieked at anti-Bush
sites" (209).

For a time, Cogswell follows her partner to Paris, and Cogswell finds
that she misses New York greatly. She recalls, "My god, I missed the
wilderness of New York" (84). The book of course, not only documents
the wilderness of New York but also Cogswell's own wilderness and
that, more broadly, of the Avengers. It is a first-person account of an
"ungentrified" White lesbian on the stage of an ungentrified city. She

mourns sexual and political opportunity associated with both a time of unbridled (read: "ungentrified") activism, and of the ungentrified city. The reader is called to mark the loss of the sexual and political energy of ungentrified New York, and those, like the Avengers, whom it nourished.

In Michelle Tea's *Valencia*, also a memoir, one can reach out and touch how San Francisco is about to change, and, with it, the dyke culture that rooted itself in the early 1990s Mission District (the same time and space that Chloe Sherman's aforementioned exhibit features). Tea writes of her time as part of a confederacy of 1990s Mission dykes: "We sat outside on the front stoop, a great place to sit, maybe the best in the city. You were connected to the absolute hub of 16th Street, but you sat in a dark corridor, apart, quieter, like 16th Street was this incredible secret, and *my street was the moment before you told it*" (2000, 76–77; emphasis added). Already, in 2000, when the book was published, Tea predicts the Mission's demise as a hub of dyke life and institutions: "I left this hysterical message on Ashley's machine, and she called me back right there at the bar, the Casanova, a great bar, dingy and red, the bathrooms smelling like vetiver. It's gone now. Swallowed up by the yuppies who are swiftly ruining my neighborhood" (103).

Tea's portrait of abundant one-night stands; dyke marches; the drama of encountering exes at bars; occasional sex work to make ends meet; day jobs at the sex toy company Good Vibrations and at coffee shops and bars; and of a rotating cast of roommates and of ubiquitous drugs and alcohol, is a tour of lost places and people.

Tea herself now lives in Los Angeles with her spouse and child, regularly touring to promote her books.[34] And Valencia Street is rife with upscale boutiques and expensive coffee shops and restaurants whose primary clientele is tech workers. The eponymous Valencia Street is, in essence, gone, and so too is the Tea who lived there. As with other books of its kind, the reader is meant to mourn the now-extinct Mission and the dykes who called it home. It is plausible that this book, together with those marking LBQT+ urban life in earlier decades, such as works by Eileen Myles and Audre Lorde, helped ignite the genre of nostalgic 1990s works that this chapter profiles.[35]

Other texts mention *gentrification* in passing, suggesting that the term is recognizable and powerful enough that even its brief evocation carries meaning for readers. Take, for instance, Mattilda Bernstein Sycamore's *The Freezer Door* (2020). The author frames a book, which engages themes of queer loneliness, by evoking *gentrification* on the first page. She writes, "One problem with gentrification is that it always gets worse" (9). Lest the reader think she is writing only of literal gentrification, two pages later Sycamore writes, "I remember when faggots kissed hello. We had so much to fear and so we feared nothing" (9), adding, another two pages later, "How strange to think that in the early-'90s, when it felt like everyone was dying, we were less fearful in certain ways" (13). Here, to "gentrify" is to become more fearful, cautious, and conservative, much like the gentrified city itself. Indeed, Sycamore dedicates her book to "everyone who still dreams of the city; to everyone who still dreams in the city; to everyone who still dreams." By evoking *gentrification*, she joins a chorus of others who imply that sexual and gender minorities are less and less "urban"; that fewer and fewer are dreamers; that more and more are "gentrified." The moral lesson at the heart of such a parable is that we sacrifice "authentic" human connection when we become cautious and "gentrified."

In the words of Chloe Sherman's photography exhibit, authors like Lawlor, Tea, Cogswell, Sycamore, and Johnson imply that few gender and sexual minorities are "renegades" anymore, and literal gentrification is a vehicle they use to convince us of the same. They imply that sexual minorities have themselves "gentrified," becoming less "various" (Lawlor) and "rusted" (Johnson) with time (see Schulman 2012). In so doing, they (implicitly) grapple with a central question of our times for gender and sexual minorities: What does access and acceptance cost us?[36] By asking this, more than the other cultural objects that this chapter engages, they entertain the possibility that personal "gentrification" is a strategy that some rely on to adapt to a transforming economic, cultural, and legal landscape. They suggest that recent LGBTQIA+ legal, social, and cultural victories may partially account for why some feel drawn to adapt in this manner (Schulman 2012).

But, like so much in an era of neoliberalism, by focusing on singular characters and their personal transformations, their work individualizes that process of change, making it a story of how *individuals* "gentrify," trading in "authenticity" and community for acceptance and access. And, of course, we typically don't have access to accounts of how the authors themselves may have grappled with their own opportunities to engage in (or to resist) personal "gentrification."

Put differently, there is a tension in the works I engage. On the one hand, they signal that individual "gentrification" is situated in a historical, legal, and cultural context, presenting this personal transformation, essentially, as a collective adaptation strategy. At the same time, the texts imply, to evoke Sycamore once more, that to resist trade-offs associated with this adaptation one must simply commit to keep dreaming and cease to be afraid. More than anything else, they offer a mournful tone; they imply regret that more LBQT+ individuals did not resist opportunities for personal "gentrification," and, in so doing, retain their "authenticity," politics of resistance, and opportunities for genuine social connection.

"Gentefier": A Parable of Economic "Gentrification"

The opening scenes of the Starz series *Vida* (2018–20) lead one to believe that the show is about the literal gentrification of Los Angeles's predominately Latinx Boyle Heights neighborhood—the same neighborhood featured in *Gentefied*, which I explored in chapter 2. If one has even passing knowledge of the neighborhood then that would be a reasonable assumption; the neighborhood has seen significant recent increases in median household income and in the median value of owner-occupied homes, and certain tracts became increasingly White.[37] But the reader will be unsurprised to learn that I find that, at heart, the series grapples with personal "gentrification."

As in *Gentefied*, the characters at the center of *Vida* are mindful of how Boyle Heights is transforming. Take Marisol, a woman in her early twenties whom the viewer meets in a bedroom of the bungalow she shares with her ailing father, a retired mechanic. Marisol affixes stickers to her wall that read, "Gentrify Us" and "Gentrified Colonialism." Wearing black lipstick, a crop top, and jeans, Mari (as she's called) records a social media post about gentrification on her phone. She warns, "If you try to come in here and replace people and displace people, good working-class people, too . . ." She continues, her voice rising, "If these fuckers think we are going to take this—this occupation, this recolonization—lying down, they have another thing coming!" She warns listeners, "You will see us rise up!"

As Marisol suggests, literal gentrification is a current across *Vida*'s three seasons. The series presents images of a neighborhood undergoing renovation: workers replace metal fences with white pickets; houses are gutted; buildings are retrofitted; galleries, run by White hipsters, open; newscasters tout the authenticity of tacos; expensive bars and cafes replace old Boyle Heights standards. Nearly every character grapples with how to position themselves as the neighborhood experiences this infusion of wealth and the newcomers who usher it in. Some struggle to pay their rent; others wrestle with whether to raise the rent they charge their tenants.

Despite this, *Vida* is not, at its core, about literal gentrification. Instead, as with the books we have already encountered, it is about the "gentrification" of individuals and, more specifically, about their personal *economic* (or class) "gentrification," or about how they come to occupy a more rarified economic and cultural location, one traditionally associated with the upper-middle class.[38] *Vida* emphasizes economic "gentrification" by problematizing the economic mobility of the series' two most affluent primary characters, Emma and Nelson. The series also draws secondary attention to how the acquisition of cultural capital associated with upper-middle-class tastes and practices can, alongside the acquisition of economic capital, alienate one from one's community of origin. Given this, I use "economic" and "class" gentrification interchangeably. In so doing, I mean to communicate how the series primarily attends to economic mobility, and, secondarily, to the accumulation of cultural capital (Bourdieu 1987).

The moral question at the center of each season of *Vida* is not whether one resists or advances the literal gentrification of Boyle Heights, but, rather, about the personal and collective costs of an individual's upward economic mobility. The show presents a parable of personal "gentrification" that casts doubt on the notion that one can "better" one's self via education, lucrative jobs, and engagement with elite culture. It counters narratives about the virtues of upward mobility—cue the American dream—by displaying how personal "gentrification" harms our deepest human connections and the communities that form us. "Bettering" one's self, *Vida* warns, can keep one from "authentically" coming home and from being one's original and most empathic self.

These themes are pertinent for Mexican Americans in a place like Boyle Heights. Echoing what we saw in *Gentefied*, the show grapples with intragroup inequality among Mexican Americans, a group who, as a result of racism and xenophobia, has banded together for self-protection and survival. With new opportunities and the intragroup heterogeneity this produces, what does it mean to leave one's natal neighborhood and community in search of education and economic attainment? By presenting a world that is (despite literal gentrification) almost entirely composed of Mexican Americans, *Vida* spotlights economic disparities and associated differences in cultural capital (Bourdieu 1987) and how they shape human connection.

Psychologists report a trend of increasing guilt among first-generation racial minority college students, with particularly high rates of guilt among Latinx students.[39] They term this "family achievement guilt" or "a socio-emotional experience related to 'leaving family' . . . to attend college" (Covarrubias et al. 2021, 696). Put somewhat differently, family achievement guilt "is the socio-emotional experience of pursuing socioeconomic mobility while simultaneously recognizing that this pursuit complicates relationships with family" (696). This pursuit can complicate personal relationships, in part, because for Latinx and Asian first-generation students, economic mobility can be read or experienced as a kind of racial identity change (696).

For instance, one first-generation student told researchers about the impact of his pursuit of higher education on family ties. He "highlighted the ways in which engaging in another cultural context created tension between him and his family." Family accused him "of becoming 'White' and leaving his culture behind" (Covarrubias et al. 2021, 701). These cultural trends and tensions are the cultural backdrop against which *Vida* is set, steering much of the show's drama. By emphasizing the problems of literal gentrification, the series presents metaphorical "gentrification" in stark terms: as a process that makes one bland, inauthentic, and disconnected from one's roots.

As with *Gentefied*, *Vida* presents this "gentrification" in a paradoxical manner. While establishing that most (literal) gentrifiers are White yuppies thoughtlessly infringing on Latinx space, it posits that the most problematic gentrifiers of all are moneyed Latinx individuals who return to Boyle Heights and remake it in their own (elite) image. Of course, this flies in the face of how many think about literal gentrification in the present day. Whereas many once conceptualized gentrification as the movement of affluent Whites into ethnic enclaves like Little Italy, today dominant popular images of the process have shifted: as brick-and-mortar gentrification accelerates in historically minority neighborhoods, it is increasingly understood as a process of racial turnover.

Complicating this image, researchers have long documented how affluent racial and ethnic minorities can participate in the upscaling of a neighborhood that has historically housed working-class and poor members of their own social group (Taylor 2002; Pattillo 2009; Hyra 2008; Boyd 2008).[40] Whereas, in some instances, longtime residents might embrace such in-movers, as long as they share their racial characteristics (Boyd 2008), hoping they will bring capital and influence with them to benefit the neighborhood as a whole, others take a more cautious or even antagonistic posture (Taylor 2002; Pattillo 2009). *Vida* plays on the ambiguity that arises from these competing images of affluent racial minorities who invest in working-class neighborhoods, asking the viewer to constantly evaluate which side characters like Nelson and Emma are on. Are they (literal) gentrifiers, despite being Chicano natives of Boyle Heights, or, in the language of the series, are they *gente*? I argue that such plotlines ultimately ask the viewer to consider whether or not characters like Emma are "gentrifying" and whether we can trust those who do so.

Many of *Vida*'s scenes take place in the modestly furnished Boyle Heights apartment of Vidalia, who has just passed away when the series begins. A Chicana longtime Boyle Heights resident, Vidalia owned the building in which her apartment sits and lived with her younger wife, Eddy, who survives her. Eddy, a husky middle-aged Chicana butch whose hair is shaved on the sides and short on top and who almost always dresses in jeans and a T-shirt, is overcome with sorrow. In the first episode, a friend comforts Eddy at a table laden with dishes of food gifted by friends and neighbors. Also at the table is Vidalia's youngest daughter, Lyn, a thin young woman with delicate features. Lyn wears a flowing silk robe in bold floral patterns over leggings, and we learn that she has traveled from San Francisco upon news of her mother's death. The viewer can't help but notice that Lyn, while only slightly older than Marisol, styles herself very differently than the antigentrification activist.

However, the greatest contrast is between Marisol and Lyn's sister Emma, who returns to Boyle Heights for her mother's funeral. The viewer swiftly learns that Emma works as a business consultant in Chicago and that she was estranged from her mother. The viewer also learns that Emma—like her mother and Eddy—is queer; in the first season, she has sex with a woman she met on an app, dates her former high school girlfriend Cruz, and, occasionally, has casual sex with men.[41] She wears her dark hair in a neat bob, sports a red manicure and red lipstick, and adorns her neck with a simple silver ring on a chain. On seeing the food that covers the table, Emma says to her sister Lyn, "Seriously, what's with all the fucking flan?" Viewers have already seen Lyn, presented with a plate of enchiladas, tell Eddy, "Oh, I'm vegan."

Via these brief interactions, it is apparent that Lyn, and especially Emma, are not like Marisol. It is also apparent that they have had little contact with Eddy. They dress, speak, and eat differently than those with whom they are poised to grieve Vidalia. In other words, from the series' start, the sisters' accrual of economic (Emma) and cultural (Lyn) capital and how this estranges them from working-class Latinx Boyle Heights residents, even from those who are family, is evident.

Of course, this is a familiar story of the loss that can accompany upward mobility, but what sets *Vida* apart is how it uses the literal gentrification of a Latinx LA neighborhood to offer this parable of the costs of personal transformation. *Vida* calls us to consider that, just as a neighborhood can gentrify so much that it risks losing its soul, so too can a person—in this case Emma and, to a lesser degree, Lyn. The series' creators externalize the internal transformation and conflict of upwardly mobile characters, such as Emma, by emphasizing how Boyle Heights is (literally) gentrifying, and the conflict that this, too, creates.

Underlining parallels between literal and personal gentrification, season 1 provides vivid imagery of a neighborhood in transition. Marisol spray-paints "Fuck White Art" on a gallery storefront, drawing the ire of a White man who emerges from the gallery. Likewise, she calls a White woman with blonde hair who is on camera touting a taco shop "Becky," disrupting the recording.

Marisol tosses around phrases such as "the real multilayered tragedy of gentrification," and she and her compatriots are quick to identify how Boyle Heights residents are complicit in literal gentrification. For instance, Marisol gestures to Latino carpenters and says, "Neighborhood people—they are the ones nailing those nails to these fucking coffins." However, it is not just residents she blames for these transformations. She references "sideways fences" and another gentrification activist calls them "gentrifences. . . . They make them for rich assholes that are colonizing our hood."[42]

It is not just Marisol who notes how the neighborhood is changing. Emma, carefully made up and adorned in business casual, works on her laptop in a pasteria that has Wi-Fi and serves almond-milk lattes. An ex-girlfriend who stayed in the neighborhood long after Emma left hands Emma a pastry to eat and says, "They're not as good [as they used to be]. . . . Everything [in Boyle Heights] is slowly becoming a plastic version of what they were."

Over and again, *Vida* reminds the viewer that it is not just the neighborhood that is becoming plastic. Emma's and Lyn's bodies—toned, fed, and coifed to meet the upper-middle-class expectations of the milieus they've called home since leaving LA—are themselves contrasted with those around them. Lyn is frequently the only runner on busy sidewalks; at yoga class, in her Lululemon attire, she stands apart from pregnant mothers in sweat pants. *Vida* warns that to "gentrify" as a person is to become plastic; to "gentrify" as a person is to lose personal "authenticity" and connection to one's family and neighborhood.

Indeed, this personal transformation, rather than the literal gentrification of the neighborhood, is at the show's heart. *Vida* explores whether Emma and, to a lesser degree, Lyn, are "gente," or of the people of Boyle Heights. As the neighborhood changes, the question of who qualifies as "gente" is openly debated. At an antigentrification meeting, an organizer calls others to protest a new coffee shop. A man expresses hesitation, saying, "The owners . . . they're gente." The primary organizer says, "It doesn't matter. They can be gente and they can be from the neighborhood. It doesn't matter. They are still displacing . . . They're gentifiers." With this sentiment in mind, characters repeatedly challenge Emma and Lyn about whether they are *real* gente.

As an example, Emma seeks to hire a contractor to make repairs on her late mother's property. She indicates that she will require a signed contract. The contractor—a handsome, tattooed neighborhood resident, whom we learn has served time in prison—says, "I usually work with *gente*—you know, people from the neighborhood. So I'm not used to this whole contract thing . . . I don't usually need one. Mostly just shake on it. Look, I know you people are more business oriented, but we don't usually do things that way." In response, Emma says, "What do you mean 'you people'?" The contractor says, "I just mean Mexicans around here. We're a little more allergic to papers, you know what I mean?" Emma retorts, her voice growing angry, "Well, two things: I *am* Mexican and I *did* grow up around here. And I still require a contract." He replies, "For real? Well, you could have fooled me. The way you talk and your whole—how you look?" Emma asks, "How is that exactly?" and the contractor says, "Come on, this can't be the first time you've heard this." Her voice rising, Emma responds, "No, and it pisses me off every time." Not backing down, the contractor says, "Well, you're kind of putting it out there."

As their defensiveness indicates, Emma and Lyn wrestle internally with how to answer the question of whether they are still "gente" given their increased economic and cultural capital. At a glamorous poolside party well outside of Boyle Heights, Lyn swims, drinks, and flirts with

a wealthy, White crowd that lounges by the pool, kissing, snorting co-
caine, and jumping in the water. However, amid this revelry Lyn notices
a domestic worker, Aurora, who cleans up after the partiers, even mop-
ping one guest's vomit from the pool deck. She also winces when a
White woman admires Lyn's eyebrows, comparing Lyn to Frida Kahlo.
In this moment, we see how Lyn grapples with her proximity to (compared to the White, wealthy individuals she partied with) and distance
from (compared to Marisol and Eddy and others) the "gente" of Boyle
Heights, such as Aurora.[43] Are Emma and Lyn poised to be "gentrifiers"
in the context of changing Boyle Heights, or, because they are Chicana
and grew up in the neighborhood, are they "old-timers"?

This internal conflict is spotlighted not only by Boyle Heights's literal
gentrification but by the related central plotline, which revolves around
Vidalia's estate. Over and again, the sisters must decide whose side they
are on. Lyn and Emma first return to Los Angeles to mourn their mother
and to efficiently take care of her affairs. They swiftly discover several
factors that complicate the settling of her estate. They learn that Vidalia
was married to Eddy and that Eddy therefore has a stake in and ostensibly
a claim to Vidalia's property. They also discover that Vidalia's bar, located
on the first floor of her building, struggles to stay afloat and that the building in which it sits has been remortgaged beyond its current value.

Emma and Lyn cannot return to their former lives without selling their
mother's legacy to a predatory developer or otherwise acting against Vidalia's widow's wishes and dramatically altering her building. This sets up
the moral dilemma at the center of the series. Season after season, the
sisters leave their previous lives behind and stay in Boyle Heights, where
they conspire to take the apartment building out of the red and to make
their mother's dyke bar profitable by renaming it "Vida," seeking to attract
a broader clientele, and installing a new manager, Nico.

Class as the Ultimate Dividing Line

As these plotlines would suggest, *Vida* often seems to present a highly
intersectional portrait of its characters. After all, the series places Latina
queer women of various class backgrounds at its center, and much of

the conflict that animates episodes revolves around how characters navigate different facets of their identities among those with whom they share certain identity traits (e.g., queer and Latina, *or* Latinx and upper-middle class) and not others. Despite this, because so many of *Vida*'s central characters are queer Latinas, the main difference that is explored and played with and that animates conflicts and interactions originates not in sexuality, gender, race, or ethnicity, but in class. In this sense, *Vida* presents class as the ultimate defining personal trait—a standpoint mis-aligned with ways of thinking about identity in intersectional terms, with the weight of any attribute existing in relationship to the weight of other attributes and to the context in which a person is embedded.[44] In *Vida*, regardless of other personal or contextual attributes, it is eco-nomic position that brings a person closer to or further away from others.

The centrality of class as a dividing line is underlined by the fact that the version of Boyle Heights that *Vida* presents is, with rare exception, a utopia for Latinx LBQT+ residents. The majority of the primary char-acters are queer, from Emma to Eddy to the late Vidalia. Queer second-ary characters include the bartender (and Emma's love interest) Nico, and many of Eddy's friends, as well as the various women Emma dates. Even Lyn, who, across three seasons, has several romances with men, admits to her sister that she has "dabbled" with women.

What makes *Vida*'s Boyle Heights a queer utopia is not, though, the ubiquity of LBQ+ women in the series, but, instead, how their friends, family, and neighbors regard their sexuality, and especially their sexual difference, as unremarkable. There are few conflicts between primary characters that originate in sexual difference.[45]

Instead, *Vida* presents the warm and supportive relationship between Eddy and Johnny—a muscular twentysomething auto mechanic (who also happens to be Lyn's on-again, off-again boyfriend and Marisol's brother). Johnny tenderly cuts Eddy's hair into a shape like his own hairstyle, and, when she is bedridden, he cradles her in his arms to move her from room to room.

Johnny's openheartedness is not presented as exceptional. Again and again, friends and family embrace LGBTQ+ neighbors and relatives. A multigenerational family cheers at the wedding of two men in white suits and sombreros; upon the loss of her wife, Eddy is supported by a warm circle of Chicana older women, most of whom are ostensibly straight.

This harmonious portrait of life for sexual minorities shines a light on the crosscurrent at the heart of Vida's *gentrification* parable: the notion that the orienting difference between people, the greatest source of tension today, is rooted in economic class. Economic position, more than any other facet of the self, is the ultimate dividing line; economic heterogeneity is the only difference that cannot be overcome. By painting a picture of a Latinx queer utopia, *Vida* allows the viewer to believe that class can be isolated and extracted from a broader matrix of intersectional identities and that economic mobility is something within an individual's control.

In the Boyle Heights that *Vida* presents, muscular, cisgender, heterosexual auto mechanics forge lasting and intimate friendships with butch lesbians; straight locals hang out in a struggling dyke bar; and an entire building comes together to support Eddy when she loses her wife. Yet, despite this open-armed approach to sexuality, some of these same characters attack one another, overtly and dramatically, because of their economic differences.

Johnny, who is so tender with working-class Eddy, occasionally pokes at the class differences between himself and his sometimes-lover Lyn. He says of her, following an argument after having sex for the first time in years, "How did I forget? Miss Superior-Ass Linda Hernandez." Likewise, Lyn recalls that, in high school, Johnny's fiancée Karla "used to call me Abercrombie & Bitch. I hated her so much." In this manner, the characters do not hold back when it comes to antagonizing one another about class differences. These antagonisms stand out, especially against the backdrop of the acceptance of sexual difference that *Vida* depicts.

Why might a show like *Vida* present class difference as the ultimate dividing line? There are two possible reasons. First, this representation resonates in a moment of growing class inequities.[46] While the United States, and much of the globe, grapples with rising income and wealth inequality, specifically a growing gap between the poor and the wealthy and a shrinking middle class, *Vida* presents class as a lightning rod and a source of distinction that, presumably, feels familiar to many viewers.

Second, and most importantly, class differences function as an orienting source of conflict because *Vida* presents this type of class difference—acquired in adulthood, with effort associated with higher education (Emma) and cavorting with the wealthy (Lyn)—as something one can control or choose; opt in or out of. Like the sexual "gentrification" of the self that is presented as at least somewhat optional in my archive, individuals "gentrify" as they choose to acquire more economic and cultural capital (associated with the affluent). Again, this presents an individual as responsible for their own fate; it represents a neoliberal sensibility that looks away from the collective and structural roots of any person's opportunity (or lack thereof) for mobility.

It would, of course, be more impolitic to present sexuality or race as similarly under one's own control or as otherwise malleable, but *Vida* can present class in this manner because Americans tend to think of class as a mutable difference. Indeed, the whole notion of the American dream rests on the idea that one can, with hard work and intention, pull one's self up by the bootstraps.[47]

The inverse of this, of course, is the idea that becoming upwardly mobile or pulling oneself up by the bootstraps is *voluntary*; that one does not *have* to do so. The parable at the heart of *Vida* suggests that the better or higher choice is to stay home; to remain closer to friends and family, and even the (original, authentic) self. The literal gentrification of Boyle Heights is a platform through which *Vida* explores this idea of personal "gentrification" as voluntary because we tend to think of literal gentrification, like personal "gentrification," as driven by individual actors and as potentially avoidable rather than as attached to a broad rearrangement of wealth and the reordering of the economic engines of cities.

Turncoats Versus "Good Working-Class People"

Given this frame that presents personal "gentrification" as avoidable, the moral arc of characters, which is an essential part of any parable, is mapped out in relation to how they approach upward mobility and whether their newfound privilege compromises their loyalty to neighborhood residents. Consider that the series' most unambiguous villain is Nelson, a man who grew up in the neighborhood but who now uses local connections to aid and abet the developers who are transforming Boyle Heights, evicting residents, and transforming the commercial landscape. In season 1, we learn that he cajoled Vidalia into remortgaging her building, placing her—and now her heirs—in financial peril. Nelson unapologetically embraces his own "gentrification."

After Vidalia's death, in an effort to force Vidalia's daughters and wife to sell their property, Nelson has construction vehicles park in front of Vida's bar, and he reports loose wires in the bar to the fire marshal—who levies fines and mandates closure. The series presents Nelson as an unambiguous traitor to his neighborhood. Indeed, Lyn and a friend discover Nelson's dating profile; on the dating app, Nelson describes himself as "Hispanic, slim, and a lead project manager for a development company on the East Side. We turn these dog shit infested streets into something palatable for the upwardly mobile incomers."

Painted thusly as a turncoat, Nelson appears even more vile than the developers for whom he brokers deals, or the White realtors, gallery owners, and gentrifiers moving into Boyle Heights. Indeed, early in the series Nelson tells Emma that he can "be a bridge" between her and developers. Throughout the episodes, it is Emma's refusal of this offer that redeems her moral character.

Nonetheless, if *Vida* were centrally about the literal gentrification of Boyle Heights, then Marisol, the series' primary antigentrification activist, would be presented as Nelson's virtuous counterpart. However, because the series' central moral dilemma is more about personal "gentrification" than literal gentrification, this is not the case.[48] Instead, Marisol is presented as a complicated figure. She often berates *Vida*'s primary characters and is even occasionally violent toward them. Encountering Emma and Lyn outside of a taqueria, Mari calls them "gringas." Emma retorts, "I'm not a fucking gringa," and Mari shouts, "Yeah, I remember this bitch [Emma]. She used to walk around all bougie and stuck up." In another episode, Marisol, anxious about how Emma will change Vidalia's bar, spray-paints "Chipsters" on its exterior. This type of name-calling and the tagging that goes along with it are not isolated. This is a constant through line across episodes, and the series does not shy away from how Marisol's insults injure Lyn and Emma.

This is not to suggest that the viewer should dislike Marisol; after all, she voices the well-earned rage of a neighborhood in which displacement and appropriation are everyday realities. However, *Vida* stops short of calling one to celebrate Marisol's treatment of her neighbors.

Instead, the characters who are routinely presented as best-hearted are those who have had the opportunity to leave the neighborhood and have come home anyway—without fully "gentrifying" themselves. They are still openhearted toward and comfortable around those with whom they grew up. Notably, despite their time away, they also are not economically affluent and thus are neither "gentrified" nor (literal) gentrifiers.[49]

Take Nico, a queer freelance writer and bartender in her late twenties or early thirties. In season 2, we learn that when she was young Nico left to join the military and to study writing, but today she holds traditionally working-class service industry jobs. In one scene, she corrects Emma, instructing her that she thinks of herself as a *bartender* rather than as a "mixologist." Nico is presented as both literally bilingual—speaking English and Spanish—and as a class polygot; she moves with ease between the different worlds that Boyle Heights contains. She is as at home with the working-class Eddy as she is with the business executive Emma.

Likewise, in contrast to Emma, Lyn is celebrated for not being totally divorced from the neighborhood. She engages in a long-standing relationship with working-class Johnny and seeks *curanderismo* from a neighbor. Lyn forges a friendship with her mother's widow, Eddy, long before Emma does so, and she forgoes some of her San Francisco habits in favor of Boyle Heights traditions, such as eating cheese enchiladas after saying she is vegan.

Crucially, both Lyn and Nico have acquired cultural capital—Nico mixes fancy drinks and recognizes the market value of an old Coke sign at a yard sale—and Lyn knows how to present "old Mexican toys" as precious antiques and, early in the series, speaks of plans to market a line of "Aztec-inspired lotions"—but neither has achieved financial success in the manner of Emma. In the parable of *Vida*, such economic limitations keep one humble and better-connected to the "gente" of Boyle Heights. Lyn tells Emma that she worries about what will happen to undocumented tenants in their building if they sell, saying, "What kind of Mexican would I be if I didn't care?" Yet, at the same time, Lyn is not unambiguously "gente"—at a local yoga studio, on finding that the class she was prepared to take isn't being offered, Lyn stormily says: "Y'all should think of investing in some kind of online scheduling system that does notifications!"

Eddy and Johnny serve as a next layer of goodness. They neither fight nor propel literal gentrification, and they are crucial, if somewhat neutral, bridges between Marisol (and others like her) and the characters, such as Lyn and Emma, who have left and tried to come home. They are morally neutral filters who provide a backdrop for the antagonism between the Marisols and the Emmas of the series. They do not soften the class conflict that populates so many scenes, but they rarely propel it themselves. They are, in Marisol's terms, "good working-class people."

In the queer utopia that *Vida* presents, you can be "gentrified" without becoming a gentrifier. You can find your way home, eventually. This is what the series hopes for Emma over and over again. She meanders between aligning herself with those like Nelson who seek personal gain by capitalizing on, and transforming, the place where they come from, and those like Nico, who master moving between worlds without asking either world to change. In some scenes, Emma finds herself tempted to collude with Nelson, while at other times she aligns herself with Marisol (staring, with Marisol at her side, in disbelief at a building that Nelson helped to redevelop). One might cheer for Emma in the moments in which she turns down opportunities for personal advancement in favor of keeping her family's bar and building afloat, or when she strikes a balance, such as by working with her sister Lyn to market their bar to newcomers without painting over bathroom graffiti.

Indeed, many plotlines revolve around Emma's growth as she becomes a person who, despite her education and her economic capital, is increasingly able to reestablish connections with neighbors and family in Boyle Heights. When Emma first arrives in Boyle Heights, she is openly critical of many who live there, including her own late mother. When Lyn comments on Emma's impeccable Spanish, Emma responds briskly, "What [you're surprised] that I went out and learned how to speak actual Spanish—unlike mother," whom she calls a "pocha"—or a Mexican American who does not speak fluent Spanish. Likewise, she calls her mother's bar a "piece-of-shit bar." In contrast, at the end of season 2, Emma recounts what Vida's bar was like when Emma's grandfather was alive. She admits, "God I was so stupid to think I could make it like it was. No, actually I thought I could make it better than it was." By the end of the series, Emma no longer believes she can make Boyle Heights "better." Instead, she is more aligned with Marisol's effort to keep it as it is and, in so doing, to come home to her community and to herself.

Vida is a cautionary tale about how *people* "gentrify" by changing their class position and the costs thereof for long-term relationships. It calls upwardly mobile individuals like Emma to recognize their linked fate to their community of origin, and it questions their loyalty to that community.[50] *Vida* tells us to guard against personal "gentrification" in favor of staying true to our original, "authentic" selves and those who helped to build them.

While this is an impressive array of issues for a series to wrestle with, it leaves untouched the risks of presenting a process of political-economic transformation—the literal gentrification of Boyle Heights—as a stand-in for how anyone might evolve and grow as a person. It presents one kind of change (neighborhood) as, despite the efforts of Marisol and others, largely unstoppable, and another kind of change (personal) as within an individual's control. Boyle Heights might (literally) gentrify despite the best efforts of Marisol, but Emma is meant to come home and to stop her own personal upscaling by leaving her corporate job behind and reestablishing ties with working-class family and neighbors. Of course, this does not acknowledge how each type of *gentrification*—literal and personal—is tied up in broader systems of inequality that might lead someone like Emma on a path

away from home to school and work in Chicago and that might pro-
hibit others, such as Marisol and Johnny, from following in Emma's
footsteps. It turns our attention away from how Latinx neighborhoods
like Boyle Heights were long stripped of economic resources and opportunities that might help to keep someone like Emma closer to
home.

We risk thinking of literal gentrification as voluntary, rather than systemic, when we use *gentrification* as a parable for individual change. We
also risk adopting a neoliberal sensibility that overlooks how structural
inequalities propel some to go to great lengths to achieve basic personal
security—pushing someone like Emma, a Latina queer individual, away
from home.

Vida, like other parables of personal "gentrification," will resonate
with those familiar with cultural narratives about the costs of upward
mobility for person, family, and community. However, we must ask,
when we tell these stories through Latina, queer characters, whose
privilege do we normalize and whose privilege do we problematize?
Such parables, however compelling, present intragroup inequalities as
a personal, private problem to be solved by resisting financial success,
and the economic mobility of members of traditionally marginalized
groups as a moral failure.

This closely parallels how cultural producers often present literal gentrification: as a morally questionable practice advanced by individual
urbanites rather than as a problem of contemporary urban policy and
late-stage capitalism that is rooted in racialized urban histories, such as
urban renewal and White flight, which opened the door for massive
economic reinvestment in city centers.[51] By offering a close reading of
Vida, I draw our attention to the risks of personalizing systemic inequalities. I argue that presenting the upward mobility of individuals from
historically marginalized groups as a morally fraught form of metaphorical "gentrification" exacerbates tendencies to individualize
inequality (and privilege), turning attention away from the systemic
roots of both literal gentrification and of the (perceived) problems of
personal "gentrification."

"Selling My Soul for These Tokens": *The Forty-Year-Old Version* and the Parable of Racial "Gentrification"

Multiple *gentrifications* coalesce in the 2020 award-winning film *The Forty-Year-Old Version*. Radha Blank's film not only captures the literal gentrification of Harlem but also the "gentrification" of art and the near-"gentrification" of a Black woman artist. As the film unfolds, wealthy White power-brokers shape the production of a play, *Harlem Ave*—a play that itself documents Harlem's literal gentrification. I argue that the film also grapples with the "gentrification" of the self as Blank, playing herself, seeks to avoid selling out for money and fame and losing her "authentic" self in the process. Specifically, it grapples with the threat of the "gentrification" of one's original or (what the film presents as) one's "authentic" racial and artistic identity.

In the world that *The Forty-Year-Old Version* sketches, literal and metaphorical *gentrification* are each to be understood, simultaneously, as a process of economic and racial turnover.[52] In Blank's New York, affluent Whites move into Black spaces, whether Harlem or a theater production. They even try to direct how a Black playwright thinks about herself, establishing (narrow and stifling) notions of "success" that Blank ultimately rejects. Again, we encounter another parable of the "gentrification" of the self; one that uses a backdrop of literal gentrification and artistic "gentrification" to offer a parable about the risks of a kind of racial "gentrification." In this version of our parable, for fear of losing her artistic "authenticity," a Black woman artist must steer herself clear of a racialized personal and artistic "gentrification" that would ensure her financial security and status in a rarified art world.[53] Of course, this type of narrative draws attention away from the structural conditions that reward certain kinds of art and certain kinds of artists at the expense of others, presenting the choices Radha must make as personal and individual. It is not happenstance that "success" is associated with becoming enmeshed in a White-dominated theater world.

Setting the film in New York's Harlem allows Blank to explore themes of how racial and economic transformation entangle. In the first two decades of the twenty-first century, the historically Black neighborhood has seen a marked increase in its White population, which rose from 2 percent to 17.5 percent.[54] The demographic transformation of what was, for at least a century, a predominately Black and low-income neighborhood, is a result of both institutional expansion (perhaps most famously that of Columbia University and the Clinton Foundation) and an influx of White gentrifiers.[55] Equally crucial for the film's subtext about how economic opportunities alter racial identities, this influx of White gentrifiers followed earlier decades in which affluent Blacks participated in Harlem's gentrification; this in-movement was welcomed by some, who regarded the return of the Black gentry as promising much-desired economic reinvestment, but, for others, it created intraracial class conflict that some ethnographers documented.[56]

For Blank, to be "ungentrified" is not only to resist the economic upscaling that *Vida* emphasizes but also to resist Whites dictating how a Black playwright makes art and calling the shots about what makes art—or a person—successful. As the plot develops, the viewer is instructed that personal (and racialized) "authenticity" can be nourished and maintained via resisting the "gentrification" of art and, in turn, of the self. Just as a neighborhood might remain ungentrified by resisting the in-movement of White middle-class populations, so too might a person remain "ungentrified" by resisting co-optation by the (White) middle and upper class and by seeking companionship in a less gentrified and less White-dominated sphere of New York.[57] For Blank, to resist racial and artistic "gentrification" is to resist letting affluent Whites set benchmarks for her art and to resist permitting them to become her artistic community. As the film progresses, Blank's moral integrity is restored when she realigns herself with Black artists in Brooklyn, eschewing the rarified White theater world of Manhattan.[58]

The "Gentrification" of Art

The degree to which these (racial and economic) nesting dolls of literal and metaphorical *gentrification* are entangled becomes particularly explicit when we learn that insecurity about her ability to survive financially in contemporary, hypergentrified Manhattan drives Blank's impulse to sell an account of literal gentrification on Broadway.

Early in the film, Radha's agent, Archie, who is her lifelong best friend, has shared her script, *Harlem Ave*, with an older White gay theater producer. The smug and elitist producer offers her feedback, telling her, "I asked myself, did a Black person write this?" His notes for revision include emphasizing the racial dynamics of literal gentrification, instructing that "this is a Black Harlem shifting under a White hipster land grab." He also implies that she ought to play on negative stereotypes about Black neighborhoods, saying, "There's something there. I just wish you hadn't shied away from darkness." While his language is veiled, Radha understands that he's urging her to tell stories of urban "disorder" and to further emphasize so-called Black urban culture. The final script, adapted to address his criticisms, includes intermittent gunshots and a chorus of young Black men who beatbox.

In addition to urging Radha to play on the above stereotypes, the producer instructs that the script should more prominently feature White newcomers. He says: "Gentrification. It shouldn't be this thing that is happening out there. We need to *personify it* in the play." He adds: "If we have a Black couple facing gentrification in Harlem we need to know exactly *who* is gentrifying . . . You have to grab your core audience and if you want to do that you have to write them into the play."

Essentially, he calls for her to "gentrify" her play about literal gentrification; to insert affluent White residents so the production can be populated and financially boosted by White individuals. Ultimately, he succeeds in pushing Radha to produce a "gentrified" version of *Harlem Ave*; that is, a version that presents gentrifying Harlem through White eyes for a White audience. Her new script is further interpreted by a White director who ignores concerns raised by Black cast members, such as about why a young Black New Yorker is speaking in the vernacular of the early-twentieth-century rural South.

When it reaches the stage, *Harlem Ave* centers how (literal) gentrification pressures play out for a Black couple who own a corner store in Harlem. A theme song includes, "Harlem Ave, Harlem Ave. You might find love on Harlem Ave . . . You just might get shot on Harlem Ave.

Harlem Ave, hub of Black and Brown life. Where a culture once ripe changed like the speed of light. Got your culture for sale, got your vultures that's pale. But the pulse of the city keeps raging on."

Throughout the play, the plight of the aforementioned Harlem store owners is dramatized as they struggle to keep their business afloat as rents rise in rapidly gentrifying Harlem. The wife (speaking in the vernacular to which the actress playing her objects) says, "Baby I'm not saying I want to go back down South." The husband asks, "So what are you saying?" and the wife responds, "I'm saying it is getting too expensive to stay here. We gots to figure it outs."

Meanwhile, following the producer's recommendation, the play also features a White woman who has recently moved to Harlem. She finds that the store doesn't carry products to which she is accustomed and demands that the shopkeepers change their inventory to suit her tastes. To great laughs from the audience she says, "What's a girl got to do to get some soy milk around here?"

Ultimately, this White customer forges an unlikely alliance with the shop owners, rallying to try to keep the store from closing. She clasps hands with the owners and proclaims, "This is *our* neighborhood and *our* store," adding, "This shop means everything to me." Despite her sympathy and support, before the curtain falls the store owner takes a check for half a million dollars from a White man in a suit, ultimately caving to the pressures of literal gentrification that make it impossible for him to remain in business in his transformed neighborhood.

At *Harlem Ave*'s opening, Radha retreats to a dressing room and, later, to a bathroom, as the above scenes unfold. She periodically cringes and sips a drink, especially in moments when the audience responds with applause and laughter. While White audience members dance to the theme song, Radha hides away, overcome with embarrassment at how she has capitulated to the demands of a White-dominated theater world. Radha is deeply uncomfortable with her script's final shape; she wishes to disavow the "gentrified" version of the play, as well as the path of morally dubious compromise that its success promises to set her on. Has she, like the fictional storeowner she penned into being, compromised her integrity for money and success?

"Gentrification" of the Racial Self

But the Forty-Year-Old Version is not just a story of the "gentrification" of art. It also presents a story of personal "gentrification," specifically of the "gentrification" of a Black artist. In Radha Blank's rendering, a Black artist worries that she must capitulate to a White theater world to secure economic stability. This parallels how Vida's core characters seek to support themselves by pursuing economic "gentrification" outside of their natal communities. The Forty-Year-Old Version, like Vida, presents such capitulation as coming at a very high cost.

The Forty-Year-Old Version draws on real-life anxieties about what qualifies and disqualifies membership in a community of individuals assigned to the same racial category, or, in other words, about what characteristics one must share with others to belong to a "community" with them. Scholars suggest that these anxieties are particularly paramount for Black Americans, a group who has experienced a threefold expansion of the middle class since the 1960s (Hyra 2007, 75).[59] While this growth has expanded opportunities for many Black Americans, it has also produced increasing within-group economic heterogeneity (75). As a result, as the sociologist Mary Pattillo suggests, "class, status, and lifestyle" have emerged as "real axes of distinction in the black community" (1999, 209).[60]

Some researchers paint these heightened inequalities among Black Americans as sources of intraracial conflict.[61] Continued racial residential segregation partially drives this conflict, as Black Americans continue to face housing discrimination and barriers to mortgage lending and, as a result of these enduring racialized obstructions, are much more likely than other racial groups to share neighborhoods with Black people of varying classes.[62]

Against this backdrop, as we have also seen to be in true in Vida's Boyle Heights, changes in personal class status can have consequences for how one understands one's self and one's connection to other members of one's racial group (Thomas 2015, 193). For middle-class Black people, this can also result in experiences of exclusion from middle-class White social circles and from those of Black people with whom one no longer shares a similar class position.[63]

The consequences of class heterogeneity are particularly vivid in places like gentrifying Harlem, where the *Forty-Year-Old Version* takes place, as poor, working, middle, and upper-class Blacks live side by side, rendering class distinctions particularly visible.[64] In such settings, "class differences become potent symbols of a threat to a unified Black identity and political coalition" (Pattillo 2005, 315). While gentrification is not the only context in which Black people of different classes share space, it is one context in which this occurs, especially in historically Black neighborhoods that have experienced influxes of affluent Black newcomers, such as Harlem (and Chicago's Bronzeville).[65] Therefore, while literal gentrification is just one instantiation of mixed-class Black neighborhoods, gentrifying Harlem is a potent symbol for exploring the broader dynamic of economically heterogenous Black communities, the (relatively recent) economic ascent of a segment of Black Americans, and, at the same time, what it means for place-based racial identity when White gentrifiers move into a historically Black neighborhood.

In the *Forty-Year-Old Version*, Radha Blank has not (yet) experienced substantial financial mobility, but she is highly educated and begins to consider strategies for upscaling (or "gentrifying" herself) in the year after her mother, who was a struggling artist, passes away. She worries that her mother wasn't successful and therefore that her mother's dreams went unfulfilled.

As an example, as Radha and her brother discuss putting some of their late mother's paintings into storage, Radha muses, "She came to New York to become a famous artist and what does she have to show for it?" Without pause, her brother challenges Radha's view of success, saying, "*Us*, you dummy. She said that *we* were her greatest creation."

As the film progresses, Radha seems to take her brother's perspective to heart, rethinking what it means to be "successful." At *Harlem Ave*'s opening, she tells the audience: "Every playwright hopes . . . Every playwright hopes they don't write a piece of shit like this play," adding, "My mother raised me to be fearless. And I guess when she died that's when I started getting afraid."

Just as novels and memoirs feature sexual "gentrification," Blank isn't just gesturing to the temptation to seek economic upscaling. Instead, she worries that she, like a gentrified Harlem, will become estranged from an "authentic" racial self she associates with her childhood (in Brooklyn) and her young adulthood (in Harlem); that she, like the transforming Harlem that her play depicts, will become increasingly aligned with White culture, interests, and, ultimately, money. Of course there isn't actually any one "authentic" way to be Black—or to be anything else. "Authenticity" is a social construct that individuals and social groups rely on to set boundaries, communicate values, and assess sincerity.[66]

Still, for any of us, the idea that there is an "authentic" version of us that may be more or less closely aligned with our social identities can feel quite real and powerful (e.g., the notion that one can be a "real" woman or "authentically" gay).[67] And the parable of Radha's "gentrification" rests on the notion that her real, true, or "authentic" Black artist self is at risk of being "gentrified" out of existence by the White, upper-class theater world of Manhattan.

This thread of the "gentrification" of the racial self becomes especially apparent when Radha and her agent, Archie, conflict over whether she should accept how a White producer has transformed her play. In his elegant apartment, which is decorated from floor to ceiling in white, Radha tells Archie, "You keep me around because it makes you feel better about yourself." Archie asks, "About what?"

Without pause, Radha quips, "Paying $5,000 a month for your apartment. About taking trips to Greece in your thongs and shit. About acting like you're not even really . . ." Radha pauses before continuing, seeming to second-guess what she is about to say. Archie, his voice slightly raised, asks, "What? *Korean*?" To which Radha replies, "I didn't say that." Archie then tells Radha that she's not above being a sellout like him.

This makes it clear that there is not just an economic divide separating Radha from Archie. In an earlier scene, Archie had cast it as such, calling Radha from outside her empty apartment to complain: "You've got me waiting in your not-gentrified-enough-for-me-yet part of Harlem getting harassed [by an unhoused man]." When Radha confronts Archie in his luxurious Manhattan apartment, Radha implies that Archie's transformation hasn't just been economic, but also, in her view, has included the transformation of his Korean-ness or his racial identity. Notably, the film is absent of any signals that the viewer ought to worry about whether Radha is herself a literal gentrifier; instead, the film's moral arc centers around the question of whether she will "gentrify" as an artist and a person.

As Radha is compelled to alter her script and fighting with Archie about whether she is a sellout, the film pursues a second plotline. While *Harlem Ave* is in production, Radha chases a long-standing dream by traveling from Manhattan to Brownsville (in Brooklyn) to record herself rhyming. In Brownsville, she works with a younger Black DJ/producer, D, who appears to be in his late twenties and has long braids. When she first visits, she spends hours on a couch in his small, dark apartment, surrounded by young African American men smoking weed, waiting for a turn to record with D.

This foray into Brooklyn is crucial for Radha's art and, more significantly, for her sense of identity and her connection to a younger, more "authentic" version of herself—a version of Radha that grew up in ungentrified Brooklyn. Against the backdrop of her "gentrified" play, her forays into Brooklyn and her new art form constitute an attempt at self-redemption. Indeed, at *Harlem Ave*'s debut, she raps:

> I got really afraid. Scared of the choices and the bullshit I made. Thinking I wouldn't get paid. But I'm Carol's daughter so that shit don't stain. I gotta tell you, a nigga was chokin'. Tired of selling my soul for these tokens, these coins. But guess what, I made a different choice. Because it's time to FYOV. Find your own voice. FYOV. FYOV. Forty-year-old-version, indubitably. FYOV. FYOV. Not telling truth just don't make sense to me. Holding back from who you should be. FYOV. Fund your own vision. Fill your own void. Find your own voice. Fuck you old vultures. Forty-year-old version. That's who I be. I'm out.

For Radha, finding her own voice occurs via collaboration, both artistic and romantic, with D. Her true voice and vision, she reveals, is not to be found on Broadway in a White-dominated theater, but in a modest apartment in an ungentrified part of Brooklyn, with the support of her Black artist-lover, D.

In her initial interactions with D, Radha asserts her credibility as a Black urbanite, insisting that he not read her as a "gentrified" Manhattanite. The second time she meets him, she tells him, "Nigga I'm from Brooklyn, too. I grew up on Mother Gaston. In the '90s. By aroma alone, I can tell the difference between three grades of crack, so don't go treating me like I'm some White newbie hipster exploring the Black terrain when I'm fucking *from* here." Mid-film she brings him home for the night after he has taken her to a rhyming competition that takes place among Black women in a boxing ring. Thus, she explores her voice and romantic love with D, whom the film presents as an introspective, humble, talented, and "ungentrified" Black artist. Here, Black artistic "authenticity" is cast as connected to class and to being apart from White-dominated artistic spheres; to be an "authentic" Black artist, Radha must associate with—and remain—working class and spend time across the river from White-dominated and upper-class Manhattan.[68]

In one scene, D appears unannounced at a script reading for *Harlem Ave.*, and Radha has to intervene when D is confronted by a White security guard. This scene further underlines the degree to which Radha experiences herself as straddling two worlds: the racist, affluent, and White-dominated theater world, and the more working-class, creative, and Black world of rhyming (in Brooklyn) in which she feels at home. Seeing D blocked from entry to her rehearsal signifies how Radha is, herself, not completely welcome in the "gentrified" theatrical space in which her play about literal gentrification is being developed.

The *Forty-Year-Old Version* ends with Radha in the elegant attire she wore to her premiere, walking with D in Brooklyn. He beatboxes while she rhymes, and she begins with "I think I just saw a rat . . ." Thus the film leaves Radha walking happily on an ungentrified street with her "ungentrified" Black artist partner. This leaves the viewer with several possible lessons, including the impression that one can only find true love when one becomes one's own authentic, "ungentrified" self; that, such as Radha's mother found, resisting personal "gentrification" may not lead to financial gain, but that it leads to alternate rewards, such as love and companionship.

In short, after having been single for a long time—made obvious by an unhoused man who lives on Radha's block who regularly harangues her for not having a lover—Radha turns her back on fame and money and finds love with a Black DJ from Brooklyn. This fairy-tale ending instructs not that love will lead one to other rewards, such as wealth or fame, but, instead, that walking away from wealth and fame and personal "gentrification" leads to love. This love is embodied by D, but, really, the *Forty-Year-Old Version* tells the story of Radha coming to embrace and accept herself as she is, as a Black artist, not as those (White power-brokers) who hold the purse strings wish for her to be. By coming to accept her "authentic" self, Radha has narrowly averted her personal "gentrification."

Conclusion

Radha Blank's film falls in line with other works that present personal "gentrification" as a moral issue. While, *Vida* aside, the novels, memoirs, television series, and film that I engaged in this chapter do not emphasize the virtues of resisting literal gentrification, they outline the high moral ground of resisting the "gentrification" of the self.[69] They use "gentrification" to present parables that highlight the significant trade-offs of individual upscaling. They suggest that personal "gentrification" risks sacrificing one's "authentic" or original self and one's connections to friends and family, unbridled sexuality, and even one's "real" artistic voice.

The *Forty-Year-Old Version*, for instance, proposes that what makes Radha not only a hero, but also, literally, lovable (by D and by herself), is that she turns her back on the opportunity to "gentrify" her art—and herself. Parables like the *Forty-Year-Old Version* instruct that the *right* or *authentic* version of a person is the one who resists "gentrification" (of the self) to pursue that which some like to think of as outside of or as otherwise untainted by capitalism and pressures to conform to mainstream expectations, such as true love (whether romantic or familial), "authentic" sexuality, community, family, and art. The film signals minimal concern with whether Radha, by reorienting her life around Brownsville, might engage in the literal gentrification of the Brooklyn neighborhood. Instead, it emphasizes the costs of personal upscaling or "gentrification."

As we have seen, not all parables of the "gentrification" of the self present the same dimension of a person as at risk of "gentrifying." In the *Forty-Year-Old Version*, Radha turns her back on a White-dominated theater industry, embracing artistic expression traditionally associated with Black urbanites. Thus, if *Vida* is principally about resisting economic "gentrification," and *Stray City*, *Valencia*, and *Eating Fire* are parables of sexual "gentrification," then the *Forty-Year-Old Version* is, foremost, about resisting a racialized form of "gentrification."

To be sure, parables of personal "gentrification" can evoke more than one kind of change. While *Vida* primarily champions resistance to economic "gentrification," it also more subtly celebrates resistance to sexual "gentrification" (e.g., to monogamy and compulsory heterosexuality).[70] However, it ultimately presents economic "gentrification" as the greatest moral dilemma that the show's primary character faces. Likewise, in the *Forty-Year-Old Version*, while the "gentrification" of a kind of racialized artistic identity is at the center of the narrative, sexuality plays a role too. After all, Radha's "prize" as she walks away from Broadway is a Black, working-class DJ in Brooklyn who supports her "ungentrified" art. By preserving herself against the "White vultures" about which she rhymes, she has found love with a Black artist (like herself).[71]

Of course, a danger of the notion of personal "gentrification" of any kind is that it individualizes change, presenting personal transformation as an individual responsibility and as a moral dilemma rather than as a response to structural and cultural conditions that are much bigger than any one individual. I have suggested that this individualization is apparent even in cultural objects that seek to acknowledge how broadscale changes in opportunity structures encourage individual transformation, such as for sexual minorities. The "gentrification" of the self is, of course, a fitting metaphor for an era marked by neoliberalism; as a society, we tend to individualize responsibility for everything, from material to emotional well-being to cultivating community. Should we doubt Emma's moral integrity in *Vida* when she seeks personal financial security, or criticize the "authenticity" of Radha's art when she adapts her script for a Broadway audience? Would they have to make such difficult choices if the arts received more governmental support or if rent-control policies vigorously protected affordable housing? Do we characterize choices oriented around securing financial security and increasing one's economic and social status as "gentrification" when White men or other more privileged actors make them?

I do not believe that it is a coincidence that White, middle-class men are absent from narratives of the "gentrification" of the self in my archive. More often than not, cultural producers approach the mobility and *suburbanization* (literal and metaphorical here) of White, cisgender, heterosexual men as not only unexceptional, but also as *expected*—like purchasing a house in a "good" neighborhood that is sure to steadily gain equity over time, versus speculating on a fixer-upper and therefore participating in (literal) gentrification. Thus, it should not surprise that so many of these accounts of succumbing to or of resisting personal "gentrification" feature the least privileged among us— mostly women or nonbinary individuals, LBQT people, and racial minorities. It is perhaps easiest for cultural producers to depict how personal "gentrification" changes a person when that person began with fewer resources than more privileged members of society.

I do not mean to suggest that cultural producers ought to avoid engaging such themes. After all, their parables engage timely issues that emerge when select members of a group achieve new opportunities and mobility, whether college-bound Latinas, White cisgender queer individuals, or a Black playwright whose work catches the eye of a White-dominated theater world. I want to be clear that any concern that I raise is rooted in my view, as a sociologist, of how these cultural objects, together, forward a collective message. Taken individually, the pieces that this chapter features aren't problematic. I might even call them admirable. But when we look at them as a body we can see that they forward a common narrative thread that communicates a neoliberal sensibility of personal responsibility—both for establishing one's personal security and for avoiding morally perilous trade-offs associated with the individual quest for that security.

In addition, collectively, narratives of personal gentrification that focus on women and on sexual and racial minorities risk advancing the notion that the acquisition of resources by some is unremarkable or expected (in the American context), while, for others, it can be the center of moral dilemmas, conflict, and a site of tension. Indeed, collectively, narratives of personal "gentrification" risk presenting the acquisition of resources by the less privileged as remarkable and as a morally complicated choice that one can opt in or out of.

It is in this sense that parables of personal "gentrification" carry a certain degree of risk. After all, they celebrate those who have historically had limited access to many privileges and opportunities when they *walk away* from those privileges and opportunities in the name of personal "authenticity" and in order to stay connected to those with whom they share a defining trait. Our collective appetite for consuming these stories might emerge from ambivalence about capitalism or current modalities for thinking about sexualities, racial identities, or even community. They might also stem from a long-standing association of "authenticity" with those outside of dominant spheres of power. However, they might also relate to discomfort—among the privileged—with how some who have traditionally been excluded from certain opportunities now have access to them, as well as tensions among members of groups that have traditionally been marginalized when some individuals acquire new resources, and others do not.

Above all, these narratives put dominant ways of thinking about literal gentrification in sharp focus. Collectively, narratives of the "gentrification" of the self shine a light on how cultural producers view literal gentrification—namely, as a process driven by individual actors (i.e., as driven by gentrifiers) that strips places of "authenticity," threatens community, destabilizes identity, and prioritizes personal gain over collective good. Of course, there are risks associated with thinking of literal gentrification, like personal "gentrification," as an individual moral issue or choice rather than as a collective issue. After all, whether or not any individual participates in literal gentrification does not alter the legacy of policies of White flight, urban disinvestment, and suburban investment that, among other factors, such as the scale of the baby boom generation, opened cities for literal gentrification in the 1970s and 1980s. Placing the moral burden of literal gentrification on individual urbanites does not create robust planning approaches and urban policies that would ensure affordable housing and other forms of equity in the contemporary city. It is little wonder, then, that some of the problems of contemporary approaches to thinking about literal gentrification filter into how cultural producers wield *gentrification* as a metaphor.

4

Gentrification as a Political Metaphor and Heuristic

I DO not believe there is a "correct" way to use the term *gentrification*. Of course, I have my own favored way of defining literal gentrification, but I also believe that, as with any other word or concept, *gentrification* means what we, individually and collectively, hold it to mean. Like any other word or idea, *gentrification* is a cultural construct that people use to describe dynamics that they observe or perceive. Therefore, it is unsurprising that the precise meaning and significance assigned to *gentrification*—whether meant literally or metaphorically—will vary by individual, time, place, and other contextual factors.

I also don't want to suggest that everyday people and the cultural producers among them are misusing *gentrification*, and that academics sit above the fray, deploying *gentrification* only in the most precise terms. Indeed, as this chapter reveals, I do not mean to suggest that scholars who write about *gentrification* are always referencing literal gentrification (Schulman 2012).[1] I demonstrate, instead, how some academics use literal gentrification as a metaphorical heuristic while others use *gentrification* as a heuristic. For some journalists and academics, *gentrification* operates as a heuristic that efficiently conveys concerns about how facets of political-economic systems contribute to social inequalities.

Thus, this chapter turns the lens on academics like myself, and on journalists and other nonfiction authors who write about *gentrification*, as well as on social movement activists who evoke *gentrification*. Just as

I have of artists, novelists, commemorators, and others, I ask what academics, nonfiction authors, and activists mean when they deploy *gentrification* and what work the term accomplishes for them. In this chapter, I especially consider why and how both literal and metaphorical gentrification can operate as an efficient carrier of meaning or as a heuristic. In so doing, I broaden the understanding, developed across this book, of the feelings, meanings, and political analyses that *gentrification* evokes.

Journalistic books and newspaper articles, written for a general audience, tend to present literal gentrification as a social problem. Catchy titles, such as Peter Moskowitz's *How to Kill a City* (2017), Jeremiah Moss's *Vanishing New York* (2017), Richard Florida's *The New Urban Crisis* (2017), and the *New York Times*'s "Gentrification Might Kill New Orleans before Climate Change" (2019) sound alarms.[2] However, this chapter will demonstrate that, like other narratives that conjure *gentrification*, some such evocations of *gentrification* are not narrowly sounding alarms about literal gentrification. This is, in large part, because they are not narrowly about literal gentrification (Schulman 2012). Instead, they rely on *gentrification* to decry facets of political and economic systems that shape life well beyond urban neighborhoods. They use *gentrification* to communicate analyses of late-stage or corporate capitalism, growing income inequalities, and a neoliberal state that holds individuals responsible for their fate.

For some, literal gentrification is a window into problems that arise from such systems, for others it is a metaphor, a heuristic, or even a metaphorical heuristic that sheds light on structural inequalities and on their sources, such as those above. That is, these cultural producers, on the surface, seem to engage literal gentrification, but their central argument is actually about something else, typically about the political and economic systems that uphold inequalities.

This becomes evident, in part, when we consider how rarely some of the books about *gentrification* that this chapter features engage academic debates about the scale and consequences of literal gentrification, and, despite presenting *gentrification* as a problem, dodge explicit discussion of gentrification mitigation strategies. This lack of specificity emerges in part from a tension between the books' purported subject—brick-and-mortar gentrification—and the critiques of much broader political-economic systems that drive them and that the texts amplify. Just as is the case for certain novelists, filmmakers, and sculptors, *gentrification* is a shortcut some academics and nonfiction authors rely on to conjure inequalities for their audience and to diagnose their roots in capitalism and neoliberalism.

In a time of intensive inequality, perhaps it should not surprise us that some cultural producers are in search of shortcuts for gesturing to what the sociologist Robin Bartram (2022) refers to as "stacked decks"—or the sense that social and economic systems advantage the privileged and disadvantage those with fewer resources. Among the other meanings that it carries, *gentrification* efficiently gestures to the notion that a broad, metaphorical land grab is afoot.

Still other books include *gentrification* in their title but aren't *really* about literal gentrification at all. Indeed, increasingly, scholars in a variety of fields rely on "gentrification" as a metaphor to capture the appropriation and increasing exclusivity of various facets of contemporary life—from music to memory. Here, they self-consciously adopt *gentrification* as a metaphor or build an argument not about urban change, but about appropriation, capitalism, and de-democratization.

In the pages that follow, I profile two books that belong to the first camp; that is, each author frames their book as being about *gentrification* but ultimately wants to make a different and bigger point about the dynamics of specific economic markets and the problems of late-stage capitalism. For them, *gentrification* serves as a metaphorical heuristic that gestures to these broader themes. Next, I profile three books that do, to varying degrees, engage literal gentrification, but that rely on that engagement to diagnose the source of a grander set of problems. For them, discussion of literal gentrification is a heuristic that sheds light on their true concern: social inequalities and the political and economic systems that foster them. This works because, for many, literal gentrification is the most powerful contemporary posterchild of elite cooptation of something significant to a lower status group and, in more general terms, of how power-holders transform resources for their own narrow enrichment and benefit. In this sense, for them, literal gentrification stands in for systemic inequalities and exploitation of the marginal; they evoke literal gentrification as a heuristic that brings those inequalities, and the systems that foster them, to mind.

Next, I spotlight scholarship that relies on *gentrification* purely as a metaphor. Authors can use *gentrification* in this manner because the term is at once evocative and nebulous. Thus they can write with ease about the "gentrification" of objects and processes that are quite distant from literal gentrification, including tattoos and music. For this camp, "gentrification" is a metaphorical heuristic for appropriation and related upscaling, often of an object once associated with the working class.

By profiling these different usages, the chapter reveals how *gentrification* can, in some cases, serve as a shorthand for signaling how macro-level forces shape meso-level processes and dynamics (and not just those related to literal gentrification). For instance, accounts of *gentrification* can forward an argument about how corporate capitalism and neoliberalism shape territorial practices and cultural communities or how elites have coopted and possibly harmed something valuable to a group with fewer resources. In this sense, this genre is much more ambitious in seeking a source for the problems they identify than some work that is more narrowly focused on literal gentrification. That is, those who write about *gentrification* in this manner don't just call us to fix literal gentrification, but, instead, rely on *gentrification* to shed light on the bigger forces that they believe produce literal gentrification and other related social problems. By using a term that traditionally refers to a process of neighborhood change, they seek to turn attention to the much bigger social and political issues that *gentrification* evokes.

The pages that follow consider the powerful subtexts of some academic and nonfiction works on literal gentrification. They also imply a set of questions that I will grapple with more fully in the book's conclusion. For instance, how do these literatures, penned by experts, feed into the ambiguous meaning of *gentrification* that allows commemorative activists, artists, documentarians, filmmakers, and novelists to liberally and nimbly deploy the term?

To begin to explore this question, I demonstrate how a variety of social movements rely on *gentrification* for political purposes. These include Black Lives Matter, Trans Liberation, Dyke March, and the People's Climate March. This is just the tip of the iceberg, though, in terms of how people rely on *gentrification* to convey a range of political positions—as my research on Reddit conversations suggests. On that social media platform, users engage in conversation about, to name just a few examples, the "gentrification of the rainbow Pride flag,"[3] the "gentrification of democracy," and the "gentrification of the term code-switching."[4]

This political deployment of *gentrification* parallels the pattern evident in academic and nonfiction works; *gentrification* efficiently encapsulates and communicates positions on more than just literal gentrification. Therefore, the book serves as a call for more research on how a variety of movements and everyday actors deploy *gentrification* to communicate positions on political issues that are not precisely about literal gentrification.

I close by asking whether it is possible that *gentrification* has, in part, been liberated for this kind of usage because of uncertainty, debate, and ambiguity among gentrification experts about how to measure and define literal gentrification and its consequences. I reveal that these debates, which have long characterized the literature on literal gentrification, themselves emerge from the fact that even scholars who take literal gentrification as their primary subject stake a variety of positions by writing about the subject. These include positions on the purpose of social research, the validity of different types of data, and the value of embedding ourselves in the contexts that we study versus adopting a posture of scientific distance. Of course, these debates are not the only source of *gentrification*'s new life, but I believe they play a role.

In the pages that follow, the reader might wonder whether I think anyone is ever *really* writing or speaking about the thing they say they are writing or speaking about. After all, if even scholars aren't always *really* writing about literal gentrification when they write about *gentrification*, who is?

Of course, there are extraneous meanings and subtexts attached to any word or idea, so the reader would not be entirely wrong to identify an argument about cultural relativism in these pages. On the other hand, though, this chapter continues the work of the previous chapters by elucidating why *gentrification* is *particularly* adaptable for a variety of purposes. As some of the authors that this chapter features explicitly state, *gentrification* works to tell other stories and achieve other aims because of its recognizability, ambiguity, and entrenched association with emotions and with the political and economic roots of social inequalities, and because it is popularly recognized as producing or exacerbating social problems. *Gentrification* is a powerful idea and, as this chapter reveals, it does a lot of work (quite efficiently)—for activists, journalists, authors, and academics alike.

"Gentrification" as Metaphorical Heuristic

Jessa Lingel's 2021 book, *The Gentrification of the Internet: How to Reclaim Our Digital Freedom*, uses *gentrification* as a metaphor and, ultimately, as a heuristic to capture how the internet has become increasingly privatized.[5] By *gentrification*, Lingel, a communications professor at the University of Pennsylvania, evokes a project of appropriation and de-democratization. More than anything else, she seeks to capture how the internet has become an elitist enterprise. "The internet is increasingly making us less democratic, more isolated, and more beholden to corporations and their shareholders," Lingel writes. "In other words, the internet has gentrified" (1). For Lingel, to call the internet "gentrified" is to rely on it as a metaphorical heuristic that efficiently evokes how it has become, as she says, less democratic and more corporate.

Lingel identifies characteristics of literal gentrification that she believes map onto the contemporary web, including displacement and isolation. To capture this symmetry, Lingel uses literal gentrification to guide the reader. That is, literal gentrification serves, at first, as a metaphor for the "gentrification" of the web: "Over time, gentrification results in pockets of isolation where longtime residents are boxed in by new neighbors who are often wealthier and have different ideas about who and what belongs in the neighborhood. Neighbors can wind up deeply segregated" (12). She argues that a parallel process has occurred on the web and that, as a result, the web, like a gentrified neighborhood, is increasingly commercialized (12). The original web, like a neighborhood before literal gentrification, has been appropriated by a more powerful class of actors, eroding its "authenticity" and the community it once generated.

What exactly does she mean, though, when she suggests that the internet has "gentrified"? She writes that, "like urban gentrification, development of digital culture supports the needs and tastes of a wealthy minority" (17). Lingel's point is that the internet is far from egalitarian and that it is inherently capitalistic and increasingly elitist. Beyond this, she also relies on *gentrification* to gesture to social and cultural facets of how the internet has transformed; Lingel depicts a re-norming of the internet, associated with the increasing influence of the internet's new "gentry." She builds such an elaborate case for how *gentrification* can be extended, metaphorically, to the internet that, eventually, *gentrification* serves as a metaphorical heuristic or shortcut that conjures the elite co-optation and privatization of something that was once accessible to a broad spectrum of people.

Lingel makes some effort to identify a causal link between the upscaling of the internet and brick-and-mortar gentrification. Here, the book briefly veers into being about literal gentrification. She offers examples of "digital redlining" and tech industry headquarters leading to literal gentrification. In my view, this piece of Lingel's argument—about how the "gentrified" web contributes to the literal gentrification of the city— is less robustly documented and argued than the rest. Specifically, the causal relationship that she maps between literal and online gentrification is more lightly evidenced than the rest of the book.

I do not mean this as a criticism. Instead, I offer this as evidence for my reading of how and why Lingel uses *gentrification* to explore the problems of the contemporary web. Lingel, I propose, did not put *gentrification* in her subtitle because her book sets out to build a direct argument about the relationship between tech and what she refers to as "urban gentrification" (39). Of course, an argument about how tech enables literal gentrification in some spaces (e.g., San Francisco) can certainly be made, but Lingel sketches this argument in light strokes because it is not, for the most part, the reason why she deploys *gentrification* in her book.[6]

Instead, for Lingel, *gentrification* principally operates as a metaphor and heuristic, or a metaphorical heuristic, that allows her to explain how and why the internet—rather than urban neighborhoods—has changed. Indeed, she writes, "When I call the internet gentrified, I'm describing shifts in power and control that limit what we can do online. I'm also calling out an industry that prioritizes corporate profits over public good and actively pushes certain forms of online behavior as the 'right' way to use the web, while other forms of behavior get labeled backward or out of date" (1).

To be sure, Lingel turns to *gentrification* to diagnose how elites have transformed the internet and to outline strategies for repairing it. She writes, "By calling the contemporary internet gentrified, my goal is to diagnose a set of problems and lay out what activists, educators, and ordinary web users can do to carve out more protections and spaces of freedom online" (3). She outlines solutions, again drawing parallels between literal and metaphorical gentrification: "I'm going to argue that for gentrification to stop taking over the internet, companies are going to have to change their relationships to profits" (66). She also suggests that the government has a role to play in mitigating both online "gentrification" and brick-and-mortar gentrification: "Like urban gentrification, one key element for dealing with gentrification infrastructure is regulation" (84).

I wish to explore a question that Lingel herself poses: *"Do we really need the word* gentrification *to talk about this?* Aren't we really just talking about capitalism?" (16). Lingel more or less acknowledges that, in fact, she does not "need" *gentrification* to talk about how the internet has changed. Lingel explicitly instructs that she relies on *gentrification* precisely because it is an evocative, powerful, and *politicized* term.

In other words, Lingel uses *gentrification* as a metaphorical heuristic *because* the term is, in her words, "loaded" (1), rather than because it is a precise fit for thinking about how the internet has transformed. In her book's introduction, Lingel writes, "Is it useful to think of the internet as gentrified? I'll argue that it's precisely because the word gentrification is so loaded that it's a good starting point for thinking about the politics of the internet. By leaning into the conflicts around urban gentrification,

we can make sense of the political realities of the internet. Gentrification gives us a metaphor for understanding how we got to the internet
we have now and how it could be different" (1–2).

Lingel wants us to think of *gentrification* as a political term that carries
a punch by evoking systemic inequalities. She writes, "I focus on gentrification because I want to address the race, gender, and class politics
involved in how the internet has transformed over time" (16). This is
part of what *gentrification* means to her and therefore part of what *gentrification* communicates for her and why it is a useful tool for building
her argument. She writes elsewhere, "[A]s urban studies researcher Neil
Smith insists, 'For those impoverished, evicted or made homeless in its
wake, gentrification is indeed a dirty word and it should stay a dirty
word'" (51). For Lingel, *gentrification* is "dirty" because those with less
privilege, specifically those with less economic and racial privilege, lose.

Because it best evokes the political power of the elite associated with
gentrification, the literal gentrification that Lingel evokes is an advanced
gentrification, one driven by developers. "Urban gentrification doesn't
happen spontaneously, it requires local policymakers to side with developers over longtime residents" (72). The *gentrification* that works as
a metaphor for Lingel is a Manhattanized version of literal gentrification, a "gentrification" driven by established developers and fueled by
"massive amounts of cash" (66). She writes, "Urban gentrification is also
tied to monopolies. . . . In many neighborhoods, gentrification is driven
by a small number of powerful developers. Able to operate at scale, raise
massive amounts of cash, and negotiate directly with local policymakers, these developers hoard resources and exclude smaller, local players
from entering the market" (66).

Why focus on this advanced "gentrification"? For Lingel, it serves as
a particularly powerful metaphor because it closely parallels the landscape she observes with technology companies. In the tech realm, she
observes community-based ISPs, or internet service providers, getting
pushed out by "national conglomerates" (73). Indeed, she sets up the
metaphor of "gentrification" by detailing how big, powerful firms have
taken over the tech neighborhood: "Within the industry, the biggest
players have monopolized digital culture, pushing out smaller

companies and older platforms. In this process of displacement, main-stream platforms get to define what online interactions are normal and what online interactions are problematic. Condensing this much control goes beyond a reduction of consumer choice; it's a form of technological gentrification" (3).

And, after all, Lingel is in search of a metaphor that will advance her argument. *Gentrification*, and especially advanced literal gentrification, works for her not only because of the synergies she identifies between it and the current state of tech, but also because of how evocative *gentrification* is today. Lingel herself writes, "If we're not precise about what the word gentrification means, then all we have is the anger and confusion associated with it" (9). It is precisely the anger and confusion behind *gentrification* that Lingel harnesses to engage the reader and motivate them to action.

What does Lingel want the reader to do? She is not concerned with stopping literal gentrification, but, instead, her book sounds a call for reform of the internet. She wishes for a movement to emerge that will fight to re-democratize the internet for all, turning to policy as a crucial tool in this battle. A crucial device that Lingel leverages in this effort is calling the internet "gentrified." Her book positions *gentrification* as a metaphorical heuristic that evokes inequality and co-optation and de-democratization, and, thus, the term accomplishes much for her.

It is worth pausing for a moment to acknowledge that Lingel positions *gentrification* as a term powerful enough to serve as a call to action—but not as a call to action oriented around actually stopping or mitigating literal gentrification. I call our attention to this because I believe that it raises crucial questions about whether such usage might either diffuse, or capitalize on the existing diffusion of, the power of *gentrification* to evoke literal gentrification and therefore its ability to call out resistance to brick-and-mortar upscaling. In other words, works like Lingel's inspire a set of questions that I believe are worthy of contemplation and debate. Has the rebirth of *gentrification* as a metaphorical heuristic drained it of some of its weight and significance as a signal of specific urban inequalities and social problems associated with literal gentrification, such as displacement and the loss of affordable housing?

On the other hand, are cultural producers, whether academics or screenwriters, so sure that their audiences will recognize the problems of literal gentrification that they trust that it might call people to action on issues as distant from literal gentrification as the de-democratization of the internet? I mean to suggest that it is possible that the increasingly dominant viewpoint that literal gentrification is a social problem may contribute to the term's increased salience as a heuristic that can be leveraged for other movements—and, partially as a result, may call attention away from work oriented around addressing the problems of literal gentrification.

———

In his book *Renovating Value*, Robert Goldman, professor emeritus of sociology at Lewis & Clark College and a scholar of the media, argues that while HGTV doesn't ever say *gentrification*, the home renovation shows that are the network's bread and butter are, in fact, truly all about literal gentrification.[7] Goldman suggests that by zeroing in on the transformation of an individual house, HGTV looks away from how renovation and reinvestment alter not just a home but the broader neighborhood context in which homes are situated.

Of course, this argument about HGTV's silence about literal gentrification is nearly the inverse argument that *The Death and Life of* Gentrification makes; instead of suggesting that we use *gentrification* to convey meanings that are not directly related to literal gentrification, Goldman proposes that HGTV represents and promotes literal gentrification without identifying it by name. Indeed, Goldman's book warns of the possible consequences of depicting literal gentrification without calling it what it is.

Goldman implies that it is dangerous for HGTV to represent literal gentrification in this silent, stealth manner. The silence means that we can't call it when we see it, even when the Property Brothers advocate for how an open floor plan will boost a home's value, or when the married hosts of *Fixer Upper* take a shabby home in a disinvested neighborhood and transform it to farmhouse chic. *Gentrification* even goes unmentioned on *Flip or Flop*, which features homes—which, uniformly, have seen better days—that the hosts purchase at auction.

But, also, like other academic books of its ilk, *Renovating Value* is more interested in revealing some of the problems of late-stage capitalism than literal gentrification itself. In this sense, Goldman's book does the same kind of work that I have traced throughout this book: it uses *gentrification* to tell a broad story about capitalism and value in contemporary society. In this sense, Goldman evokes literal gentrification, but in so doing he, like Lingel, relies on *gentrification* as a metaphorical heuristic for the dynamics of late-stage capitalism, particularly its reliance on value extraction.

Like much else that I trace in the chapters that came before this, Goldman's reliance on *gentrification* to tell his story is value-laden. Indeed, Goldman dedicates his book "to the principal of housing as a human right." He takes issue with late-stage capitalism and with the performance of value extraction that he regards as the bedrock of HGTV. He is particularly perturbed by the educational posture of this performance, writing that "HGTV envisions a path for viewers to follow and learn how to find and extract new value from housing properties" (1).

Goldman writes that he is not interested in the nuts and bolts (no pun intended) of these shows or, put differently, in how hosts and their clients rescue houses from decay or decline. Instead, Goldman is "interested in a *different type of rescue,* the ideological rescue of value amid the extinction of affordable housing and the perpetuation of systemic housing inequalities" (5; my emphasis).

Put differently, Goldman is generally concerned with financialized capital and, crucially, not only as it relates to housing market inequalities. He writes, "On HGTV we can binge-watch efforts to culturally salvage and distance the neoliberal model from the precarity of financialized capital and its appetite for perpetual indebtedness" (5).

For Goldman, this is not really about houses per se. Instead, it is about "salvage consumer capitalism, in which value can be sought by making old objects pretty again" (7). Elsewhere he echoes this, writing that "HGTV endorses a neoliberal solution to a neoliberal paradigm in crisis" (8). In this instance, the solution and crisis are housing related, but the broader pattern extends not only beyond *gentrification* but beyond the realm of housing itself.

Part of what makes it evident that this book, despite having *gentrification* in its subtitle, is using *gentrification* as a metaphorical heuristic to tell a broader story is that Goldman himself is uncertain that HGTV is truly capturing *literal gentrification* (Schulman 2012). If it is literal gentrification, it is what Goldman himself calls a "generalized" and geographically diffuse gentrification. As he notes, shows like *Property Brothers* and *Flip or Flop* typically feature suburban locales; spaces scholars only sometimes consider eligible for literal gentrification (because, in theory, they have not experienced the same processes of disinvestment that opened the door for gentrification in many central city and some rural locales).[8] He writes, "This logic of abstracted geography pushes the principles of rent-gap gentrification into the suburbs. In this way, HGTV supports an impression of generalized, geographically nonspecific gentrification" (35). Goldman even suggests that on HGTV literal gentrification is so "general" as to not involve neighborhoods at all; houses, as independent units, "gentrify" without the viewer gaining insight into the broader neighborhoods in which they are situated.

The leaps that Goldman takes are part of how we know that his book is not *really* just about literal gentrification, or even much about literal gentrification at all. *Gentrification,* in this instance, ultimately serves as a metaphorical heuristic for the idea of how capital is manipulated for the benefit of some at the cost of others. It represents how value and wealth can be wrung out of the devalued; it is an example of increasingly desperate and creative attempts to secure capital from that which has otherwise been discarded (*Junkyard Empire* and *Antiques Roadshow* are other examples of this).

What fascinates Goldman is how HGTV pursues the idea of realizing profit by rescuing that which has been devalued. This is a logic that, indisputably, underlies literal gentrification. However, I suspect that Goldman uses *gentrification* as a metaphorical heuristic for this broader point because it is the best-known contemporary rescue operation. He writes, for instance, that "HGTV proposes a generic rent-gap model of gentrification" (9).[9]

By offering this reading of Goldman, I do not wish to contest the idea that HGTV offers representations of literal gentrification or that, in other instances, it depicts a cousin of literal gentrification that may, in turn, inspire spin-off literal gentrification. However, as Goldman suggests, HGTV's gentrification is a "silent" and "generalized" gentrification; one stretched nearly to the limits of what many might traditionally think of as literal gentrification. Indeed the book stretches *gentrification* so far that it is worth interrogating whether the book is really about HGTV and literal gentrification, and, even more so, whether the author means for it to be such.

Ultimately, more than anything else, for Goldman, what he refers to as the *theater of gentrification* "reinvigorate[s] a value theory of labor" (11), and that is what he wishes to teach us by proposing that HGTV engages with literal gentrification. *Gentrification* works for Goldman because it is evocative of "rescue" capitalism (5). In other words, *gentrification* earns a place in the title of Goldman's book less because he is actually writing about literal gentrification (despite the fact that he uses the term and writes about the rehabbing of homes) and more because the term is a charged way of making the capitalist dynamics he actually diagnoses tangible and meaningful for the reader. The fact that Goldman is able to make this different point about rescue capitalism while using the term *gentrification* and engaging a network that features home renovation TV shows goes to show just how nimble and evocative metaphorical "gentrification" can be and how readily accessible it is as a heuristic that communicates critical perspectives on appropriation, exploitation, and value extraction, whether pertaining to home renovation television or the internet.

It's Literally a Metaphor

This is not to suggest that all academic books that purport to be about literal gentrification are really about something else. Some books rely on *gentrification* as a metaphor and heuristic to make a broader intellectual argument or to convey a grander argument or position while also engaging with literal gentrification. In most cases, they do this because they believe that literal gentrification is representative of a broader pattern, dynamic, or issue, or symptomatic of a more far-reaching problem. Thus they attend to literal gentrification but only partially because they wish to explore it as its own discrete phenomenon; they rely at least as much on *gentrification*'s metaphorical power.

Gentrification is multivocal; it communicates multiple meanings, and academics, like others, harness this multivocality for their specific, individual purposes. Of course, many words contain multiple meanings, but *gentrification* is not only multivocal; it is also weighted with political punch, recognizability, and has had an impressive shelf life since Ruth Glass first coined the term in 1964. Thus, by virtue of possessing this dynamic set of attributes, it serves as a weighty conveyer of an author's intended meaning—and, in some instances, even works for authors to build simultaneous arguments about literal and metaphorical "gentrification."

Consider *Capital City*, by Samuel Stein, which Verso published in 2019. The book, which is subtitled, "Gentrification and the Real Estate State," engages more directly with literal gentrification (and the scholarly literature about it) than the aforementioned books. For instance, Stein deftly addresses long-standing debates about production versus consumption explanations for literal gentrification—or the question of whether markets and governments create gentrification or whether gentrifiers' tastes and demands generate brick-and mortar gentrification.[10] He also relies on the late geographer Neil Smith's rent-gap explanation—or the idea that literal gentrification emerges when the value of land drops well below the potential profit to be made by building on or improving that land—to contextualize how gentrification arises in cities.[11]

This is not just a matter of engaging with academic literatures on literal gentrification. In a few places in the book, Stein attends to specific instances of literal gentrification as they unfold in New York City, such as the redevelopment of the Atlantic Yards and the Lower East Side.

Despite this engagement with how literal gentrification unfolds and the author's apparent genuine concern about the state of literal gentrification in places like New York, at heart Stein's book is really about the field and profession of planning, and, even more specifically, about its role in facilitating what he terms the "real estate state." In point of fact, the book is a seething indictment of the planning profession's role in advancing the real estate state, and Stein uses literal gentrification, together with Donald Trump's family's long history in real estate development, to illustrate his argument.

By the "real estate state" Stein refers to "a political formation in which real estate capital has inordinate influence over the shape of our cities, the parameters of our politics and the lives we lead" (5). He posits that real estate increasingly controls other domains of social life: "As real estate values have risen to absurd heights, so has the political force of real estate capital" (5). Put succinctly, for Stein, the real estate state is "a government by developers, for developers" (38).

But the book does not only impugn the real estate state. Stein builds a case for the crucial role that planners have played in facilitating this state. He suggests that the tradition of planners upholding the interests of the real estate state is older than the field of planning itself, writing that "proto-planners enabled the country's murderous westward expansion, and mapped the rail networks and other infrastructure that made it possible" (15). More recently, in New York, planners led planned shrinkage in 1975 aimed at shutting down certain city services "to encourage poor people of color to exit the city" (25). Of course, these are processes that extend, both temporally and in geographic range, beyond literal gentrification.

More than anything else, Stein suggests that planners rely on zoning as a key tool, particularly in cities like New York (21). In turn, this becomes a primary method by which planners enable the real estate state, whether they intend for this to occur or not. He writes that the problem is bigger than any individual planner: "Most planners do not seek to line the pockets of wealthy elites or displace the poor. Yet, this is exactly what has happened, again and again, in city after city" (26).

Stein proposes that at this stage, planning is intractable from the real estate state. He writes that the New York Planning Commission is peopled by planners with intimate connections to development (38), and he argues that even planners with intentions of intervening in the real estate state often inadvertently advance the goals of real estate capital accumulation by the wealthy: "In the real estate state, planners can create marvelous environments for rich people, but if they work to improve poor peoples' spaces they risk sparking gentrification and displacement" (40).

As the above suggests, Stein devotes particular attention to (and expresses frustration about) planners' role in advancing literal gentrification, which he presents as a key mechanism of contemporary capital generation by the real estate state. He defines *gentrification* as "the process by which capital is reinvested in urban neighborhoods, and poorer residents and their cultural products are displaced and replaced by richer people and their preferred aesthetics and amenities" (41).

When it comes to literal gentrification, he indicts planners for engagement in a set of zoning, land use, and tax policies that facilitate the process. Stein writes, "Part of what planners do, then, is ensure that both sides of the relationship are present by luring gentrification's producers with land use and tax incentives" while inviting its consumers through race- and class- inflicted neighborhood initiatives" (43).

Presented thusly, he calls his reader to see literal gentrification not as an accident but as quite intentional, writing that it is "planned by the state as much as it is produced by developers and consumed by the condo crowd" (43). However, Stein does this less to build an argument about the origins of literal gentrification and more to illustrate how planners have blood on their hands when it comes to literal gentrification and so much else. Literal gentrification is a key example of the problems of contemporary planning and of its close association with the real estate state. Presented thusly, literal gentrification is a metaphor for how planning has embedded itself in systems of capital accumulation that benefit the few at the cost of many.

While Stein relies on literal gentrification as a primary example, in actuality it is only one among other urban processes and policies for which he holds planners accountable. For instance, he writes about how redlining and urban renewal policies left many US cities poised for reinvestment in the 1970s. Still, he proposes that planners are to blame for what came next. "It would take planners, however, to scale up gentrification from a neighborhood phenomenon of renovation and re-invention to a larger process of displacement, demolition, and development" (56). This, he suggests, is not because planners have a particular aim of advancing literal gentrification, but rather because "the job of planners, then, is to keep business booming as long as possible, and when land and property values ultimately fall, to get them back up as quickly as possible" (56). As a result, "planners have increasingly used zoning to facilitate gentrification" (61), and they alternatingly channel resources toward gentrified space or inadvertently encourage reinvestment in disinvested space by encouraging the reallocation of resources to those areas. Ultimately, he concludes that under the real estate state, "planners . . . have little incentive to do anything resulting in lower land values" (168).

Ultimately, Stein's book is not about how to undo literal gentrification, nor (despite writing about literal gentrification) does it really present an argument about literal gentrification at all. *Gentrification* is a vehicle for impugning planning; a charged metaphor for how planners have colluded with capital again and again.

In other words, Stein relies on an insightful account of four decades of literal gentrification in New York to build an argument about how planning as a field and practice should be reenvisioned. Literal gentrification is an example or metaphor in service of Stein's true argument, about the imbrication of planning and capitalism. For this reader, this was notable, given how often friends and colleagues described Stein's book as being (only) about literal gentrification.[12]

Why use literal gentrification to tell this story? It would be easy enough, for instance, to use other dark chapters, such as urban renewal or the ghettoization of public housing, to indict planning. After all, Jane Jacobs and others have fundamentally altered how many people think about cities by highlighting midcentury missteps in planning (1961). But, in the end, literal gentrification is, arguably, the best and most efficiently evocative contemporary example of the true problem—of the collusion of the planning profession with the real estate state—that Stein wishes to uncover.

However, according to Stein's own account, that is not the only reason he relies on literal gentrification to illustrate his point about planning. At least in the present day, *gentrification* is especially evocative; even infamous urban renewal is not as charged as *gentrification*. Indeed, Stein writes that "the clunky term 'gentrification'" is "a household word" (5) and presumably, therefore, easily retrievable and recognizable to the general, educated audience he writes for. In other words, it is both a useful example and metaphor of the failures of planning, and an easily accessible heuristic.

Scholars like Stein can use *gentrification* as a tool to advance their arguments precisely because *gentrification* is at once "clunky" and powerful while also being "a household word." *Gentrification*, as an idea that can be used to evoke and develop other, related ideas, presents a forceful and dynamic combination of charged recognition, multivocality, and divisiveness. No one is quite sure what *gentrification* means, but everyone is quite certain that it means a lot. This emboldens those like Stein to use it to build their adjacent arguments, with all of the recognizability and elusiveness that *gentrification* brings to bolster their case.

———

I find a similar reliance on *gentrification*—as a literal, concrete, urban process and, at the same time, as a method for gesturing to the structural roots of cultural changes—in certain nonacademic texts. Consider, for instance, a memoir that addresses literal gentrification but also uses the concept to diagnose how and why queer culture and politics have changed.

Tom Eubanks's *Ghosts of St. Vincent's* attends to the literal gentrification of Greenwich Village, but mostly it wrestles with how a gay male subculture of which he was once a part has transformed since the last decades of the twentieth century.[13] Unsurprisingly for a book titled after a now shuttered hospital, *Ghosts of St. Vincent's* very much engages death; the death of cities as sites of refuge and cultural experimentation; AIDS-related deaths; and, foremost, the death of a way of being queer that Eubanks positions as having perished with AIDS, literal gentrification, and increased social acceptance of gender and sexual minorities.[14]

Like the other books we have encountered, there are passages in Eubanks's text that might lead one to surmise that literal gentrification is the author's principal subject. For instance, he writes, "I never thought I would live to see the hospital [where he nearly died from an AIDS-related illness] that kept me alive replaced by 200 condominiums and five townhouses for 'slumming' celebrities, hedge fund bros, and the offspring of oligarchs. . . . Before the entitled lived here exclusively, the marginalized died in droves" (2017, 11).

However, this is not just another book about how New York has died.[15] Rather, it is an account of a broader set of losses that Eubanks has experienced, some directly related to AIDS, which took many of his intimates and threatened his own life, and some related to the changing social position of those who composed the vibrant queer subculture he encountered in New York in the late 1980s. Eubanks relies on the twin figures of St. Vincent's hospital, and the changes that it has itself endured, and of literal gentrification, as guideposts for this broader personal and cultural transformation.

To be sure, this is not merely a descriptive argument. Eubanks is building a case for—despite widespread and unfiltered celebration of LGBTQIA+ victories—mourning a time before gay marriage and other markers of increased LGBTQIA+ acceptance, when he and his queer compatriots maintained a vibrant, close, and provocative community. In this sense, the book builds an argument—akin to some we encountered in chapter 3—about the costs of homonormativity for queer culture and community.[16] In so doing, it crafts a strong rejoinder to narratives of unambiguous progress for sexual minorities and gestures to how the adoption of norms and practices once sequestered by heterosexuals has altered the community he experienced as a young man.

What, precisely, is the cultural transformation that Eubanks seeks to capture? Eubanks was born in 1968 to a Midwestern Catholic family. He writes, "Two years later, Stonewall would open the floodgates of human sexuality. In hindsight, it is clear I was on a collision course with AIDS" (12). His childhood was marked by homophobia and his certain knowledge that he could not speak openly about his sexuality. He describes, for instance, an incident at a movie theater with his father and brothers in the 1970s. The film they watched featured two men kissing. Eubanks recalls the audience making sounds of disgust. He writes, "I couldn't bear to check my father's reaction. I lowered my head and shrank into my seat. Deep down I knew I was condemned to desire the kiss of another man and certain to be greeted by a violent chorus of boos and jeers—even worse—if that desire was ever made public" (16).

Eubanks sought to leave this homophobic world behind as swiftly as he could, moving to New York City for college and delighting in the public life and community he discovered there. For instance, he writes, "I met Raven at the boy bar, a deliberately lowercase asylum of joy located on rough and raggedy St. Mark's Place. Part drag club, part twink bar, the two-story building—not counting the illegal basement dance floor . . . showcased fierce performers who worked fags into a froth" (50). He misses not only these institutions but also how Greenwich Village itself served as an institution; one that served as a crucial resource for sexual minorities. Eubanks writes: "On July 11, 1964, the day Vito turned 18, he made his great escape from the Hell that was Lodi, New Jersey, to Greenwich Village, to recreate himself" (176). Via such accounts, Eubanks builds the case that he was not alone in fleeing from the Midwest (and other such places) to the West Village for respite from a homophobic world; and, crucially, that one could find just that there.

Today, Eubanks instructs, St. Vincent's is gone, and so too is Eubanks. The West Village is no longer a place that he can call home or even recognize. He writes: "Twenty years have passed since my winter on the 7th floor at St. Vincent's, another lifetime. . . . These days, I live uptown, at the northern end of Manhattan. It was time to move. The West Village became an open-air mall, a celebrity chef food court for the rich and the aspiring. The neighborhood that once housed abattoirs, artist lofts, nightclubs, sex clubs, and Restaurant Florent has been erased by the haute hotels and high-end retailers. And tourists wait in line to wander the revamped Highline" (211).

This is not just a complaint about literal gentrification writ large, but, instead, about how queer culture and institutions—both formal and informal—have transformed too. Eubanks names some of these: "The piers I roamed as a troubled young fag have been redesigned as lush parkland with glass towers multiplying in size and number along the West Side Highway. . . . Where boys carried on in the bushes and queens did runway among the ruins, moneyed brahs lug golf clubs to Chelsea Piers and leery-eyed nannies push trust fund children in pricey strollers" (211). He goes on to write, "St. Vincent's is a phantom, virtually undetectable in its new role as another Habitrail for the one-percent" (212).

When I first read Eubanks's memoir, I had the vague notion that I should write about how books that aren't explicitly about literal gentrification are, after all, *really* about literal gentrification. It seemed to me that literal gentrification was everywhere, in all kinds of books. Over and again, I would pick up a novel or a memoir because it intrigued me, only to find that literal gentrification stood out prominently in its narrative. Could we read the story of literal gentrification and perhaps even document its progress and dynamics in fiction and memoir, I wondered. Were writers a secret legion of ethnographers, collecting data about the city as they went about their lives and recording insights in their novels and memoirs? Might I write something about what literal gentrification means to cultural producers, just by reading their accounts of their lives (or of the affairs of their fictional characters) in contemporary cities?

As I read Eubanks's memoir (and a few others like it), I came to realize that my hunch was, at least partially, wrong. Books that evoke brick-and-mortar gentrification are not always *really* about literal gentrification. That is, books that make literal gentrification central to their narrative are not always telling a story about or explaining literal gentrification. Nor are they always looking inward to explain personal transformation.

Instead, in books like *Ghosts of St. Vincent's*, literal gentrification plays a relatively prominent role because it serves as a metaphor for a different kind of change (often change that occurred parallel to, and even intersected with, literal gentrification) that, at heart, is most central to the book. Authors, like Eubanks, often turn to literal gentrification as a shorthand or heuristic to make a causal argument about the loss of cultural vitality at the hands of elites, whether developers and those who aid and abet them, governments who deny AIDS care and research, or the strictures of heteronormative society. In contrast to the memoirs, films, TV series, and novels we encountered in chapter 3, in a work like

Ghosts, gentrification is evocative of how broadscale systems, spanning from the legal to the political to the economic to the cultural, shape the most intimate facets of our lives, such as the possibility of forging queer community. That is, Eubanks does not hold himself responsible for the losses he has experienced; instead, he lays blame on the systems in which he is embedded. And, for him, literal gentrification serves as a metaphor that helps him to make that point.

Like others of its ilk, *Ghosts of St. Vincent's* is meant to counter the view that the movement toward gay marriage and homonormativity is unambiguously positive.[17] It is meant to make us stop and think about what is lost in our cultural landscape when we seek to erase that which make us different—whether via literal gentrification or via cultural assimilation (a.k.a. "gentrification").[18]

For instance, Eubanks writes, "I'm smart enough to know that AIDS is not over by any means. It's merely lost its punch. But then, so has being gay. We're no longer criminals. We serve openly in the military. We won the right to marry. Western society has begun to embrace the fluidity of sexual identity and the flexibility of gender lines" (214). He blames this change, as much as AIDS and literal gentrification, for the loss of boy bar and the Chelsea Piers and all of the other places that made his early adulthood meaningful and free and that connected him to others. Eubanks writes, "If I were in the hospital today I wouldn't have nearly as many visitors as I did back then" (215). The reason for this, he suggests, is not just AIDS, but, rather, because what it means to be queer has changed and that change has weakened connections on which he once depended.

Eubanks himself implies that *gentrification* works for him as a device that facilitates his ability to mourn and feel pain about the loss of an earlier queer culture and the neighborhood in which it was situated for him. In other words, thinking about the tragedy of literal gentrification allows him to access the tragedy of the transformation of queer culture that he has experienced: "I know it's sick to be sick about a time when I was sick, but St. Vincent's destruction haunts me. . . . The neighborhood's transformation and my banishment from it only heighten my yearning" (213). Just as literal gentrification emerges from political and economic systems, the "gentrification" of queer culture has, too.

Of course, his yearning is less for an ungentrified West Village and more for a culture that existed there pre-hypergentrification and pre–gay marriage. Thinking about how the West Village has changed materially provides fodder for his nostalgia for how New York—and the subculture constituted by other gay men like himself that he once found there—has changed culturally, socially, and politically. Thus, he wants the reader to think, with him, about the loss of St. Vincent's and of the broader West Village so that we can *feel with him* a different (but parallel in time) loss: the loss of an earlier, renegade queer culture and community.

There is a lesson here in how Eubanks reveals that literal gentrification allows him to access pain and nostalgia for a different (albeit not totally unrelated to literal gentrification) loss. This sentimental resonance is part of what gives *gentrification* its political potential and fervor, and it is part of what makes it such a resonant heuristic. *Gentrification*, at least in the current cultural moment, is emotionally evocative; we have encountered, in chapter 1, how talk of *gentrification* evokes nostalgia, and, in chapter 2, how it calls out mourning. This emotionally evocative nature nurtures *gentrification*'s utility as a storytelling device, especially for those who wish to spur action with their words.

Of course, *Ghosts of St. Vincent's* also reveals that it is not just academic authors and journalists who leverage literal gentrification as a metaphor and heuristic, and, often, to diagnose the structural roots of the problem they examine. *Gentrification* is such a widely accessible symbol, one that many are very conversant and comfortable with around the globe, that it should come as no surprise that memoirists, novelists, and others also leverage it to call for change or to challenge dominant narratives, such as those about the unambiguously happy progress of the LGBTQIA+ movement.

———

Once we recognize that authors sometimes pair literal gentrification and metaphorical "gentrification" in the manner of Eubanks and Stein, we can see how books that are even *mostly* about literal gentrification also rely on *gentrification* to make a broader set of points. In other words, some books devote significant space to literal gentrification while also relying on *gentrification* as a metaphorical heuristic that gestures to social inequalities borne of political and economic systems.

Take the author and psychoanalyst Jeremiah Moss's book, *Vanishing New York: How a Great City Lost Its Soul* (2017). Without a doubt, Moss's book is about the literal gentrification of New York City, but it is also about more. While the book was heralded by newspaper reviews, celebrities (Sarah Jessica Parker, Andy Cohen), and academic blogs alike as elevating a national conversation about literal gentrification, *Vanishing New York* impugns not just literal gentrification but neoliberalism and late-stage capitalism more broadly.[19] Moss presents neoliberal governance and late-stage (or corporate) capitalism as driving literal gentrification, as well as other problems of contemporary life. Whereas in chapter 3 we saw how a neoliberal sensibility sometimes assigns responsibility for personal "gentrification" to the individual (rather than situating uneven opportunities for upward mobility in broader systems), in Moss's account *gentrification* is evocative of a neoliberal political system rooted in a capitalist economy. That system, characterized by deregulation, individualization, and privatization, holds individuals accountable for their fate, erasing safety nets and coloring over how individuals' opportunities are enabled and constrained by economic and political systems.[20] Moss has a problem with late-stage capitalism reliant on neoliberalism, and literal gentrification is a way, conceptually, into that problem. To be more precise, literal gentrification is a metaphorical heuristic for the problems of late-stage capitalism under neoliberalism.

In this sense, for authors like Moss, *gentrification* is multivocal. Because *gentrification* is so recognizable and so resonant, authors like Moss can write about literal gentrification and their books can underline problems associated with it while also relying on literal gentrification as a metaphorical heuristic for the source of systemic inequalities. That is, one can read books like *Vanishing New York* in at least two ways: as narrowly impugning literal gentrification, and as using *gentrification* as a productive example to identify bigger systemic issues (in Moss's case, neoliberalism and late-stage capitalism). This, of course, echoes the work that Samuel Stein's book accomplishes, but Moss goes one step further to engaging with literal gentrification in the service of his broader argument about the problems of neoliberalism and late-stage corporate capitalism.

Aren't most books, mostly, about more than one thing? Perhaps so, but *gentrification* is evocative in a particular manner. Consider, for instance, how Moss evokes literal gentrification while simultaneously arguing that New York's soul has been in peril for a century. He suggests that the "battle for New York's soul" originated in the 1920s, therefore predating the timeline by which most of us think about literal gentrification (which, after all, was first coined by Ruth Glass in 1964) by several decades.[21] For instance, he writes, "The death of industrial New York was planned by a privately organized group of bankers and real estate developers. They didn't like having all of those blue-collar multiethnic people taking up space on valuable Manhattan land. . . . Starting in 1922 [they] schemed to destroy working-class New York by zoning away industrial areas" (62).

For Moss, this history culminates, eventually, in neoliberalism (of course, I am skipping huge stretches of historical development to which Moss is attentive), which "is neither new or liberal" and is "the invisible engine that drives hyper-gentrification" (103). He goes on to write that "neoliberalism is that shadowy shark devouring cities across the globe" (103).

The "corporate model" that aids and abets neoliberalism, Moss argues, insists on relentless growth (285), seeking individual profit rather than shoring up the collective good. For him, it is this broader model, the engine of neoliberalism—and not literal gentrification per se—that has disappeared New York City.

I would be taking my argument too far to say that Moss's book isn't about literal gentrification, but *Vanishing New York* is polemical on a much broader scale than anything narrowly related to a single process of urban transformation. The implications of his argument and of the changes that he suggests are required to save places like New York from extinction extend well beyond antigentrification planning and policy. Centering literal gentrification provides Moss with a powerful and recognizable metaphorical heuristic to make bigger and bolder claims:

about neoliberalism, corporate culture, and a century-old war against the working class.

Of course, some of the dynamics to which Moss ultimately wants to draw our attention began before literal gentrification emerged (in the 1960s and 1970s), and *all* of the issues he engages relate not only to literal gentrification but to a range of other issues, processes, and dynamics, too. For instance, Moss might have told his story about neoliberalism, the war on the working class, and the rise of corporate culture by highlighting homelessness or even the proliferation of unpaid internships.[22]

Does it matter whether literal gentrification brought Moss to these broader concerns or whether the broader concerns brought him to *gentrification*? After all, Moss writes movingly of having been inspired by his own personal gentrification losses—from beloved delis and corner stores, to people. Should one care whether Moss or any other author that this chapter features uses *gentrification* instrumentally, when the argument closest to their heart engages a broader systemic issue, such as neoliberalism? The reader may disagree with me, but I am agnostic. Regardless of the author's initial intentions, a reader of *Vanishing New York* will walk away with a different sense of what the problem at hand is and of what relevant solutions might be than they would if the book narrowly diagnosed literal gentrification as having killed New York. Thus, while *Vanishing New York* is a timely, lively, and insightful account of how cities have changed, a reader would be mistaken to pick it up as a primer on literal gentrification in New York or anywhere else.

Put differently, Moss offers a compelling vision of how literal gentrification is entangled with other forces and histories, which is incredibly valuable and follows in the footsteps of some of the luminaries of gentrification studies (e.g., Neil Smith's book *The New Urban Frontier* referenced a couple of times earlier). Perhaps it is an accident, then, that the scope of the book and its argument extends so far beyond literal gentrification, but the effect, for an attentive reader, is the same. In the end, we learn from Moss that literal gentrification is an example of a much broader problem rather than *the* problem itself. This is yet another way in which literal gentrification serves as a metaphorical heuristic to tell a different (even if related) story.

"Gentrification" as Metaphor
for Upscaling and Appropriation

Not only scholars and other authors who write about cities engage *gentrification*. Scholars, including musicologists and sociologists, have adopted *gentrification* as a metaphor to forward a variety of arguments about the appropriation of working-class culture by the professional classes. Still others use *gentrification* in a similar manner but close the loop by suggesting that the "gentrification" of cultural components, like music and memory, can in turn lead to the literal gentrification of place.

As an example of the first camp, an emerging field of scholars writes about "musical gentrification," which a recent volume on the subject conceptualizes in the following terms: "Cultural objects of relatively lower status, in this case popular musics, are made objects of acquisition by subjects or institutions of higher social status, thereby playing an important role in social elevation, mobility and distinction" (Dyndal et al. 2021, 1).[23]

The editors of a volume on "musical gentrification" (Dyndhal et al. 2021, 14) suggest that the notion of "musical gentrification" emerged in the 1990s, when sociologists Richard Peterson and Roger Kern suggested, in a highly influential article, that elites were adopting popular or folk music for their own purposes and, in a sense, "gentrify[ing] elements of popular culture" (1996, 906).[24]

Petter Dyndahl et al., the editors of the volume on musical gentrification, acknowledge that in studies of musical gentrification, *gentrification* operates as a metaphor (15) and that some are critical of the use of terms originally coined to describe a particular set of circumstances for such purposes. For instance, they note that some object to calling schools "colonized" (15) when the authors don't refer to colonization in a literal sense.[25]

Despite acknowledgment of such concerns, Dyndahl et al. indicate that *gentrification* nonetheless works for them, because, as with other usages of *gentrification*, the notion of musical "gentrification" is not value-neutral. For them, as for others, *gentrification* communicates a type of appropriation that benefits the appropriator at the cost of the appropriated. They write, for instance, that "these processes strongly contribute to changing the characteristics of particular musical communities as well as the musics, practices, and cultures that are subjected to gentrification" (Dyndahl, Karlsen, Skårberg, ad Nielsen 2014, 54).[26]

In a manner similar to that of scholars of musical gentrification, other scholars identify a broad applicability of *gentrification* to the professional classes' appropriation of cultural practices traditionally associated with the working class. For instance, Karen Halnon and Saundra Cohen write that "gentrification processes are applicable to a new frontier: the 'symbolic neighborhoods' of the lower classes in popular culture.... [W]e aim to show how muscles, motorcycles and tattoos ... have been objects of investment, invasion, transformation and displacement" (2006, 33).[27]

The authors make clear that they do not mean literal gentrification when they use the term, writing that "what is novel about the kind of gentrification discussed herein is that it refers to relatively elusive symbolic terrain dispersed across popular consumer culture today, rather than specific geographical territory, as in gentrification proper" (Halnon and Cohen 2006, 36). They adopt this metaphor, in part, because it provides a framework for considering the "consequences for the gentrified" (37) of such appropriation. In other words, relying on *gentrification* allows them to communicate their critical perspective on the adoption of working-class cultural practices, such as tattoos, weight-lifting, and motorcyles, by the professional classes. Here, metaphorical "gentrification" is so evocative of appropriation that it operates for scholars as a heuristic.

The above examples of how some academics adopt *gentrification* as a metaphor and heuristic are subtly distinct from how another camp of scholars relies on *gentrification*. This second camp turns to *gentrification* as a metaphor to describe how the gentrification of something, such as music or memory, leads to the literal gentrification of place.

Take the research of Gillian Turnbull as an example. She writes that "the predominantly middle class desire for an imaginary Calgary is fueled by and dependent on the presence of a roots music soundtrack in gentrified regions of the city and that this music helps to create a simultaneously modern, urban identity as well as a traditional, rural one. The roots music scene of the city is directly connected to the perpetual quest for a definitive Calgarian identity, and is *essential to the reconstruction of neglected neighbourhoods*" (2009, 24)[28] Put differently, the "gentrification" of roots music plays a role in the literal gentrification of Calgary.

I highlight these texts to contrast arguments about how musical appropriation fuels neighborhood appropriation with those that, instead, rely on *gentrification* purely as a metaphor to facilitate a critical evaluation of the transformation of popular music.

Following Turnbull's scholarship on Calgary, some scholars argue that literal gentrification is partially produced via cultural narratives or frames. Among those who make this type of argument are some who suggest that ways of thinking—culture—can itself "gentrify"—and that, in turn, "gentrified" culture can advance literal gentrification. For instance, Guiseppe Tolfo and Brian Doucet write of the "gentrification of memory" (2022) and how it advances narratives of livability in Vancouver and therefore the literal gentrification of a neighborhood.[29]

The authors write: "Livability discourse requires the *gentrification of memory*: the methodical and deliberate eviction of marginalized communities' histories, in service of capital accumulation and dominant class interests" (288). Here again, for the authors the metaphorical "gentrification" of memory plays a role in the literal gentrification of a city.

These examples illustrate the intentionality with which some scholars adopt *gentrification* as a metaphor. While some believe that figurative "gentrification" can produce literal gentrification, others quite explicitly use *gentrification* purely as a metaphor to describe a process of change and appropriation that they regard as unambiguously distinctive from literal gentrification. *Gentrification*, for them, is a metaphorical heuristic in their communication arsenal that expresses the cultural appropriation of marginalized groups' cultural practices by elites. For such scholars, because *gentrification* is so familiar and charged, it works to communicate the idea that the transformation they model is an injustice; it marks how the marginalized face involuntary change and cultural appropriation. This indicates the degree to which some cultural producers are confident that their audiences will recognize that literal gentrification is often perceived as a problematic, exploitative process. After all, *gentrification* only works as a metaphor for them if it evokes exploitation, and none of the authors whom I have engaged have to devote much work or space to make that case. With little effort, *gentrification* signifies appropriation.

We will see in the next section how confidence in this meaning of *gentrification* extends beyond authors—whether academics, memoirists, or journalists—to the realm of social movement activists. Activists present *gentrification* as a rallying cry that has the potential to mobilize and extend their appeals to a broader audience that might respond to the symbolic significance of *gentrification*. Here, yet another set of actors capitalizes on *gentrification*'s emotional evocativeness and its utility for signaling the structural roots of social problems.

Gentrification as a Social Movement Resource

Authors are not the only individuals who rely on *gentrification* to make arguments that are not, narrowly, about literal gentrification. Indeed, stepping away from books and academic articles, I invite the reader to consider how some activist groups use *gentrification* for purposes that are not directly or specifically aimed at stopping literal gentrification. That is, they use them to advance political causes that are not explicitly connected to literal gentrification. This, of course, echoes how some scholars rely on *gentrification* as a metaphor or heuristic because the term efficiently evokes the systemic roots of certain social problems.

In the summer of 2020, the United States grappled with a pandemic, and after the violent death of George Floyd at the hands of Minneapolis police officers, protests against racist police violence rippled across the country. At some such protests, *gentrification* became a rallying cry. In both Brooklyn and Louisville, Black Lives Matter activists chanted "Fire, Fire Gentrifier," and antigentrification graffiti appeared at other Black Lives Matter protests.[30] At one San Francisco protest, an activist carried a sign that read: "Gentrification = police brutality."[31]

Of course, the aim of such protests was to combat racism and the violence that upholds it, with a particular emphasis on racist state violence. However, for these protesters, *gentrification* presumably communicated a parallel racial injustice and a form of violence of its own kind. Thus, in the case of Black Lives Matter, evocations of *gentrification* may work to extend the frame of racial injustice associated with police brutality, broadening the notion of the fragility of Black lives and of what it means for them to *matter*.

In other words, such protests convey the idea that forced displacement, housing segregation, and the separation of families and other caregiving networks as people are priced out of gentrifying neighborhoods are their own kind of racialized violence. They also sometimes leverage *gentrifier* as a metaphorical heuristic for how those who hold power misuse it and exploit others—hence "Fire, Fire Gentrifier!" As a result, activists potentially extend the salience of Black Lives Matter by broadening movement frames from police brutality to another highly recognizable and charged issue: literal gentrification.

A few years before the events of 2020, the Chicago Trans Liberation Coalition conducted a radical action aimed at shutting down the city's annual Pride Parade.[32] Among their demands was a call for "divestment from gentrification, displacement, and white-cis supremacy!"[33] They decried "the violent systems of gentrification and segregation in Chicago, echoing racist practices of redlining that have shaped the human geography of this city."[34] Here, echoing dyke bar commemorators who find that *gentrification* evokes a unifying sense of marginality, trans activists evoked literal gentrification without presenting it as a trans-specific issue.

By doing so, they presented one of their grievances—*gentrification*—in very general, recognizable, and relatable terms. *Gentrification* evokes structural inequalities writ large; as we have already seen, *gentrification* is a heuristic for inequalities that emerge from political and economic systems that benefit a few at the cost of many. For all of these reasons, by evoking *gentrification*, intentionally or not, Trans Liberation activists positioned themselves to render their suffering more relatable; their claims-making in this instance is not only about the specific burdens of being transgender in a hostile society but also about the more general and highly relatable problem of suffering from the consequences of *gentrification* (read: from the burdens of social inequalities that emerge from unequal political and economic systems). While, presumably, they aimed to show how issues of transgender bias and exclusion and literal gentrification intersect, making transgender Chicagoans especially vulnerable to gentrification-related displacement, *gentrification* simultaneously serves as a metaphorical heuristic that has the potential to make transgender activists' concerns accessible to a broad audience.

Still earlier, climate change activists relied on talk of *gentrification* at the 2014 New York People's Climate March. A contingent of activists carried blue tents imprinted with the words "DISPLACED" and "DISPLACING WORKING PEOPLE." Using "rising tides, rising rents" and "our city, our homes," as rallying cries, they married concern about climate change and literal gentrification.[35] Here, they play on the idea of the insecure renter, familiar to many because of literal gentrification, and extend that idea to the broadscale insecurity of climate change. In other words, they seem to aim to convey the notion that if literal gentrification makes some insecure, we ought to imagine what climate change will do to an even greater swath of people. Displacement associated with literal gentrification is familiar; they prime their audience for an even broader climate-change-driven "gentrification" (a.k.a. mass involuntary displacement).

In 2019, the Dyke March took place in Washington, DC, after a decade of inactivity. The theme of the march was "dykes against displacement." Organizers aimed to raise money for two nonprofits, one of which has worked on housing justice and the other on antidisplacement.[36] Despite the theme of the 2019 march, protest signs and chants generally did not evoke *gentrification*.[37] In keeping with the formal theme, there were a few exceptions, including a chant at the beginning and the end of the march. Organizers called, "Displacement means . . ." and the audience called in response, "We've got to fight back!" A few signs also gestured to literal gentrification. One read "Dykes for Rent Strikes," and another "Dykes against Rent Hikes." However, press coverage suggests that more than anything else, the march, like most other dyke marches, emphasized dyke pride and visibility rather than housing justice or urban reform.[38] For instance, marchers chanted, "Go dykes, go!" and "Hey, hey. Ho, ho. Transphobia has got to go." Signs read, "Black Dykes Matter" and "Queer as Heck."[39]

Why frame a march as engaging issues of literal gentrification if organizers' core goal is dyke visibility and pride? As we have already seen in chapter 1, in some instances *gentrification* brings people together, uniting them around a shared sense of vulnerability. In other words, *gentrification* sometimes works as a hook to draw people together. Moreover, it helps to demonstrate how what matters for dykes matters for other social groups, too—and therefore helps to render the concerns of dyke march participants broad and relatable. In this spirit, the march also included many signs on the theme of "Black Lives Matter."

This brief survey of protests that evoke *gentrification* suggests that *gentrification* is sometimes deployed as a political resource by movements. While there are certainly activists who resist literal gentrification, working to block specific developments and/or to advocate for affordable housing, rezoning, and increased density, a distinct subset of activists engage *gentrification* not to mitigate literal gentrification, but, instead, to advance issues that are not narrowly related to place or to neighborhood change.[40] In other words, some certainly lobby against literal gentrification, but there are also activists who leverage *gentrification* as a rallying cry to serve distinct aims.

Paralleling the work of authors such as Jeremiah Moss, this liberal usage of *gentrification* by activists is, at least in part, spot-on social analysis: they recognize and name how literal gentrification emerges from and perpetuates the same political and economic systems of inequality that propel climate change, trans exclusion, homophobia, systemic racism, and racist state violence. On the other hand, we see again how *gentrification* is an effective metaphor and heuristic for communicating a sense of "us" versus "them," or of how the decks are stacked against some and in favor of others (Bartram 2022). *Gentrification* is, more and more, an every-person's social problem, and therefore it can support a variety of causes in a variety of ways—from serving as a hook to securing sympathy from a broader audience to boosting the relatability of a marginalized social group.

In the book's conclusion, I will address directly the question of whether this adoption of *gentrification* is good or bad, accurate or inaccurate. For now, though, I will highlight what this widespread adoption signals about the significance, recognizability, resonance, and malleability of *gentrification* in contemporary US society. Cataloging some of these usages and identifying patterns in how authors, activists, and memoirists deploy *gentrification* brings us closer to understanding what the term means today.

For instance, by looking at how people rely on talk of *gentrification* to advance other projects we see the broad systems, such as neoliberalism, late-stage capitalism, and the homophobic and racist state that writers and others have come to see as entangled with literal gentrification. In the case of Black Lives Matter, we learn how activists regard literal gentrification in racial terms, and their confidence that others will see "gentrification" in similar terms, too. Literal gentrification is among the most recognizable social issues of our times, and therefore it is a powerful reminder of broad inequalities and of their roots in our political and economic systems. This is so much the case that *gentrification* is a rallying cry for movements that are not primarily—or even at all—aimed at advocating for a specific urban future. This is because *gentrification* effectively carries other meanings with it, including a general if vague set of feelings and political orientations related to rallying for the underdog, decrying systemic injustices and inequalities, and marking the displacement, both literal and symbolic, of marginalized peoples from various realms of public life.

Conclusion

I would be remiss if I closed this chapter without acknowledging how scholars who write about literal gentrification, much like the authors, academics, and activists whom this chapter profiles, also engage in the work of connecting *gentrification* to broader issues. Here, I mean something different than the broader issues I have identified thus far in the chapter. While some scholars rightly underline how literal gentrification connects to broader political-economic systems, in their work on literal gentrification scholars often also stake claims to positions on still other issues.

While, more often than not, I suspect they do not set out to research literal gentrification to make parallel claims about the "right" way to conduct research or analyze data, many scholars, in writing about literal gentrification, nonetheless end up engaging in parallel conversations about how we know what we know and about what our responsibilities are to the people whom we study.[41]

There is an enormous body of academic scholarship on literal gentrification—a body of work that is notably fractious.[42] Some scholars argue that gentrification is gravely consequential for contemporary urbanites, particularly those with the fewest resources.[43] Others suggest that we have overstated its direct effects.[44] Some explicitly define literal gentrification as a process of racial turnover while others insist that we think of it, more narrowly, in economic terms, with class operating as the defining feature of "gentrifiers" and "long-timers."[45] One set of researchers explores brick-and-mortar gentrification in nonurban locales, including small villages and suburban areas; another insists that it is a strictly urban process.[46]

I have argued elsewhere that, like some of the treatments of *gentrification* that this chapter has profiled, academic arguments are often not just about literal gentrification at all.[47] Instead, scholarly debates about literal gentrification are simultaneously debates about how and why we conduct research, whom we believe, and what data best represents social reality. For instance, scholars debate ad nauseam whether displacement is best captured via quantitative census data or via engaging with people on the ground in gentrifying places.[48] They also engage in debates about the role of the researcher (as advocate versus neutral scientist); about whether the "truth" is best captured by looking at things closely or from a greater distance; and about the degree to which there is veracity in everyday accounts versus in detached, expert analysis.[49]

In short, increasingly, literal gentrification is a front on which scholars wage battles about grander intellectual issues. Thus, when they evoke *gentrification* not even experts on literal gentrification always communicate, narrowly, about only literal gentrification.

Is anyone harmed if we use *gentrification* to debate broader philosophical issues about truth, objectivity, distance, and advocacy? Beyond this, is anyone harmed when authors and activists use *gentrification* as a heuristic or metaphor in support of arguments about inequalities and the political and economic systems that produce and sustain them?

This chapter cannot thoroughly answer that question, but it does reveal the degree to which a range of cultural producers and activists feel quite comfortable deploying *gentrification* to offer critical analyses of broader problems, dynamics, and systems, such as late-stage capitalism and neoliberalism. After all, the chapter highlights the ambitious manner in which a variety of people leverage *gentrification* in support of their arguments, either by relying on literal gentrification as a heuristic or by deploying "gentrification" as a metaphor (that is so recognizable and resonant that it, too, can serve as a heuristic).

Beyond the social movements I have written about above, this is apparent in the work of the scholars whom I have profiled. For instance, Jessa Lingel hopes that using *gentrification* to talk about the transformation of the web will lead people to resist the corporate domination of the internet, and Samuel Stein uses *gentrification* to advocate for a vision of a socialist city and for how urban practitioners might distance themselves from capitalist projects that narrowly serve the wealthy. Even humanities scholars who deploy *gentrification* as a metaphor do so to offer criticisms of the co-optation of working-class culture by elites.

Together, the examples I have highlighted in this chapter reveal that when a word becomes as charged, weighty, and as loosely defined as *gentrification*, it serves myriad purposes. And when it becomes as recognizable as *gentrification*, it becomes a highly effective heuristic. It is plausible that, today, *gentrification*—as a word and an idea—actually accomplishes more as a flexible symbol than as a representative of a specific process of urban change.

Of course, *gentrification* is not just deployed randomly. There are patterns evident in how writers, scholars, journalists, and activists deploy *gentrification* as a metaphor, heuristic, and metaphorical heuristic to support their arguments and advance their political causes. Specifically, they tend to rely on *gentrification* to diagnose the source of systemic inequities and to highlight the plight of the underdog. They also rely on *gentrification* to gesture to the appropriation of marginalized peoples' culture and space by elites and resultant experiences of loss. More often than not, they use *gentrification* to illustrate problems associated with political-economic systems, whether pertaining to late-stage capitalism, neoliberalism, rescue capitalism, or the perils of racial capitalism. Thus, while references to *gentrification* are increasingly endemic, they are not haphazard. Authors, activists, and academics especially rely on both metaphorical and literal gentrification to mark and diagnose the sources of involuntary changes that benefit a few at the cost of many.

In part, *gentrification* accomplishes this because people who evoke *gentrification*—whether in a protest, a memoir, or an academic article—recognize that literal gentrification is entrenched in broader social and economic systems. However, they also present *gentrification* in this manner because *gentrification* carries messages—many of them about the political-economic roots of social problems—very effectively. In addition, as Tom Eubanks suggests, *gentrification* is an effective signifier of meaning, in part because it is so evocative of *feeling*. Of course, *gentrification* is emotionally evocative because of the durability and visibility of both the term *and* of literal gentrification. Who among us has not witnessed or at least considered the pain of displacement and of the involuntary transformation of community and home that literal gentrification so often engenders?

However, familiarity with literal gentrification is not the only reason the term is evocative. Part of why *gentrification* makes many people *feel* is because *gentrification*, as a concept, is not only multivocal, but also multiscalar. As we have discovered in earlier chapters, *gentrification* evokes the upscaling not just of urban neighborhoods, but of the self, the community, and the social group. In other words, it evokes involuntary change writ large, and, often, involuntary change operating at multiple scales simultaneously. Mercifully, only some have experienced gentrification-induced displacement, but most of us have experienced change that we did not wish for. Whether our parents' divorce, a job loss, the end of a friendship or of a romantic relationship, or even our own evolution—political, psychological, or otherwise—most people have experienced the feeling that the ground is shifting beneath one's feet even as one wishes it would remain steady. This recognizability renders *gentrification* a potent, resonant, and accessible symbol that authors, activists, and academics can readily deploy to communicate a variety of meanings and to gesture to appropriation and inequalities that operate at multiple scales.

Of course, despite the flexibility of *gentrification* as a symbol, across all of the diverse usages that this book engages there is one foundational shared assumption evident in how cultural producers present *gentrification*. That is, all of the usages of *gentrification* in my archive rest on the (often unarticulated) premise that literal gentrification is a problem, or, at the very least, that it produces or exacerbates social problems, including exploitation, displacement, co-optation, the breakdown of community, and commercialization. To "gentrify" as a person, for instance, is not to acquire resources and opportunities that make one an unambiguously better person or that one should otherwise celebrate. Talk of *gentrification* only brings bar commemorators and their audiences together to forge community because of a shared belief that literal gentrification is problematic; indeed, commemorators assume that their audiences will regard literal gentrification as a threat. And, as this chapter documents, *gentrification* works as a heuristic that evokes, among other things, the problems of contemporary capitalism and neoliberalism because the operating premise is that literal gentrification is itself a problem.

If *gentrification* is so evocative of both feeling and politics and if so many cultural producers present it as symptomatic of social problems or as a social problem in its own right, why isn't there more broadscale mobilization against literal gentrification? If a diverse set of authors and activists engages *gentrification* in pursuit of other arguments and causes—using the implication of inequality and capitalism gone awry that *gentrification* implies to forward their own causes—why aren't there masses in the street signaling their frustration with and resistance to literal gentrification?

One possible explanation, which I will pursue more directly in the book's final pages, rests in the fact that, despite a shared foundation in the idea that literal gentrification is problematic, the meaning of *gentrification* is significantly diffuse and flexible. *Gentrification* carries much weight, significance, and feeling, but the word *gentrification* increasingly conveys diverse meanings and does not always evoke literal gentrification. Indeed, some of the cultural producers whom this chapter features directly acknowledge that *gentrification* works for them as a metaphorical heuristic because the term is deeply evocative while its precise meaning is vague (Lingel 2021). Thus, to resist literal gentrification is, in a sense, to resist a moving target and, more and more, to resist a symbol rather than a concrete, indisputable, easily identified process of urban transformation. We seem to be entering an age when *gentrification* is more evocative of feeling than it is of action; at least action oriented toward the literal transformation of urban neighborhoods and other upscaling locales.

How did we get to this place? In other words, how did *gentrification*—as a term that evoked a very specific process of urban transformation—perish? This chapter suggests that part of the answer rests in how *gentrification* is evocative of emotion, particularly of feelings of loss and dispossession. It also suggests that *gentrification* is politically charged, in part because it works to identify the roots of social problems in broader political and economic systems, without specifying a specific political platform.[50] Part of the answer to the question of why so many rely on *gentrification* might rest in the degree to which so many people seem to yearn for language that captures their sense of deepening inequalities and of how the decks are stacked against those with fewer resources (Bartram 2022). The conclusion continues to consider how and why *gentrification* has taken on a new life, looking more closely at the role that academic debates about literal gentrification have played in the rebirth of the term as, among other things, the heuristics, metaphors, and rallying cries that we have encountered in this chapter.

Conclusion

IN THE book's final pages, I have two primary tasks. In a moment I will address the consequences of the broad and flexible usage of *gentrification* as metonym, parable, metaphor, and heuristic that the book's chapters have documented. First, though, I will elaborate on arguments I presented in the introduction about how and why *gentrification* works so well as a communication tool. As part of this elaboration, I turn the lens on academics (like myself) who research literal gentrification; this is a component—albeit far from the only one—of explaining how and why *gentrification* is multivocal and therefore why it was well positioned to find a new life.[1] While there are multiple reasons why *gentrification* is broadly resonant and highly retrievable, as a longtime scholar of literal gentrification, I would be remiss if I did not close this book by reflecting on the relationship between the meaning scholars of literal gentrification assign to the term and the role of *gentrification* as a metaphor.

In the last chapter I entered related territory by looking at scholars who write about *gentrification* without studying it empirically (or by only loosely studying it empirically). Specifically, I highlighted work by journalists and scholars who rely on *gentrification* as a metaphor, heuristic, or metaphorical heuristic for systemic inequalities and the political and economic systems that support them. But that isn't quite sufficient.

It isn't sufficient because I need to take up a possibility that I raised in the book's introduction. At the outset, I suggested that I suspect there is a relationship between the broad adoption of *gentrification* in popular culture and ambivalence, among urbanists, about allegiance to the term and concept of *gentrification*. I also suggested that it is possible that end-less academic debates about *gentrification*—what it means, when to apply the term, whether there is one or multiple gentrifications, what gentrification's consequences are—help to create a haziness about *gentrification* that has helped to free the term to be taken up as a metaphor by novelists, songwriters, sculptors, television writers, filmmakers, activists, social media users, and so many others.[2] In short, from the book's start I promised to consider how scholarship on literal gentrification might help to feed into the ambiguous meaning of *gentrification*.

In the pages that follow, I will do just that, before revisiting additional explanations for the death and rebirth of *gentrification* and before turning to the consequences thereof. To do so, I must take the reader through some muddy and fractious territory to unearth some of the fission that characterizes scholarship on literal gentrification. My aim is not to thoroughly review a vast literature, but, rather, to illustrate how that literature presents a knowledgeable reader with competing maps of the breadth, temporal limits, severity, and consequences of literal gentrification.

In the first decades of gentrification research, scholars came to figurative blows over literal gentrification's causes. Most famously, the geographer Neil Smith theorized that markets are what create gentrification, specifically a "rent-gap" between current and potential rent on properties and land in the central city.[3] That is, by "getting in early" on lower-cost property, one could gain profits in the long term, particularly in neighborhoods in which property values had fallen as a result of systemic disinvestment. By this logic, members of the gentry, alongside real estate investors and developers, were destined to take advantage of that gap; in essence, urban markets compelled them to seek advantageous housing and investment opportunities in the central city. In contrast, others, like Ruth Glass, argued that literal gentrification emerged from a transformation of the tastes, preferences, and attitudes of the professional classes. In rising numbers, they rejected their parents' suburban lives and appreciated the density, grit, and "authenticity" of urban life. For scholars in this camp, the emergent cultural tastes of this growing class of highly educated professionals, some of which were rooted in the countercultural politics and tastes of the 1960s and 1970s, gave birth to literal gentrification. If their parents fled the central city for White, middle-class suburbia, gentrifiers, in Ruth Glass's verbiage, rejected their parents' "suburban aspirations" in favor of a return to the demographically heterogeneous, architecturally "authentic," and culturally rich central city.[4]

The specific contours of this debate between production (read: markets) and consumption (read: cultural tastes) explanations for literal gentrification do not particularly matter for my purposes. Instead, I revisit these debates, which animated the early decades of gentrification studies, to convey two things. First, from its start, gentrification scholarship has been fractious. And, second, from the beginning, scholars debated fundamental facets of the process and disagreed about foundational explanations for literal gentrification's existence, such as why and how it emerged and about the fundamental significance of the role of the gentry (or the professional classes) in this process of urban reinvestment.

Today, gentrification scholarship is just as divided and fraught, but the debates that are front and center have moved away from those oriented around its causes. Today, scholars of literal gentrification present competing images of gentrification's breadth and of its severity and significance. They debate the racial dynamics that characterize literal gentrification (i.e., whether gentrification is always or mostly characterized by the movement of White gentry into the spaces of racial minorities or if, instead, gentrification ought to be primarily characterized by the class differences between newcomers and longtimers); the temporal stretch of gentrification (i.e., whether it existed before Ruth Glass coined the term in 1964); and the geographical expanse of gentrification (i.e., whether a term, first developed to describe changes in London, ought to be applied to reinvestment processes in the Global South, for instance). Increasingly, they debate the suitability of *gentrification* as a term or concept that captures urban dynamics around the globe.

Underlying these debates are deep and far-reaching questions about what literal gentrification *is* and about the degree to which it shapes the contemporary city. Some present literal gentrification as a nearly un-stoppable force bearing down on cities that exacerbates economic and racial inequalities and plays a prominent role in the spatial reorganiza-tion of urban life. In contrast, others present literal gentrification as less monolithic and as of only modest consequence for poor and working-class residents, particularly racial minorities. Still others regard literal gentrification as a mere symptom or tool of more consequential pro-cesses and dynamics.[5] To be clear, these are not, for the most part, criti-cisms that are lobbed at scholars of literal gentrification from outside of the field, but, rather, criticisms that scholars of literal gentrification di-rect at one another.

Why devote space to these academic debates and criticisms in the final pages of a book that has, more than not, explored an archive of cultural objects that are (seemingly) at a far remove from seminar rooms and conference halls?

At the outset, I hinted that my reading of the objects in my archive suggests that cultural producers' deployment of *gentrification* is not iso-lated from the vicissitudes of academic discourse. This is, in part, because academic debates do not exist in an ivory tower. Researchers interface with a variety of constituencies, from students to community partners to journalists—and, increasingly, with the broader audiences they reach via social media and public-facing op-eds and talks.

As one example, a recent study, conducted by Princeton University researchers, found limited evidence of an uptick in evictions as literal gentrification advances in neighborhoods.[6] On its face, this seems to trouble the idea that direct displacement is fundamental to literal gen-trification, despite the fact that Ruth Glass, when she coined the term, suggested that, by definition, literal gentrification entails displacement. I do not know whether the authors wish for their findings to be inter-preted in that manner, but the article certainly could, in theory, be in-terpreted as unsettling a conceptualization of gentrification that pre-sents displacement as an essential feature.

Even I, an infrequent social media user, noted how a post from one of the paper's authors about their results stimulated significant debate on X. In the same week, I happened to engage with a journalist from a major newspaper who volunteered that he was aware of the article on eviction and that he was trying to make sense of what it meant for his conceptualization of literal gentrification and for how he can write about the subject for his newspaper. If he saw the author's social media post, and the diverse (social media) responses thereto by other gentrification scholars, he was well positioned to absorb and, potentially, to recommunicate to his own audiences, discordance about what many regard as a core feature of literal gentrification: displacement.

This is all to say that while debates among scholars of literal gentrification never existed in a bubble, thanks to social media the dispersion of such debates is increasingly obvious. As someone who sometimes speaks with journalists about literal gentrification, it is clear to me that, regardless of social media, at least some reporters follow trends in the literature and that they are well aware of some of the impasses within gentrification studies. Consider the local television news host, who, in 2014, told me that he kept a copy of my reader, *The Gentrification Debates*, on his office shelf. Consider also members of the cast of a 2013 New Haven production of the play *Clybourne Park* who told me that, at the instruction of their director, they read a handful of academic texts on literal gentrification, including the aforementioned book, to prepare for their roles. These are mere anecdotes, of course, and they are examples I have personal access to, but they are signals of how academic frames of *gentrification* enter broader circulation.

Why does this matter? It matters, I think, because scholarly debates do not occur in a vacuum. Our debates are consumed and reinterpreted by journalists who are positioned to reach broad audiences, and, in turn, journalistic representations may inform how the cultural producers of the films, television series, novels, memoirs, and artwork I have engaged in this book interpret *gentrification*.[7] I suspect that some of *gentrification*'s flexibility, and therefore its availability for adoption as metaphor, metonym, heuristic, and parable, emerges from the breadth and heterogeneity of scholarship on literal gentrification—a body of scholarship marked by enduring debate.

Of course, I cannot and do not aim to definitively establish a causal argument about how academic discord shapes public engagement with *gentrification.* I will not attempt to do so, nor is that my goal. Indeed, scholars who trace the careers of multiple academic concepts or of academic figures note that isolating a singular explanation for the popular adoption of academic concepts or figures is a challenging, if not impossible, task (Hallett et al. 2019; Lamont 1987). To accomplish this, one would need to craft a study that charts how academic discourses, journalistic reports, and artistic representations of gentrification have evolved across time. Ideally, one could eventually determine how change in one type of discourse (e.g., academic) produces changes in discourse in another realm (e.g., print media), eventually seeping into film, television, and fiction.

Even if such analyses confirmed that academic debates influence journalistic accounts, which then shape how *gentrification* appears in popular culture, we would struggle to capture whether those academic debates are themselves informed by the fact that some scholars of literal gentrification (like me) watch *Vida* and *Last Black Man in San Francisco*, read *Ghosts of St. Vincent's*, and take in a sculpture commemorating Boston's triple deckers.[8] I might, quite unintentionally, carry insights from *Vida* into conversation with graduate students about the racial characteristics of literal gentrification, or images from *Ghosts of St. Vincent's* into a conference presentation on the literal gentrification of gayborhoods.

In other words, I do not want to make a neat causal argument, because I do not believe there is a singular reason why *gentrification* has been reborn as a metaphor (indeed, below I reengage some of the other reasons why I believe that *gentrification* has a new life). Moreover, if this book accomplishes anything, I hope it provides a window into how different realms of discourse bleed into one another; indeed, that, rather than any kind of neat causal explanation, is at the heart of this book's argument. Across four chapters, I have charted how an academic idea has taken on new life in a variety of realms of popular culture. This book reveals that the lines between the academy, television, journalism, art, fiction, memoir, and film are porous; we are talking with or at least engaging with one another more than some might expect. The cast of a play that engages themes of literal gentrification might read academic texts on the subject, but, then, scholars of literal gentrification also consume such plays. I do not mean to suggest, for even a second, that scholarly representations of literal gentrification direct *all* representations of *gentrification* out there in the world. On the contrary, I perceive a messy feedback loop, one that parallels similar feedback loops that play out today, such as between scholars who study subjects such as gender or critical race theory and the cultural producers and publics who take up their concepts, assigning new meaning and significance to them.[9]

That entirely sincere caveat about causation aside, I would be remiss if I closed without attending to the fact that academic debate—which can, sometimes, be construed as academic uncertainty—about what literal gentrification *is*, why it exists, and how it unfolds, likely plays some role in the new cultural life of *gentrification*.

Below, I briefly highlight key areas of debate among scholars of literal gentrification: about how to define, conceptualize, and measure literal gentrification; about the related question of the geographic and temporal breadth of literal gentrification; and the centrality of displacement to gentrification processes.[10] Of course, this is not an exhaustive review of contemporary debates, of which there are many. Rather, it highlights a few key areas of divergence that help to render *gentrification* a multivocal object readily deployed to convey a range of meanings and to forward a variety of purposes, from the political to the sentimental.

The Gentrification Debates Continue

First, scholars remain divided about how to define, conceptualize, and measure literal gentrification. To provide an example, a 2017 article seeks to map the breadth and spatial location of literal gentrification in New York and Chicago. The authors suggest that by 1980 many of Chicago's North Side neighborhoods were not available to gentrify because their median income was too high, therefore qualifying them as "ungentrifiable."[11] As a result, the authors do not measure subsequent changes in those neighborhoods, excluding them from their count of neighborhoods that gentrified. I raise this not because I take issue with the article or with the authors' decision to exclude those neighborhoods. Indeed,

they follow standard practice among quantitative scholars of literal gentrification and the article is penned by scholars I admire.[12]

Yet, as an ethnographer who has studied the gentrification of Chicago neighborhoods and who is quite familiar with others' work on the
same, I am mindful that, because the authors suggest that a neighborhood has to be below a certain income threshold to gentrify, they exclude from their analysis some of the very neighborhoods that qualitative scholars of gentrification rely on for case studies of gentrification,
such as Uptown, Edgewater, Boystown, and Andersonville.[13]

I don't believe these differences should be read as unambiguous error
on the part of either those who study or who bracket such neighborhoods. Must a neighborhood be resolutely working class to gentrify?
Or, in the present day, might some lower-middle-class or more economically heterogeneous neighborhoods gentrify? That is, might they, too,
experience class turnover, with wealthier residents replacing those who
were there before them? These are weighty and worthy questions that
scholars are right to wrestle with.[14]

However, these different perspectives on what counts as a *gentrifiable*
neighborhood underline significant gulfs in contemporary gentrification scholarship.[15] Some of us have busied ourselves documenting (eth-
nographically) the gentrification of neighborhoods that other gentrification scholars suggest have been *ungentrifiable* since 1980! More than
fifty years after Ruth Glass coined the term *gentrification*, scholars continue to debate, both implicitly and explicitly, how to define the process.
Partially as a result, scholars study different places, different time periods, and call different conditions *gentrification*.[16]

That said, impasses about how to measure literal gentrification, or
how best to select indicators or measures of gentrification, suggest that
debate does not merely emerge from the heterogeneity of gentrification
out there in the world. Some scholars consider neighborhoods to be
gentrified if they have experienced both economic *and* racial turnover,
whereas others only consider economic turnover.[17] Many consider
changes in education levels, whereas others limit their attention to
changes in median household income. Some examine changes in home
values or mortgage lending patterns; others do not.[18] Some evaluate

commercial and other nonresidential changes, whereas others focus narrowly on residential transitions.[19] Likewise, some qualitative scholars study slow-moving or intermittent gentrification, whereas others attend to ascendant gentrification.[20]

There are also differences in the spatial scales that scholars examine. Most quantitative analyses turn to census tracts that sometimes do not align with recognized neighborhoods or do not coincide with the areas studied by qualitative scholars because they are either too broad or too narrow.[21] This may turn their attention away from smaller pockets of intensive or muted gentrification, perhaps partially explaining competing accounts of gentrification's consequences. There is also variation in how researchers select neighborhoods for inclusion in their studies; some determine which tracts they will examine by considering the economic and demographic conditions of a tract relative to other tracts within a central city, metropolitan statistical area (MSA), or county.[22] Other scholars rely on how residents present a neighborhood as gentrified or not, whereas others rely on census indicators.

As I suggested above, these measurement differences emerge from both implicit and explicit disagreement and uncertainty about how to define and set conceptual parameters around literal gentrification.

Some of this gulf likely emerges from some scholars' desire to have their conceptualization of *gentrification* keep pace with literal gentrification's advancement; that is, to include what my colleague Loretta Lees terms "super-gentrification" (2003): the movement of financiers and other highly affluent individuals into already gentrified neighborhoods.[23] It likely also emerges from efforts to trace gentrification's increasing geographic breadth by studying rural villages and looking beyond the US and European capitals that most researchers initially studied.[24]

In other words, some of the discord about how to define and measure literal gentrification might reflect the heterogeneous nature of the process, or what the geographer Damaris Rose referred to as gentrification's "chaos."[25] Cumulatively, empirical research presents evidence of quite varied literal gentrification processes, from the early-stage gentrification of Chicago's West Side (Douglas 2012) and the stalled gentrification of Washington, DC (Williams 1988), to the advanced gentrification of parts of Manhattan and Brooklyn (Butler and Lees 2006).[26] Research also reveals substantial variation in the breadth of gentrification within cities and especially across cities.[27] Gentrification has surpassed all expectations in Manhattan's Greenwich Village and London's Notting Hill, but it has taken different shape in parts of Pittsburgh and Providence.

As a result of both the empirical heterogeneity of what scholars call *gentrification* and divergent approaches to defining and identifying the process, scholars increasingly study different places undergoing different stages of literal gentrification while nonetheless using the same language of *gentrification*.[28] This means, more and more, that there are fairly significant differences in the geographical scope of places that scholars of literal gentrification investigate. It is little wonder, then, that they sometimes rely on distinct definitions of the process and describe the contours of literal gentrification and the outcomes it produces in disparate terms.[29]

Discord is not limited to the question of how to define and measure literal gentrification. Indeed, the most overt area of division in gentrification scholarship rests in how scholars study, count, and present displacement. A 2010 article refers to the "politics of measurement" (Wyly et al. 2010, 2603) of displacement, by which the authors mean debates about how to calculate and quantify gentrification's harm.[30] This "politics" has emerged because scholars offer sharply contrasting views of the scale and severity of gentrification-induced direct displacement.

A spate of publications in the early years of the twenty-first century suggest that low-income renters in tracts that scholars identify as gentrifying exit the neighborhood at rates comparable to those of low-income renters in nongentrifying neighborhoods.[31] At its core, this research suggests that low-income residents of urban neighborhoods tend to move frequently regardless of literal gentrification; their housing situation is generally tenuous.[32] Thus, this research suggests that low-income renters would be "replaced" when more affluent residents move in behind them rather than "displaced" (Hamnett 2003).[33] This, of course, counters a common claim about literal gentrification's risks and consequences for the contemporary city as well as definitions of literal gentrification that position displacement as a core feature of the process.

Scholars have, for decades, gone around and around on questions of just how prevalent displacement is in processes of literal gentrification, as well as about how to measure direct displacement.[34] What is *gentrification*, some might wonder, if not a process that uproots marginalized populations? If scholars can't agree that rampant displacement along the lines of what Ruth Glass described in her original definition—that "once this process of 'gentrification' starts in a district, it goes on rapidly until all or most of the original working class occupiers are displaced, and the whole social character of the district is changed"—is essential to literal gentrification, then what is *gentrification* after all?[35]

I could go on. And on. Suffice it to say that explanations for, definitions of, approaches to measuring, and assessments of outcomes of literal gentrification are openly debated and are subject to frequent change and revision. It is little wonder, then, that *gentrification* has found new life as a metaphor, heuristic, parable, and metonym. As authors like Samuel Stein and Jessa Lingel acknowledge, *gentrification* works as a symbolic device because it is a highly recognizable term and process, but also because the term's meaning, much like literal gentrification itself, is somewhat "chaotic."[36] I believe that, in part, we have a fractious and voluminous academic literature to thank for this conceptual slipperiness.

What Does *Gentrification* Mean After All?

That said, the term's elusiveness is not the only explanation that Stein and Lingel and others offer for *gentrification*'s utility as a communication device. Stein and Lingel also note that *gentrification* conjures debate and even conflict. Broadly speaking, in my archive *gentrification* often serves to communicate concerns with inequalities, exploitation, appropriation, and, in the most general terms of all, with economic and political systems that benefit some at the cost of many. *Gentrification* carries worries about social inequalities with it, particularly those that people tend to code as *urban*, such as racial and economic inequalities and the marginalization of gender and sexual minorities. Indeed, we might take *gentrification*'s ubiquity as a signal of how cultural producers and everyday actors grapple for language that captures the sense that a broader (metaphorical) reappropriation is afoot.

On top of this, the memoirist Tom Eubanks instructs that *gentrification* makes one feel. Of course, he implies that *gentrification* makes one feel sorrow. This is because *gentrification* conjures loss and, at least for Eubanks, even death. It is little surprise then that my archive reveals again and again how *gentrification* communicates a wistfulness that often takes the form of nostalgia for the past. Over and again, *gentrification* signals feelings of loss that cultural producers associate with social change, whether the change that occurs when a neighborhood becomes more upscale and exclusive, with a social group leaving its natal neighborhood as it experiences increasing economic mobility, or with the declining sense of shared identity and marginality among a group of people as they become less ostracized.

Thus, if elusivity (partially born of the academic literature on literal gentrification) renders *gentrification* multivocal, and the notoriety and ubiquity of literal gentrification render the term highly retrievable, *gentrification*'s strong association with *both* politics and emotion helps to render it resonant. It is so resonant, in fact, that, in its new life, *gentrification* has moved into our houses and into our heads. It is on our televisions and social media platforms, and it is in the books we read, the articles we skim, and the art we consume. For some, it might seem that literal gentrification is everywhere and that its abstraction, *gentrification*, is everywhere, too. Metaphorical "gentrification," much like literal gentrification, manages to claim more and more cultural territory, remaking it to forward a variety of communicative goals.

This combination of multivocality, recognizability, ubiquity, and resonance would render any term powerful. Some of *gentrification*'s power certainly emerges from the evocativeness of literal gentrification itself and from the close proximity of so many of us to the brick-and-mortar process, as the displaced or as gentrifiers or as mere spectators to neighborhood transformation. Yet this book also reveals that some of *gentrification*'s power comes not just from literal gentrification, but from the term's association with a set of other terms that are also, in their own right, quite resonant. *Gentrification* carries other timely and charged ideas along with it.

What are some of the ideas that *gentrification* comingles with? And what do they suggest about *gentrification*'s meaning? Across the chapters, I have done my best to trace the feelings that cultural producers rely on *gentrification* to convey, and the political positions and polemical stances that they communicate (intentionally or otherwise) by relying on *gentrification*.

Without repeating myself, I will devote some of this book's closing pages to highlighting a few terms that appear again and again in my archive and that entangle with *gentrification*'s enduring and powerful connection to notions of the *urban* and to *change*, which I mentioned at the book's outset. I do so, because the powerful association of *gentrification* with other weighty carriers of meaning is part of what makes *gentrification* so charged and abundant today. Their meaning is so tied up with *gentrification*'s meaning that if we want to truly understand what *gentrification* means today, we have to examine the words that walk alongside it.

My archive reveals a powerful association between *gentrification* and *community*. Specifically, cultural producers rely on talk of *gentrification* to underline the loss, fragility, or transformation of communities, or, in the case of dyke bar commemorators, to facilitate the rekindling of community. As the social critic Raymond Williams long ago noted, *community* rarely has negative associations (1976), and so evocations of *gentrification* made in relationship to *community* evoke nostalgia, mourning, and feelings of loss (of community). Because of the intractable relationship between literal gentrification and place, it is little wonder that *gentrification* so often forwards positions and sentiments about *community*. Of course, not all communities are place-based, but, more often than not, *gentrification* works to conjure communities of people who share social traits and common physical space, whether a neighborhood, a house, or a bar.

At the same time, *gentrification* is associated with involuntary transformation. Across the chapters, my archive reveals how this transformation can take different forms. In some cases, it is an institution, such as a bar or a family's house, that transforms. In other cases, it is a whole community of people, like Boston's North Enders or the young generation of a Chicano family in Los Angeles's Boyle Heights. In chapter 4, I introduced academic literatures that propose that some cultural objects, such as music or tattoos, undergo involuntary transformation as a more affluent set adopts them. We see echoes of this in social media posts that decry the "gentrification" of "authentic" cultural forms. In yet other instances, it is the *self* that involuntarily transforms, typically becoming more mainstream or upscale.

In reference to both community and involuntary transformation, *gentrification* communicates *loss*. This is true, too, when cultural producers rely on *gentrification* to communicate the cultural appropriation of working-class objects and traditions, particularly those belonging to racial and ethnic minority groups. When the more privileged among us "gentrify" cultural objects, ordinary people lose treasured bars, connection to family members, a common sense of identity, the old neighborhood, feelings of community, and cultural goods that marked a group's distinction and sense of interconnectedness. Often, cultural producers imply that *gentrification* induces the loss of "authenticity." Indeed, loss is so prevalent in representations of *gentrification* that it is one of the primary meanings or, to borrow from Eubanks, *feelings*, that the term carries.

When Raymond Williams suggested that *community* has only positive associations, he also suggested that we tend to regard *community* as outside of capitalism and, often, outside of cities (1976; see also Williams 1975). Traditional views of community present it as tucked away in the countryside, at a safe remove from cities around which capital production centers (Williams 1976). As an extension of this, if *gentrification* threatens community, then, by extension, *gentrification* is associated with capitalism. Since several decades have passed since Williams sketched his argument, today literal gentrification is specifically associated with late-stage corporate capitalism and neoliberal governance. In more basic terms, *gentrification* communicates the pursuit of profit and greed at the expense of "authenticity" and "community" and other invaluable aspects of life. Put differently, *gentrification* can communicate the problems of capitalism, particularly the inequalities that it produces, without calling capitalism by name. This is, in large part, how and why so many find that *gentrification* constitutes an indispensable resource for communicating political positions—from decrying the commercialization of items that were once outside of the market to impugning how the state liases with private capital (and not just in instances of literal gentrification). In a cultural context in which many struggle to speak directly about some of the problems of capitalism, *gentrification* is a much-relied-upon vehicle for (indirectly) doing just that.

There is an additional term that, at least in my archive, comingles with *gentrification* again and again, which is *queer*. Of course, this may be because it is, after all, *my* archive. The cultural objects I draw on do not constitute random sample of references to *gentrification*. In matter of fact, some entered my archive quite unintentionally, because I'd picked up a book to read, for instance, having no idea that it would engage *gentrification*. Still, I suspect that another's archive would find a similar cohabitancy of *queer* and *gentrification*.

Why might *queer* and *gentrification* attract one another? On the one hand, the cohabitancy of *queer* and *gentrification* relate to the long entanglement of queer populations with literal gentrification (in part because marginalized populations often have to inhabit ungentrified or less gentrified spaces and then, when they achieve upward mobility, can transform the space to meet their changing needs or, intentionally or not, can signal to others their neighborhood's desirability).[37] *Queer*, like *gentrification*, is also closely associated with the urban—a refuge of anonymity and heterogeneity that pulls so many in.[38] But that's not all. *Queer*, like *gentrification*, has a reasonably nebulous, flexible meaning. This is not an accident. *Queer* is purposefully vague, as it is meant to include rather than to exclude; to embrace the fluidity of experience and identity. Thus, both *gentrification* and *queer* are well matched in their allusivity and evocativeness; they mirror for one another ambiguity and resonance.

Another reason why *queer* and *gentrification* work well together is because, as the chapters have documented, cultural producers invoke *gentrification* in relation to groups that are popularly perceived as having experienced recent "gentrification" (read: upward mobility). Among these, of course, are sexual and gender minorities. As I have already suggested, this "gentrification" (to the degree it has truly occurred) has been markedly uneven. The most privileged (and normative) among us benefit most from a changing social, cultural, and legal landscape. Still, the idea that certain LGBTQIA+ populations have achieved new legal, social, and cultural mobility is widespread and may be part of why cultural producers find *gentrification* to be such an effective and evocative tool for exploring the experiences of queer individuals and communities.

Of course, this also relates to a broader pattern I called out in chapter 3, which is that *gentrification* sometimes signals the remarkability of the social and economic mobility of certain traditionally marginalized populations, from queer women of color to Black artists. However cautious I am about that usage of *gentrification*, it signals yet another source of resonance. *Gentrification* captures the revaluing of that which society has traditionally devalued; it expresses upward mobility, viewed through a critical lens that seeks to capture that which is lost as one "advances."

In sum, *gentrification* serves as a touchstone that communicates a broad range of emotionally and politically evocative meanings, from community to transformation to capitalism to queer to upward mobility. It can do this because literal gentrification is so abundant and vivid and, in part, because scholars of literal gentrification have rendered the term's meaning opaque, and therefore flexible and adaptable. But the other meanings that *gentrification* evokes carry its significance, too. As a scholar of literal gentrification, I believe I have a responsibility to document how academic debates about how to define literal gentrification parallel some of the heterogeneous uses of *gentrification* in popular culture, but I do not mean to downplay the significance of the signals and associations that *gentrification* so successfully conveys. *Gentrification* only has new life because the ideas it carries with it are resonant and timely, too.

———

From where I stand, it seems to me that cultural producers do not rely on other urban concepts as a metaphor, metonym, parable, and heuristic, such as *segregation* or *suburbanization*, with the same frequency with which they turn to *gentrification*. Why do we use *gentrification* to tell stories about how we, as people and communities, change? Why do cultural producers rely on it to bring disparate people together; to communicate feelings; to engender support for movements; and to support polemical arguments and political positions?

Some might think it is enough to say that Ruth Glass coined a good word. After all, *gentrification* is a noun that suggests action. But so, too, are *segregation* and *suburbanization*. And I am unaware of evidence that those urban terms have caught on in the manner of *gentrification* as a carrier of much broader meaning and significance than anything narrowly related to brick-and-mortar urban processes. We could, for instance, talk about the "segregation" of the self to explain the gap between our professional and personal lives, and perhaps some do, but at least in the cultural domains that I inhabit I do not encounter such deployment with the frequency with which I stumble upon *gentrification* as a metaphor.

I won't repeat any of the explanations I have offered above and in the introduction for *gentrification*'s resonance, retrievability, and recognition. However, I do want to extend one dimension of my argument, which is about how *gentrification* communicates politics and feelings. While I have worked to elucidate some of the specific political positions, associations, and feelings *gentrification* engages, I think it would be disingenuous to overstate the degree to which *gentrification* evokes specific positions or emotions. *Gentrification*, in so many ways, exists in a sweet spot of recognizability and blurriness. We know it when we see it, even if we aren't always exactly sure what "it" is. *Gentrification* is politically charged without evoking a specific, narrow political stance. This may be, in part, because there is not yet a highly visible or cohesive antigentrification movement. Instead, there are piecemeal—but nonetheless incredibly important—methods for resisting literal gentrification that a variety of groups and individuals rely on across the globe, from political protest to community land trusts to affordable housing advocacy. In the absence of a highly visible and cohesive movement, *gentrification* evokes a kind of general sadness and loss without presenting a singular image of that sadness or loss or a singular solution for it.

In addition, while there is movement in this direction, *gentrification* does not yet by default engage racial politics in the same manner as a term such as *segregation,* or even *suburbanization* (which, in the US context, depended greatly on White flight and the concomitant ghettoization of racial minorities in the central city). In my archive, some indisputably use *gentrification* to communicate processes of racial dispossession, but we have also seen how, because the precise racial dynamics of literal gentrification vary by place and time period and because scholars debate how central racial dynamics ought to be to any definition of literal gentrification, *gentrification* can also be used to talk *around* racial and other inequalities. *Gentrification,* for many, may *imply* racial inequities, but they are not (yet) quite as central to the term's meaning, at least in my archive, as they would be, if, say, *segregation* was taken up as a ubiquitous metaphor.

Likewise, perhaps because literal gentrification has advanced so mightily as to pose financial burdens on even moderately affluent members of the gentry in places like New York, London, San Francisco, Boston, and Paris, the precise class politics that *gentrification* calls out are similarly vague. *Gentrification* is, certainly, more associated with the involuntary transformation and appropriation and loss of the working class than of any other group, but it also is not presented as narrowly pertaining to that class. Today, *gentrification* is, in a sense, an everyperson's term.

I don't mean to suggest for a moment that *gentrification* is apolitical or that it is emotionally neutral. To the contrary, as I explore below, I believe *gentrification* has reached a tipping point in the sense that its meaning is now more negative than positive. Still, *gentrification* exists in what we might think of as a comfortably negative space; more and more people might agree that gentrification is problematic, and the term may well evoke negative emotions of loss, powerlessness, and frustration, as well as political sentiments of resistance. However, I suspect that *gentrification*'s political and emotional connotations are not as negative as certain other terms, such as *genocide, imperialism,* or *apartheid. Gentrification* is a problem, but it is not popularly understood to be such a severe problem that some feel compelled to look away from it. On the contrary, my archive suggests that we look at *gentrification*, quite directly, over and again.

Gentrification as a "Dirty Word"[39]

Some impasses in the academic literature are fairly neatly transposed onto cultural representations of *gentrification*. Perhaps we see this best in the gap between parables of the "gentrification" of the self in chapter 3, which, considered cumulatively, offer a narrative that holds individuals responsible for their "gentrification," and the reliance on *gentrification* as heuristic for the broad set of systemic factors that produce deepening social and economic inequalities found in chapter 4. One view—of "gentrification" as something an individual can control—maps onto scholarly accounts of how gentrifiers themselves drive literal gentrification, whereas the other view, of *gentrification* as shorthand for systems that produce and reproduce inequalities, more closely aligns with rent-gap and other explanations that regard gentrifiers, and literal gentrification itself, as responding to market forces and the political and policy machinations that support capital accumulation.[40] Across both usages, though, is a singular presentation of *gentrification*: as negative or problematic, either because it signals a loss of "authenticity" or because it is indicative of systemic inequalities.

Part of what we learn by looking at *gentrification* as a cultural object is how cultural producers and everyday people (like those who use the term in social media posts) perceive literal gentrification. Beyond all else, it is apparent that few regard *gentrification* as unambiguously good. Despite academic debates about precisely how consequential and widespread literal gentrification is, nobody likes *gentrification*. Well, maybe some do, but they are more and more in the minority and less and less vocal, in the public sphere, about their position on the subject.

Consider an argument I had with a close friend fifteen years ago about whether literal gentrification "improves" neighborhoods. She insisted that it does, because it brings in new commerce and induces cities to invest in infrastructure, public safety, and institutions, like schools. I said, "Who gets to decide what an 'improved' neighborhood is? Who benefits from those 'improvements' and who becomes safer?" In other words, I insisted that literal gentrification does not actually better neighborhoods; it transforms them to serve a different, more privileged population, remaking the neighborhood in the process.

Despite the fact that I almost never argue with friends, our conversation became heated. We were packing books in my office as I prepared to begin a new job. I was immensely pregnant, meant to have my first child within the month, and my friend had, very generously, flown to Chicago to help me pack. She was then and is to this day one of my closest friends. Still, I remember fearing, as we seethed over literal gentrification in my office, that we might be so far apart on the issue that we might not be able to repair things; our debate about literal gentrification became so heated that I wondered if we'd be able to make things right. My point is that our conversation grew into an argument because we were each entirely sure that we were correct, and neither of us was the least bit self-conscious about our position on literal gentrification; for the twenty minutes or so that we debated, it seemed to me that neither of us could imagine establishing common ground on the subject. Fifteen years ago, literal gentrification was the kind of thing that two people who love and respect one another could argue bitterly over.

It is hard to imagine that same fight, involving the same characters (two highly educated White queer women), unfolding in the same way today. Since then, my friend has likely watched *Vida*, and perhaps *Gentefied* or *Last Black Man in San Francisco*, too. Maybe she's read *Valencia*. Certainly she's mourned the closure of bars like the Lexington. She has seen her own city gentrify and then gentrify more, until it has become almost a new place entirely. Today, while we have distinct occupations and live far apart, I can more easily imagine us shaking our heads about how we have each "gentrified" than fighting over whether literal gentrification is good or bad. Our fight belongs in another era, when *gentrification* meant something slightly different than it does today.

The reader does not need to take my word for this. Consider all of the evidence that this book presents of how *gentrified* is used in reference to the transformation or upscaling of things that are not brick-and-mortar neighborhoods; consider how, in every instance, the term is deployed not to applaud that transformation, but, rather, to criticize it. We are not meant to think that the "gentrification" of individuals or art or communities or songs are good things. Instead, evocations of *gentrification* call on us to note how something "authentic" and valuable has been lost as it becomes more upscale, rarified, and potentially mainstream.

This, of course, is because more and more people regard literal gentrification as problematic and as coming at a significant humanitarian cost (if not, as I suggest above, on the same level as *genocide, famine,* or *nuclear holocaust*). Almost twenty years ago, I presented research from my dissertation at a sociology conference. I told the assembled crowd that some gentrifiers in my sample objected to literal gentrification; they were self-conscious about their participation in the process and even worked to mitigate further investment and displacement. I called these gentrifiers, who were self-conscious about their role in gentrification and protective of longtime residents, *social preservationists*.[41] On that day, the crowd was skeptical of the notion that any gentrifiers are critical of gentrification. My analysis even seemed to offend some. Yet, twenty years later, the notion that some gentrifiers are self-conscious about literal gentrification and mindful of the harm that it causes would not surprise many. In part, this is because the field of gentrification studies has evolved, but it is also because the presence of social preservationists and others who resist literal gentrification is increasingly unmistakable—because there are more and more like them in neighborhoods all over the world as more and more neighborhoods gentrify and as, collectively, more and more people frame literal gentrification as problematic.[42]

Why might more and more cast literal gentrification in a negative light? In part, it is because literal gentrification has continued, largely unabated, for at least sixty years (if we start the clock when Ruth Glass first coined the term).[43] Moreover, literal gentrification has moved into more markets and spaces that were once protected from firsthand experience of literal gentrification's negative consequences. In this context, critical views of literal gentrification are increasingly common.

Given the advanced stage of literal gentrification, even the privileged can feel harmed by the process. Not long ago, I had lunch with a

thirtysomething assistant professor. She spoke of the struggle for housing in her gentrified small city. A half hour later, I met with the manager
of a western Massachusetts event center—an Irish American mother of
adult children who is in her mid-sixties—who spoke of how her children
struggle to afford housing in the highly gentrified Boston metro area. It
is doubtful that my former student and this older woman's politics, educational backgrounds, or incomes are perfectly aligned. One is queer;
one is heterosexual. One sports tattoos, the other a perfectly coifed bob.
They are a generation apart. Yet they each spoke with easy fluency about
literal gentrification, and neither seemed self-conscious about presenting literal gentrification as a problem. That is, neither seemed to worry
for a second that I might think literal gentrification is a good thing. More
and more, *gentrification* is something that the educated classes can agree
on; consensus is building that *gentrification* is, in the geographer Neil
Smith's terms, a "dirty word" (1996).[44]

Of course, it is also plausible that widespread usage of metaphorical
"gentrification," which is so often presented in negative terms, acerbates
critical views of literal gentrification. Thus, the symbolic deployment of
gentrification is a window into how cultural producers think about literal
gentrification (e.g., as a kind of upscaling that comes at the cost of "authenticity" and genuine community). At the same time, symbolic deployment of *gentrification* may affirm or encourage negative views of
literal gentrification by modeling a critical stance.

But that is not all. We live in a time of intensive inequalities, and, as
chapter 4 argues, *gentrification* is a metaphor and heuristic for the
political-economic roots of social problems and inequities, as well as for
cultural appropriation. Growing certainty that *gentrification* is "dirty"
(even if not the *dirtiest* of processes and terms) may emerge from increasing dissatisfaction with systems that drive literal gentrification,
such as a neoliberal state that eschews public solutions for a massive
affordable housing crisis, and strategies of capital accumulation that approach properties as investment strategies rather than as homes. In
some cases, distaste for *gentrification* may emerge from discontent with
the sense that each person is adrift, responsible for their own solution
to today's economic pressures, and meant to think of their home (if they

are lucky enough to have one) as a retirement plan (again, if they are so lucky). *Gentrification*, above all else, is a concrete method for gesturing to social structures that produce inequalities.[45]

I don't want to suggest, though, that *gentrification* has a solidified, singular new meaning and that the new meaning is altogether negative. On the contrary, in part because *gentrification* is multifaceted, its deployment as a metaphor is flexible and opaque. It has negative connotations, without conjuring any singular negative thing. This growing convergence around the idea that literal gentrification is a problem is a crucial part of why *gentrification* has found new life as a metaphor. But what are the costs of that new life?

The Costs of *Gentrification*'s New Life

One could pen an entire chapter on the myriad potential consequences of *gentrification*'s new life. For instance, as someone who has, in part, organized her career around the study of literal gentrification, I can imagine that some might be anxious about the dulling of *gentrification*'s resonance and the reduced singularity of the concept as its meaning and significance extend beyond a specific process of urban upscaling. Some might worry that all of this talk of *gentrification* in so many distinct domains stretches the term so thin that it will no longer mean much at all. Does the ubiquity of *gentrification* place at risk the evocative power and resonance that this book traces? Have we reached peak *gentrification*, even if brick-and-mortar gentrification continues apace?

These concerns are worthy of our consideration, but, in the book's final pages, I highlight two that are most front and center in my mind: how *gentrification* has become a source of entertainment, and how cultural emphasis on *gentrification* evokes a snapshot view of history. I highlight these because I suspect that they are of particular consequence for our ability to remedy literal gentrification. To do so will require many resources, but among these, I believe, will be adopting a sober approach to thinking about literal gentrification and a commitment to locating literal gentrification in a broad set of policies, politics, and histories. In my view, anything short of that risks treating a symptom, rather than a cause, and is unlikely to remedy the affordable housing shortages and commercial gutting characteristic of literal gentrification. I worry especially that the way in which many currently deploy metaphorical *gentrification* mimics narrower ways of thinking of literal gentrification—that is, as an entity unto itself—rather than as an important piece of a much bigger puzzle.

Gentrification as Entertainment

I came to this project from multiple directions, including from my ethnography of dyke bar commemoration. However, I also came to this book unwittingly. That is, this book emerged from quiet moments when I intended to be *away* from work—watching television, reading a novel, listening to music, or perusing the newspaper. Again and again, I found *gentrification*, a subject I had long studied, waiting for me in the very places I went to step away from it for a moment. *Gentrification* kept finding me.

This, is, of course, because *gentrification* is nearly everywhere and because it communicates so much so well. Consider this post from X, which appeared on January 8, 2024: "Bro we gotta end capitalism, they just gentrified smoking pot out of a can." Accompanying the post was a photo of a white ceramic beer can that was mass produced and marketed for smoking weed.[46] Fifty-eight thousand users liked the post, with many commenting on the ridiculousness of the upscaling of a free, improvised method for smoking pot, favored by high schoolers and college students for time immemorial. Consider also, another X post (from 2020), which proclaims, "This WHITE woman done gentrified Hip-Hop."[47] In a similar vein, another post reads, "'The Gentrification of DJ Screw' presented by White People Who Don't Know A Damn Thing. A horror film coming to a social media account near you."[48]

Throughout the book, I have routinely noted the ubiquity of *gentrification*, but I want to consider for a moment the fact that I often encounter *gentrification* in my leisure time; *gentrification* has made a home for itself in many of the places that people like me go when we wish to escape after work or when the kids are in bed. This spotlights the degree to which *gentrification* has become a source of entertainment, integral to many of the cultural objects that we consume for pleasure.

I do not mean that cultural producers who evoke *gentrification* in their books, films, and television series do so lightly or merely for entertainment purposes. Indeed, I suspect that some rely on the term to invite conversation and even to spur action on issues pertaining not only to literal gentrification but also to intersecting social issues, from racial dispossessions and appropriations to the weakening of social networks rooted in shared territory and identity.[49] Above all else, they may turn to *gentrification* to mark social change and associated feelings of loss and unmooring and to signal that entrenched social inequalities are afoot.

Still, if we accept the central place of *gentrification* in that which we consume as part of our leisure pursuits, we must also accept there is more and more talk of *gentrification* not only because of the term's resonance and recognizability (which I've discussed above), but also because so many cultural consumers must find *gentrification* to be entertaining. After all, it must entertain for it to propel plotlines, animate tension between actors, aid character development, and add political bite to art exhibits that consumers seek out—not when they are in search of political debate or intellectual engagement, but when they turn on the television, scroll through X or TikTok, or pick up a memoir to read on the beach or on a flight.

What are the consequences of *gentrification* becoming fodder for entertainment? Does it amplify the degree to which we take metaphorical "gentrification" seriously? Might it risk dulling our responses to literal gentrification? Might the entertainment value of *gentrification* support my suggestion above that *gentrification* is a "dirty word" (Smith 1996), but that it is not *so* dirty that cultural consumers want to look away from it?

Part of the answer to these questions depends on better understanding how people receive talk of *gentrification*. For instance, do social media posts about the *gentrification* of pot smoking or hip hop inspire resistance to capitalism and/or to cultural appropriation? In other words, does evoking *gentrification* on X or Tiktok or Instagram forward positions or causes? Or, instead, do users laugh, nod, or shake their heads, and then move on? Of course, the data necessary to answer this question is beyond this book's scope, but the ubiquity of *gentrification* in contemporary popular culture suggests that while its presence as a metonym, metaphor, heuristic, and parable accomplishes certain communicative goals (i.e., that it is a successful carrier of meaning), this does not mean that evocations of *gentrification* call people into the streets. Even if some cultural producers might hope that it will, it doesn't seem to compel people to resist literal gentrification or, as far as I can tell, even to protest metaphorical "gentrification," such as that associated with the cultural appropriation of working-class cultural goods and practices by the elite.

Just as important, I think, is the question of whether metaphorical usages of *gentrification* turn attention away from literal gentrification, or encourage us to regard it with detachment, as one part metaphor and one part entertainment. Has literal gentrification, like the *gentrification* one can passively engage via various forms of art and media, become something to nod or shake our heads about and then move on from? Might we *feel* literal gentrification less, when metaphorical "gentrification" is so evocative of emotions about evolving family ties, personal transformation, or the loss of beloved bars? And if we feel literal gentrification less, might it also call us to action less? How many, especially the privileged among us, sit and watch literal gentrification unfold, regarding it with a dangerous combination of distance and familiarity, much as we might take in a plotline evocative of "gentrification"? When we become entertained by representations of something, does the significance of that actual thing—as a brick-and-mortar process and as a cultural idea in its own right—begin to perish, and, with it, the possibility of resistance?

It is in this sense that I believe that this book stands in witness to the death of *gentrification*. What do I mean by this? I mean to suggest not that literal gentrification has died, but, instead, that there has been a death of *gentrification* both as a term suggestive of a specific urban process *and* as term that is evocative in a manner that calls one to specific action. *Gentrification* has become a highly communicative abstraction; one that many find ably captures key tensions, feelings, positions, and experiences of contemporary life or helps them to either engage or talk around issues such as systemic racism, the problems of corporate capitalism, or feelings of loss associated with social change. *Gentrification* isn't what it once was; to be sure, that old *gentrification* has perished. And yet the term very much lives on, taking new form and significance. More than anything else, *gentrification* entertains; it evokes a reliable set of tensions, actors, and dynamics that cultural producers rely on to draw audiences in.

The Risks of a Snapshot View of History

All of this attention to *gentrification* runs the risk of distracting us from a broader view of history and of the systemic forces that produce both literal and metaphorical gentrification. In chapter 2 I warned that, in some cases, attributing community transformation to literal gentrification is to take a snapshot rather than a landscape view of history. Consider the title of Tanya Golash-Boza's 2023 book, *Before Gentrification*, which documents a long history of racialized disinvestment, White flight, and the mass incarceration of people of color that set the stage for the later literal gentrification of Washington, DC.[50]

As Golash-Boza's book illustrates, *gentrification* calls attention to reinvestment without turning attention to systemic processes of disinvestment, incarceration, White flight, and ghettoization that opened up the central city and an increasingly broad set of other places for the speculation that is fundamental to literal gentrification today. Perhaps that is why the books I discussed in chapter 4 diagnose the problems of capitalism and neoliberalism but pay less attention to colonization and carcerality. I close this book by suggesting that there are risks associated with a too-narrow focus on the blip in time that is literal gentrification, and, at the same time, of a too-intensive focus on metaphorical "gentrification."

Even as a metaphor, *gentrification* risks foreclosing connections between that which literal gentrification evokes and that which gave birth to literal gentrification or that which might come after. Metaphorical "gentrification" draws our attention to upscaling but not to disinvestment.[51] For instance, it draws attention to the upward mobility of a queer Latina but not to the systemic factors, including structural racism and homophobia, that positioned her to "gentrify" in the first place. *Gentrification* also draws attention to loss but not to regeneration. It calls us to mourn the Italian American community that once flourished in the North End of Boston but not to celebrate the upward mobility and geographic flexibility that some Italian American residents experienced in the second half of the twentieth century. Nor does it, or any other mournful representation of the "gentrification" of community, acknowledge how the transformation of primordial communities, predicated on presumed sameness, can be quite liberatory for some who find themselves on the margins of that community (e.g., a transgender person in a lesbian bar circa 1970; a queer person in a heavily Catholic urban neighborhood; a Black playwright in a White-dominated arts "community"). Community transformation is not always experienced as loss, but *gentrification*, which is so deeply evocative of loss and involuntary transformation, implies that it will be.

Thus, I ask the reader to see with me how *gentrification* reveals certain insights and perspectives and, by default, simultaneously turns attention away from others. In reality, we should be talking as much about *segregation* and *suburbanization* as about *gentrification*. We should be thinking beyond "gentrification" (and literal gentrification) to evaluate a housing system based on personal responsibility and processes of capital accumulation. In other words, we ought to speak more about capitalism, racism, and neoliberalism, and less about *gentrification*. In point of fact, we ought to speak more directly about a whole range of things; the new life of *gentrification* sheds light on a growing tendency to do otherwise, because cultural producers have picked it up and deployed it for so many purposes.

———

But here *gentrification* is. It is here when I turn on the television, pick up a book, read the paper, or flip through social media. My archive leaves me quite certain that *gentrification* is very much alive, even if it isn't what it once was—and even if the work it does as a metaphor forecloses certain communicative possibilities, in favor of others.

It is hard to image that Ruth Glass could have predicted this future for *gentrification*—or, for that matter, for literal gentrification. But here we are, and if metaphorical "gentrification" is anywhere near as ascendant and unyielding as literal gentrification has demonstrated itself to be, we can anticipate the continued cultural ascent of the term; I predict that cultural producers will continue to rely on *gentrification* as a metonym, metaphor, parable, and heuristic. After all, this book reveals how metaphorical "gentrification," much like literal gentrification, has a knack for taking root in cultural rent-gaps and for satisfying the gentry's cultural proclivities. Metaphorical "gentrification" is as adept as literal gentrification at taking new territory.

I do not write this book to ask us to mourn *gentrification* circa 1964.[52] Instead, I hope it will inspire others to continue to trace how alternate academic concepts and celebrity scholars are taken up by cultural producers, coming back to us in new form and reshaping our scholarship in the process (see Lamont 1987; Hallett et al. 2019). In other words, I hope that by tracing *gentrification*'s new life we might gain clarity about how, in general terms, academic concepts circulate and evolve, as well as, more specifically, about what we (meant in the broadest possible terms) wish for *gentrification* to mean, both as a metaphor and as a way of capturing the process of urban upscaling that Ruth Glass first identified.[53] This book serves as a call not only for more research on *gentrification* as a metaphor, but for additional in-depth readings of the "careers" (Hallett et al. 2019) of academic concepts as they move away from academe and take on new life. These close readings are poised to complement the comparisons of academic terms and figures that others have undertaken (Hallett et al. 2019; Lamont 1987) by tracing the meanings that cultural producers assign to terms and by mapping how they rely on them to accomplish certain work or solve specific problems (McDonnell et al. 2017).

If I weren't so fascinated by how *gentrification* circulates as an idea, I might be tempted to end the book by identifying an opportunity for those of us who study literal gentrification to take ownership of *gentrification*, as a concept, again. But, how could any gentrification scholar not question what it would mean to "own" an idea or otherwise question such an elitist enterprise? It is better, I think, to let the concept evolve and circulate through cultural domains as it will, but we ought to watch as it does, marking what *gentrification* comes to signify and the politics, feelings, and positions that it evokes. To do anything less would leave both a death and a new life unmarked; it would be to look away from how *gentrification*, as a term and an idea, has broadened and evolved over the last half century. It would also be to forgo the opportunity to acknowledge how, when it comes to certain concepts, a wide set of actors engage in an iterative process of meaning making and remaking that spans from faculty offices to newsrooms to artists' studios to Hollywood sets. *Gentrification* isn't just Ruth Glass's anymore; it is our collective accomplishment.

For this reason, it is also our collective responsibility to mark *gentrification*'s progress and evolution; to take a step back in order to take a full view of the term's new life and meaning. To accomplish this, we will have to be urbanists and cultural analysts at the same time; others will have to do what I have attempted here, stretching beyond traditional disciplinary boundaries to find a new language with which to document and explain how a concept that was originally coined to describe a process of urban change became tremendously expansive, flexible, and charged. In other words, I call readers to continue the work I have started here of charting how *gentrification* came to belong to all of us, and to consider together how we ought to deploy it going forward.

ACKNOWLEDGMENTS

During much of the writing of this book I served as department chair. I thank all of my colleagues for their collegiality, but I owe special thanks to those who went to great lengths to ensure that I had time for writing and research. In that vein, I thank Heather Schoenfeld, Alya Guseva, Cati Connell, Arianne Chernock, Max Greenberg, and Debby Carr. I also thank Elise St. Esprit for being a wonderful department administrator, and Matthew Dineen for his administrative support. Above all else, I thank Nazli Kibria for her wise counsel and for her selfless offer to step in as chair for a year while I completed this book. I don't know how I will ever repay her kindness and generosity.

At BU, I am blessed to be surrounded by terrific urbanists. I owe thanks to Ana Villarreal and Jessica Simes for, among other things, their conversations and engagement, to Loretta Lees for her partnership in all things gentrification, particularly in the 2023 international conference on gentrification and displacement that we co-organized and on the book project and special issues that grew from it. I thank a growing cadre of urban graduate students and postdocs for their engagement, and I thank the remarkable team at the BU Initiative on Cities for supporting my Urban Inequalities Workshop, which nurtures valued conversation with students and colleagues. I also thank Landon Lauder, Andrew Ward, and Blaine Smith for their research assistance, as well as for their engagement on themes that relate to this book.

At Princeton University Press, I thank Meagan Levinson for her initial interest in and support of the book. I thank Eric Crahan and Erik Beranek for their support throughout the writing and publication process, and Rachael Levay for her generous and insightful feedback during the crucial final stages of writing and revision, as well as for her support and her thoughtful responses to my queries. I also thank the press for connecting me with Kali Handelman, a terrific developmental editor, whose comments shaped every page of this book. I offer heartfelt thanks to the reviewers for their generous and productive engagement and thoughtful feedback.

I thank the *American Journal of Sociology* and the *Annual Review of Sociology* for permitting me to build off of my previously published articles. I also owe particular thanks to the people who generously allowed me to interview them or to engage in participant observation at events that they organized as I conducted research for this book.

Debbie Becher and Sara Shostak read and provided tremendously incisive feedback on much of this manuscript. I am indebted to them for their laser-sharp recommendations, enthusiasm, and for coming along for the ride over the last several years. I also thank Debbie for brilliant suggestions on the full manuscript as I prepared to submit the book for publication. Terry McDonnell offered thoughtful feedback on my penultimate draft, and I thank him for making time to offer valuable insights. Robin Bartram deserves particular thanks, not only for reading portions of the manuscript, but also for being a steadfast source of intellectual engagement across the years. I also thank Mario Small, Kevin Fox Gotham, Corey Fields, Maggie Kusenbach, and Wendy Griswold for their support, and I thank Mignon Moore for her insightful reading of the manuscript and for her encouragement. Finally, I am grateful for ongoing conversations about gentrification with colleagues, former students, and friends, including Loretta Lees, Jackie Hwang, Derek Hyra, Maggie Kusenbach, Richard Ocejo, Jeffrey Parker, devin bunten, Zawadi Rucks-Ahidiana, Meaghan Stiman, Ladin Bayurgil, Taylor Cain, Whitney Gecker, Maria Sulimma, James Pasto, and Sarah Hosman.

I thank organizers and participants at the places where I have presented portions of this research, including UNC Chapel Hill; Boston University; University of South Florida; Georgetown; the Gentrification Stories Conference, organized by Maria Sulimma and sponsored by the Freiburg Institute at the University of Freiburg; and a media and gentrification conference organized by Stéphane Sadoux, Marie-Pierre

Vincent, Louise Dalingwater, and David Fée, which was sponsored by the Sorbonne.

I thank the BU Center for the Humanities for a Henderson Senior Research Fellowship that provided practical and intellectual support when I first began writing the papers that grew into this book. For feedback during the fellowship, I thank all of the Senior Fellows, but especially Jonathan Zatlin and Keith Vincent. I thank the BU Center for Innovation in the Social Sciences for a grant that helped me to partner with students and staff at BU Spark! to scrape newspaper and social media data on *gentrification*. I offer sincere thanks to Zeba Cranmer, Michelle Voong, and Seth Villegas, as well as the student teams with whom I worked. Finally, thanks to Kenton Card, Catalina Neculai, and Loretta Lees for collaborating with me on a 2024 gentrification and media mini-conference, which provided insights as I made final edits.

My family and friends make everything possible. I thank my parents, Pam and Mike, and their partners, as well as my amazing sisters, Jocelyn and Brooke, and their families for their support. I thank Liz, Alisa, Amit, and Emily for their enduring friendship. In Boston, I owe thanks to a terrific set of friends, but especially to Jill and Liz and to Mneesha and Josh. I am beyond grateful for walks, meals, childcare swaps, and drinks, as well as for your brilliance and levity.

Of course, I owe particular thanks to my wonderful wife, Jana. I am immensely grateful for all of the practical and ephemeral support you have provided for this project and for me as we embarked on a very full life together. I am equally grateful for all of the happy adventures that provided a respite from book writing and from everything else, from hikes to bike rides to weekends away. You make everything better.

My three terrific children, Louisa, Ezra, and Arlo, are more bighearted than I can say. When I began writing, the four of us were weathering Covid isolation together, and I thank them for giving me the time to write (at first, often during Arlo and Ezra's Zoom kindergarten sessions). Beyond all else, I thank them for the love, creativity, intelligence, curiosity, and joyfulness that they bring to everything.

I will never forget when Louisa, who was just learning to write, casually asked me how to spell *gentrification*. A decade later, I still have the envelope on which she scrawled the word in her kindergarten penmanship. That envelope is a warm reminder of the lovely ways in which the different parts of a life are interwoven. I thank Louisa, Ezra, Arlo, and Jana for so generously helping me to stitch things together. This book is, without any doubt, for all of you.

NOTES

Introduction

1. On December 25, 2023, *New Yorker* author Jennifer Wilson promoted her new article for the magazine on polyamory. She wrote, "I wrote about the gentrification of polyamory, Park Slope open marriages, and the people who'll share their lover but not their wealth. Merry Christmas!" See Jennifer Wilson (@JenLouiseWilson), Twitter, December 25, 2023, x.com /JenLouiseWilson/status/1739340611084238965.

2. Kofman 2023.

3. Finn-Olaf Jones, Jack Healy, and Derrick Bryson Taylor, "Burning Man Attendees Begin to Leave Soggy Festival Site," *New York Times*, September 4, 2023, www.nytimes.com/2023/09 /04/us/burning-man-festival-rain-mud-updates.html.

4. Griswold 2001.

5. See Duneier 2016 on the *ghetto* as an idea.

6. As I elaborate, Schulman differentiates "literal gentrification," or brick-and-mortar gentrification, from the metaphorical "gentrification of the mind," which is the primary focus of her 2012 book.

7. See, for instance, Rebecca Ostriker, Mark Arsenault, Andrew Brinker, Stephanie Ebbert, and Diti Kohli ,"Beyond the Gilded Gate," *Boston Globe*, November 1, 2023, apps.bostonglobe .com/2023/10/special-projects/spotlight-boston-housing/boston-towers-of-wealth/.

8. Glass 1964.

9. See Burke 1966.

10. On "cultural objects," which is what I regard *gentrification* to be, see Griswold 2012. For examples of work on how *gentrification* operates in specific cultural objects see, for instance, Peacock 2019; Sulimma 2023 and 2018; Rucks-Ahidiana 2024; Heise 2021; Griffin 2017; Henryson and Knittle 2023; Knittle 2019; Neculai 2014. At the time of this writing, a book by James Peacock, *Gentrification in Contemporary Fiction*, is forthcoming with Bloomsbury.

11. See Brown-Saracino 2017.

12. See bunten et al. 2024.

13. Indeed, scholars themselves debate how to define, conceptualize, and measure gentrification (Lees et al. 2008; Brown-Saracino 2017). Dennis E. Gale writes, "Put simply, gentrification has become a synonym for urban development of almost any kind primarily benefiting middle- and upper-class people. . . . As the term's meaning has become increasingly fuzzy . . . we have undercut the term's utility for understanding processes of urban growth, change, and decline" (2021, 11).

14. My archive includes systematically collected and analyzed items, such as newspaper articles and Reddit posts, and data from my ethnography of dyke bar commemoration in four cities. These complement items in my archive that accumulated before I planned to write this book and before I knew that I was building an archive—that is, novels that friends or colleagues recommended because of their depiction of brick-and-mortar gentrification, or a television show, like the Starz series *Vida*, that I sought out because it featured a dyke bar (while I was in the midst of dyke bar commemoration research). A third set of cultural objects caught my attention once I became conscious that I was, indeed, curating an archive. For instance, I sought out the series *Gentefied* and the film *The Last Black Man in San Francisco* because media heralded them for relying on brick-and-mortar gentrification as a theme. Such objects then entered my archive once I recognized that they relied on *gentrification* as a metaphor. As this suggests, while there are books, films, social media posts, and newspaper articles that simply engage literal gentrification, my archive is constituted by items that rely on *gentrification* as a metaphor. Therefore, I evaluated items for inclusion that evoked *gentrification* in some manner. However, I ultimately selected items that rely on *gentrification* as a metaphor (i.e., they relied on *gentrification* as a communication tool to articulate a message or meaning that is not narrowly linked to literal gentrification). Of course, my archive is my archive; I make no claims to its representativeness. However, its breadth and heterogeneity, together with the patterns evident across items that were systematically collected (e.g., newspaper reports and dyke bar commemoration) and those that entered my archive in a more ad hoc manner, lend me confidence that a similar pattern of usages and meanings would be found in a more random sample of cultural objects that evoke *gentrification* as a metaphor. I intend for this book to invite others to the task of exploring and refining that expectation.

15. Brown-Saracino 2021.

16. Gale writes that "definitions of gentrification have expanded to encompass virtually any form of urban development resulting in the succession of low-, moderate-, and even middle-income people—particularly racial and ethnic minorities—by those of a higher socioeconomic status" (2021, 185).

17. See Schulman 2012 on "the gentrification of the mind." In chapter 3 I further explore the relation between Schulman's concept and the "gentrification" of the self.

18. Brown-Saracino 2021.

19. Brown-Saracino 2021.

20. My title plays off of Jane Jacobs's *The Death and Life of Great American Cities* (1961). I do so because so many cultural producers frame *gentrification* as foretelling the death of cities today.

21. On divisions in the gentrification literature see Rose 1984; Slater 2006; Wacquant et al. 2014.

22. There are terrific scholars who study gentrification from a literary or film studies perspective, documenting how it is deployed in cultural objects. I do not mean to downplay the significance of that work, but, instead, to suggest there is ample opportunity for scholars of literal gentrification to more directly engage with the symbolic deployment of *gentrification* in contemporary popular culture. See, for instance, Peacock 2019, 131–56; Sulimma 2023. My thanks to Maria Sulimma for organizing a highly generative mini-conference at the Freiburg Institute on gentrification and storytelling, and to all of the terrific scholars who shared their work.

23. For discussion of these developments in literature on literal gentrification see Hwang and McDaniel 2022; Hwang and Zhang 2024; Hwang 2020; Rucks-Ahidiana 2022.

24. *Gentrification*'s multivocality lends it a kind of flexibility that it shares with other academic concepts that have found an "afterlife" in the public realm (see Hallett et al. 2019).

25. Gale writes, "When defined so expansively, gentrification suffers from a heterogeneity of meanings, which risks obscuring more than it reveals" (2008, 186).

26. See Kent-Stoll 2020; Rucks-Ahidiana 2021; Kirkland 2008.

27. I draw on Neil Smith's language of frontier here (1996). On which neighborhoods, with which racial characteristics, tend to gentrify see Timberlake and Johns-Wolfe 2017; see also Hwang and Sampson 2014.

28. See Freeman 2005; Freeman and Braconi 2004; Freeman et al. 2023.

29. For summaries of these debates see, for instance, Lees 2014; Valle 2021; Ghertner 2015; Smith 2002.

30. Rucks-Ahidiana 2022.

31. See, for instance Rucks-Ahidiana 2022; Teresa 2019; Wharton 2008; Moran and Berbary 2022; Kent-Stoll 2020.

32. In the early 2010s I served on a panel on gentrification at the Times Center in New York. The panel was moderated by a local television anchor who told me that he kept my edited volume, *The Gentrification Debates*, on a shelf in his office to reference to help him prepare for gentrification topics. Likewise, the play *Clybourne Park*, by Bruce Norris, which engaged issues of White flight and gentrification, was staged all around the United States at this time. One cast member told me they were assigned *The Gentrification Debates* by their director and that they all met to discuss it before beginning rehearsals. These are mere anecdotes, but they suggest that at least some cultural producers consume academic books representing a fractious intellectual landscape, in part in preparation for public-facing engagement with gentrification (in plays, and on the local news, etc.). This book partially explores how that dynamic has played out and what the consequences of that dynamic are for the meaning of *gentrification* today. Of course, academics consume local news and attend plays representing *gentrification*. Thus, I do not mean to suggest that the relationship between such entities is unidirectional.

33. Because this book does not take up questions about specific mechanisms, I do not directly map the history of the term. While that is a worthy task, it would distract from the book's central questions about what *gentrification* means today, how it is taken up, and what purposes it serves or problems it solves for cultural producers. However, others do ask such questions, and some research suggests that the media increasingly deploys the term in a variety of contexts (see Hochstenbach 2017; Tolfo and Doucet 2021; Knieriem 2023.

34. Nanos 2018.

35. See "Globe North Commentary," February 19, 2016.

36. Ginia Bellafante, "Must We Gentrify the Rest Stop?" *New York Times*, January 8, 2023, www.nytimes.com/2023/01/06/nyregion/thruway-rest-stops-gentrification.html.

37. Chandrasekaran 2013.

38. Gold 2013.

39. Rosenberg 2016.

40. Holland 2013.

41. Montero 2018.

42. Lloyd 2019.

43. Cotter 2012.

44. Tingwall 2013.

45. Sicha, "Farewell, My Lovely Cigarettes."

46. Roller 2016.

47. Borrelli 2015.

48. Exposito 2022.

49. Borrelli 2018.

50. Brodeur 2015. Similarly, another article refers to the cultural gentrification or "settling" or "mainstreaming" of the American West that accompanies economic upscaling: "Those often include the gentrification of the American West" (Faughnder 2021).

51. Page 2014.

52. Borrelli 2014.

53. Lapidos 2013.

54. Banks 2012.

55. Monika Krause defines zeitgeist as "a hypothesis for a pattern in meaningful practices that is specific to a particular historical time-period, links different realms of social life and social groups, and extends across geographical contexts" (2019).

56. Hallett et al. write that "each time an idea is used in any form (object or interpretant), it refreshes the cultural archive and makes it available for later use, increasing the chances of later retrievals and subsequent peak" (2019, 568). Likewise, McDonnell et al. write, "We argue that resonance occurs as cultural objects help people puzzle through practical challenges they face or construct. We discuss how cognitive distance and the process of emotional reasoning shape the likelihood of cultural resonance. We argue resonance is an emergent process structured by interactions between individuals that shape each other's interpretation of cultural objects, diffuse objects through interactional circuits, and create opportunities for resonance among people facing similarly shaped problems" (2016, 1).

57. See also Duneier 2016 on the *ghetto* and Wacquant 2022 on the *underclass*.

58. This is not the same as making an explicit causal explanation about why *gentrification* has a new life. I echo Hallett et al. 2019 who write, "We resist the siren call to explain the causes and conditions that lead to an idea's public success or failure. It is exceptionally difficult to determine why particular cultural objects—whether television shows (Bielby and Bielby 1994), novels (Childress 2017), pop songs (Askin and Mauskapf 2017), or academic ideas—'hit' and others do not. Lack of information on negative cases, multiple interdependent causes, and the role of luck make it nearly impossible to identify a formula for success. At best, scholars can point to the common features of objects that do succeed, post hoc" (546). It is also crucial to keep in mind that the success and resonance of a term depends, in part, on how it circulates in popular culture. The more it circulates, the more it becomes available for continued usage (Hallett et al. 2019; see also McDonnell et al. 2017).

59. On social capital see Bourdieu 1987 and on the creative class see Florida 2002.

60. Tuck and Yang 2012.

61. Kofman 2023.

62. Halnon and Cohen 2006.

63. Lingel 2021.

64. On resistance to the "gentrification" of the self in literature, see Peacock 2023.

65. Schulman 2012.

66. Indeed, in the year it was published, Schulman's book was referenced by the *New York Times* and reviewed by the *LA Review of Books*, and when some journalists rely on metaphorical *gentrification* they specifically evoke Schulman's book (e.g., a 2020 article on the "gentrification of the gay politician" by Adam Almeida). Within the academy, it has been cited (according to Google Scholar) more than five hundred times at the time of this writing, and, crucially, has been cited by scholars in a variety of fields of study, from urban studies to sociology to queer studies to literature to film studies. While this book closely engages Schulman's notions of "literal gentrification" and of the "gentrification of the mind," it steps back and analyzes the type of metaphorical deployment of *gentrification* that Schulman relies on (2012). That is, Schulman does not analyze how and why some rely on *gentrification* as a metaphor. Instead, she wields the term as a metaphor in a manner parallel to the other cultural objects this book analyzes.

67. "Because they are multivocal, cultural objects are never fixed, and the analyst must be able to treat a cultural phenomenon in terms of its characteristics as a process, as movement through space and time. The dynamic nature of a cultural object is perhaps most obvious in its reception, i.e., in its impact on a human agent. A parallel interaction, also dependent on culture as process, is influence—the impact of one cultural object on another" (Griswold 1987, 13)

68. McDonnell 2010.

69. Childress 2017.

70. Because my analysis is of cultural objects, rather than of the process by which objects are created, produced, and received (see Childress 2017), I cannot say for certain which actors or entities made which calls about referencing *gentrification* in a cultural object. Therefore, I rely on Griswold's concept of the "cultural producer" (1987) loosely to represent those who labor to prepare an object for consumption. In the case of a newspaper article, for instance, this might include a journalist, their informants, an editor, or even a publisher. In reality, two or more actors are likely involved in the production of any object. A formal cultural analysis of the process of production of such objects would seek to break actors into discrete categories, but that is outside the scope of this book's questions, which focus on what *gentrification* means and how it is used.

71. McDonnell 2023.

72. Brown-Saracino 2009.

Chapter 1: Mourning the Dyke Bar

1. See Mattson 2019 and 2020; Brown-Saracino 2020.

2. Zarrelli 2016.

3. Rachel Lee, "Last Call: Stories from New Orleans' Disappearing Dyke Bar Scene," *Autostraddle*, March 24, 2015, www.autostraddle.com/last-call-stories-from-new-orleans-disappearing-dyke-bar-scene-282482/.

4. Sarah Cascone, "The Spirit of Exploration Drives PULSE 2016," *Artnet*, March 4, 2016, www.news.artnet.com/market/pulse-2016-contemporary-art-fair-441008.

5. As is true throughout the book, I borrow the term "literal gentrification" from Sarah Schulman (2012), who uses the term to differentiate brick-and-mortar gentrification from what she terms "the gentrification of the mind."

6. Brown-Saracino 2017.

7. Just as I finished writing this book, a new "sapphic bar," Dani's, opened in Boston's Back Bay neighborhood.

8. Kennedy and Davis 2014.

9. Brown-Saracino 2018.

10. On the concept of "critical nostalgia," see McDermott 2002; Cashman 2006; Magagnoli 2011; Brown-Rose 2009.

11. See Davis 2003; Meyer et al. 2002; Brown-Saracino 2018.

12. Even though they evoke a problematic history, commemorative events tend to be fun, and thus further cultivate a sense of groupness and shared experience (Fine & Corte 2017).

13. See Zarrelli 2016.

14. In fact, in some instances, nostalgic representations are outweighed by critical portraits, such as at Last Call's performances. Across cities and events, critical and nostalgic portraits are often intertwined. For instance, at the *Lost and Found* exhibit, archival photographs that, left uninterpreted, might have seemed straightforwardly nostalgic were reframed in critical terms via the guide's critical commentary and by textual guides that called audiences to think critically about, among other things, bars' exclusivity.

15. On the origins of the concept of "critical nostalgia," see Boym 2007; McDermott 2002. See also Brown-Saracino 2011.

16. Commemorators have to call people together carefully because they are mindful of how past communities have been exclusionary. They echo a chorus of others in this regard. The geographer Julie Podmore writes, for instance, of how the gradual rejection of lesbian-feminist identities by young women in the 1990s and early 2000s contributed to the closure of the once-prolific lesbian bars of Montreal. Podmore writes, "While the lesbian-feminist commitment to the creation of 'women-only' spaces sustained the bars on the Plateau in the 1980s, it could not respond to new market demands from a generation of women who saw themselves as both lesbian and queer" (2006, 595). See also Stein 1997.

17. Fifteen years on from Podmore's writing, with the rising visibility of transgender identities and increasing public attention to racial inequalities, for many commemorators, the idea of a bar organized narrowly around lesbian identities—or, really, around any singular identity at all—seems problematic and, increasingly, passé.

18. On "imagined community" see Anderson 2006.

19. Of course, their framing of lesbian identity politics as exclusionary does not acknowledge how the gay and lesbian movement relied, partially, on acknowledgment of difference (Armstrong 2002).

20. From the film documenting *Eulogy for the Dyke Bar*.

21. See Ruth Glass's original definition of gentrification in Glass 1964.

22. Of course, while acceptance is increasing, this does not mean that discrimination and hate crimes do not continue. Indeed, some research suggests that hate crime rates may *increase* as points of contact increase (Levy and Levy 2017).

23. Lees 2003.

24. Bell 1997.

25. The problem that dyke bar commemorators confront—yearning for ties predicated on a sense of commonality without wanting to replicate the exclusivities and errors of identity politics or to evoke narrow or rigid group boundaries—is increasingly common among members of marginalized groups that have recently achieved new social, cultural, and legal advances. However, it may be especially acute among LBQT+ individuals, given the specific legacy of identity politics, which they inherit.

26. See, for instance, Gay et al. 2016.

27. See Gotham 2007.

28. Gentrification was discussed as a racial and economic process in New Orleans more than in the other three sites. This heterogeneity reflects debates in the gentrification literature (e.g., Bader and Krysan 2015; Goetz 2011).

29. By Angela Davis Fegan.

30. Created by the photographer Honey Lee Cottrell.

31. Again, most do not regard gentrification as the only factor contributing to bar closure. Rather, they present it—both privately and in their commemorative events—as the *dominant* cause.

32. From Isabel Farrington's documentary of *Eulogy of the Dyke Bar*. See "Eulogy for the Dyke Bar," www.maconreed.com/eulogyforthedykebar. Emphasis added.

33. As a point of reference, Glass coined the term "gentrification" in 1964 to describe changes in London. Scholarship on gentrification in the United States emerged in the late 1970s and early 1980s.

34. Schulman 2012.

35. See "Review: Wild Side West," *TimeOut*, July 28, 2017, www.timeout.com/san-francisco /bars/wild-side-west. Indeed, I had dinner with a group after a Dyke Bar Takeover gathering in a Lower East Side community garden. Over dinner, they spoke casually of their plans to attend a play party in Brooklyn; they never endeavored to explain why such parties do not, in their minds, fill the gap created by the closure of Lower Manhattan dyke bars.

36. See "Eulogy for the Dyke Bar," www.maconreed.com/eulogyforthedykebar.

37. See Lewis 2017 on literal gentrification and canaries in the coal mine. Because commemorators are reacting to gentrification on both material and symbolic levels, as something that contributes to bar closure but that also represents cultural change—or "the gentrification of the mind" (Schulman 2012)—we might anticipate the deployment of a *gentrification*-lens even in cities experiencing less intensive gentrification than the study cases. See Rafail 2018.

38. Tabak and Smith 2015.

39. In this rendering, Spike parallels the "tough bar lesbian"—working-class women who, they write, "were many in number and came from various racial/ethnic groups" (Kennedy and Davis 1993, 10). Crucially, this class "refused to deny their difference, and used confrontational tactics to deal with the heterosexual world" (10). Commemorators embrace a parallel narrative.

40. See Bell 1997 on ghosts of place. While a mythology has developed around the 1990s Mission (e.g., Tea 2000)—aptly captured by the notion of a world where everyone is named

Spike—the neighborhood's transformation largely aligns with the portrait of ascendant gentrification that informants present. Median household income in the Mission in 2016 was over $96,000; the average cost of townhouses was over $1.2 million; and the average price of condos was over $1.8 million. Inner Mission average rent was over $3,500 per month—slightly higher than the average San Francisco rent (See RentCafe, "San Francisco, CA Rental Market Trends: What Is the Average Rent in San Francisco?" accessed November 4, 2018, www.rentcafe.com /average-rent-market-trends/us/ca/san-francisco/). In contrast, in 1989, the mean market-rate rent in the Mission was $659; under 16 percent of residents had a bachelor's degree; and median income was $30,205 ($58,386 in 2016 dollars). From *San Francisco Neighborhood Profiles*, San Francisco Planning Office, 1997, 200–8.

41. See Lefebvre 1968.

42. Lees 2003.

43. Lees 2003.

44. This echoes Chauncey's argument about how early-twentieth-century public gay life was working class because middle and upper classes had greater access to private space (2008; see Kennedy and Davis 1993).

45. Lawlor 2016 (my emphasis). Here, "our cities" implicitly gestures to a particular type of city: urban locales experiencing "super-gentrification" (Lees 2002).

46. See Lees 2002.

47. On subcultures, see Fischer 1975; Fine and Kleinman 1979.

48. See Smith 1996.

49. The 2023 median income data is from the US Census Bureau, American Community Survey (ACS) and Puerto Rico Community Survey (PRCS), 5-Year Estimates, 2019–2023. Median income is in 2023 dollars. See www.census.gov/quickfacts/neworleanscitylouisiana. The 2020 data is from the Decennial Census 2000, DPE, Profile of Selected Economic Characteristics 2000. US Census, //data.census.gov/table/DECENNIALDPSF42000.DP3?q =2000+census+new+orleans. On post-Katrina New Orleans see Gotham and Greenberg 2014.

50. On the notion of being "tightly groupist" see Brubaker and Cooper 2000.

51. A New Orleans organizer said of a bar, "The Country Club used to be the spot when it was hella gay and now it's corporate gay and terrible." This mirrors Gotham's (2007) documentation of the upscaling of parts of New Orleans via corporate and city partnerships.

52. This pushes analyses of urban sexualities, which increasingly attend to how claims to queer space vary by race (Greene 2014, Hunter 2010), to seriously consider how place-based identities and class identities are embedded in contemporary images of sexual personhood. These images are gendered; that is, gay men are often presented as urban, but they are much less resolutely depicted as working class today (Chauncey 2008).

53. On yearning for community see Oldenburg 1999.

54. As previously mentioned, "ghosts of place" is a concept developed by Michael Bell (1997).

55. The advancement of gentrification partially explains why bar commemoration is happening now, versus when bars closed in earlier periods.

56. Armstrong and Crage would call these alternate institutions "other contenders for memory" (2006, 739).

57. Brown-Saracino 2015.

58. This celebration of the dive bar contrasts with dominant trends in queer commemoration, which tends to be "biased toward 'great' men and women, normative forms of 'accomplishment,' and accepted spaces of recognition" (Dunn 2016, 181). Despite counter evidence, commemorators also imagine the bar as urban (Mattson 2020).

59. Faderman 1991.

60. Hirsch 1997.

61. On "critical nostalgia" see Boym 2007 and McDermott 2002.

62. On "stacked decks" see Bartram 2022.

Chapter 2: A Funeral Mass for the Triple Decker

1. On cultural producers see Griswold 1987. Griswold posits that cultural producers play a key role in the life course of any cultural object. A producer, as the term suggests, plays a pivotal role in the production of a cultural object. Griswold provides the example of a prophet or artist, for instance (24). Other factors and actors have significant roles in the reception of objects.

2. On imagined community see Griswold 1992; Anderson 2006.

3. As I note in the introduction, I borrow the term "literal gentrification" from Sarah Schulman (2012) who uses the term to differentiate brick-and-mortar gentrification from what she terms "the gentrification of the mind."

4. On the dubious notion that community is always a positive good see Plett 2023, 87.

5. Suttles 1968. See also Plett 2023.

6. See Plett 2023 for discussion of the boundedness of community.

7. On urban renewal see Jacobs 1961; Gans 1982; Fullilove 2016; Teaford 2000; Hyra 2012.

8. Glass 1964. See also Hyra 2012 and Golash-Boza 2022.

9. See Putnam 2000.

10. On the role of community institutions, like the coffee shop, in sustaining community, see Oldenburg 1998.

11. Producers included James Pasto and Alex Goldfeld.

12. Conforti 1996; Smajda and Gerteis 2012.

13. This message may emerge, in part, from the film's chronological structure, moving forward in time, toward literal gentrification, as it seeks to capture the "old community" and thus describe how social ties in the neighborhood have changed.

14. For a collection of photographs and oral histories from the North End, see Riccio 2022.

15. These figures are based on a search of all Redfin listings in the North End of Boston on January 17, 2023.

16. Kaitlin McKinley Becker and Abbey Niezgoda, "Boston Bakery Closed This Week as Movie Starring Matt Damon, Casey Affleck Films There," NBC Boston 10, March 21, 2023, www .nbcboston.com/news/local/boston-bakery-closed-this-week-as-movie-starring-matt-damon -casey-affleck-films-there/3000628/.

17. American Community Survey, 2023 5-year estimate, "Median Income in the Last Twelve Months," S1903. Per capita income is in 2023 dollars.

18. The US Census estimates that the unemployment rate for the North End is less than 2 percent. See American Community Survey 2023, 5-year estimates, "Selected Economic Characteristics," DP03).

19. American Community Survey, "Educational Attainment," 2023 5-year estimate, S1501.

20. From "Historical Trends in the North End," Boston Planning Department, BostonPlans, www.bostonplans.org/getattachment/540eb648-42e7-4410-807e-fc2949ffd8c0.

21. US Census, "Hispanic or Latino or Not Hispanic or Latino by Race," 2020, p. 9. On the changing racial classification of Italian Americans see Richards 1999; Alba 2019; Kosta 2019.

22. From "Historical Trends in the North End," Boston Planning Department, BostonPlans, www.bostonplans.org/getattachment/540eb648-42e7-4410-807e-fc2949ffd8c0.

23. From "Historical Trends in the North End," Boston Planning Department, BostonPlans, www.bostonplans.org/getattachment/540eb648-42e7-4410-807e-fc2949ffd8c0. See also Smajda and Gerteis 2012.

24. Smajda and Gerteis 2012.

25. This is not to suggest that immigration from Italy altogether stopped. See Pasto 2016.

26. Hartman 1963.

27. See Waters 1990. Of course, increased access to resources has been uneven across the social group; I do not mean to suggest that all Italian Americans have experienced upward mobility.

28. See media coverage of rising prices in neighborhoods such as the North End in the years before the film was released: Deirdre Fenandes, "Tiny Condos Fetch Hefty Prices in Prime Boston Spots," *Boston Globe*, July 15, 2015, and *Boston Globe*, "Recent Home Sales, Boston and Cambridge (Dec. 5)," December 10, 2017.

29. See also Amanda Reetz, Olivia DiRenzo, Luke Macdonald, "The North End: Demographic Change in an Ethnic Landscape and the Threat of Sea Level Rise: A Neighborhood Under Siege," Story Maps, November 16, 2022, storymaps.arcgis.com/stories/b1037ea250184 090952da884c31d26f5.

30. BPDA Research Division 2017.

31. BPDA Research Division 2017.

32. Beauregard 2009.

33. Cathy Cohen 2019; Rothstein 2017; Jackson 1987.

34. Teaford 2000; Carmon 1999; O'Connor 1995; Cohen 2007; Jackson 1987; Edel and Sclar 1975; Rothstein 2017.

35. Fullilove 2001.

36. On the court-mandated desegregation of Boston public schools and subsequent busing initiatives see Formisano 2004; Eaton 2001; Theoharis 2001.

37. The percentage of White residents in Boston public schools declined from 1964 until the 1974 phase 1 of court-ordered school desegregation and continued to decline in 1975, when phase 2 was launched. But Christine Rossell (1975) and others argue that this pattern was already in motion before school desegregation (see also Rossell 1977).

38. BPDA Research Division 2017.

39. These figures reflect the proportion of residents reporting ancestry. See the American Community Survey, 2023 5-year estimate, "People Reporting Ancestry," B04006, for reported ethnic heritage of Medford residents. On Boston's Italian American population see American Community Survey, 2023 5-year estimate, People Reporting Ancestry, B0 4006.

40. American Community Survey, 2023 5-year estimate, "People Reporting Ancestry," B04006.

41. Gans 1982.

42. BPDA Research Division 2017; O'Connor 1995.

43. Small 2004; Fisher & Hughes 1992.

44. Alba 2023. See also Krase 1990.

45. While the time period the film captures is not explicitly delineated, my read is that the film captures life there circa 1950–80.

46. On redlining generally, see Hillier 2003. On the redlining of Boston's North End, in which housing mortgages were unavailable for a portion of the twentieth century because of the neighborhood's density and high proportion of working-class, foreign-born residents, see Digital Scholarship Lab, University of Richmond, "Mapping Inequality: Redlining in America," dsl.richmond.edu/panorama/redlining/map/MA/Boston/context#loc=11/42.3138/-71.0811&adview=full.

47. It is plausible that the filmmakers did not intend to place such emphasis on literal gentrification. However, *gentrification* stands out because it so resonant and recognizable as a method for diagnosing social problems and also because literal gentrification enters the scene (so to speak) as the demise of community takes center stage. This conflagration presents an implicit causal argument for viewers to pick up on.

48. Alba 2023.

49. Alba 2023.

50. On cultural objects, see Griswold 1987.

51. Alba 2023.

52. As well as how the answer to this question may vary by person and household.

53. Hannon 1984; Masur 2008.

54. See Pasto 2010.

55. BPDA Research Division 2017.

56. BPDA Research Division 2017.

57. US Census 2020, "Hispanic or Latino and Not Hispanic or Latino by Race," 9.

58. American Community Survey, 2023 5-Year Estimates (in 2023 Inflation-Adjusted Dollars), S1901.

59. From "My Demographic Viewer," Boston Planning Department, BostonPlans, maps.bostonplans.org/census/#/demographicviewer2024.

60. On educational attainment see "My Demographic Viewer," Boston Planning Department, BostonPlans, maps.bostonplans.org/census/#/demographicviewer2024. On employment status see American Community Survey, 2023 5-Year Estimate, "Selected Economic Characteristics," DP03.

61. See this 2020 article that remarks on the surprisingly "low" cost of a Jamaica Plain triple decker condo unit: Tom Acitelli, "Jamaica Plain Two-Bedroom with a Renovated Bathrooms Drops for under $530,000," *Curbed*, April 9, 2020, www.boston.curbed.com/2020/4/9/21214401/jamaica-plain-two-bedroom-renovated-bathroom. See, also, Anthony Flint, "Boston's Beloved Triple-Deckers Are Next-Level Affordable Housing," *Bloomberg*, May 17, 2023, www.bloomberg.com/news/features/2023-05-17/three-cheers-for-the-triple-decker-boston-s-iconic-cheap-housing.

62. Sharon Cornelissen, "Rethinking the American Dream: Small Multifamily Housing Remains Popular among Immigrant Owners," Joint Center for Housing Studies at Harvard

University, June 26, 2023, www.jchs.harvard.edu/blog/rethinking-american-dream-small
-multifamily-housing-remains-popular-among-immigrant-owners.

63. Jennifer Smith 2018.

64. Aalbers 2016.

65. Geismer 2013; Massey and Denton 1988.

66. I use Falco's name with his express permission.

67. See Gorel 2019.

68. Gorel 2019.

69. Aiden Stein, "A Boston Artist's Critical Solutions to the Housing Crisis," *The Scope*,
December 15, 2021, www.thescopeboston.org/7410/news-and-features/features/boston-artists
-provide-critical-solutions-to-the-housing-crisis/.

70. Pat Falco, "Mock," www.illfalco.com/mock.

71. Pat Falco, "Mock," www.illfalco.com/mock.

72. On hypergentrification see Hackworth and Smith 2001.

73. Edel et al. 1984.

74. In most Boston neighborhoods, gentrification did not begin to take significant root until
1990, with gentrification increasing substantially each decade since, both in terms of gentrification stage within neighborhoods and the expansion of gentrification across the city. See Vigdor
et al. 2002; Wyly and Hammel 1999; Cain 2020.

75. BPDA Research Division 2017.

76. Jennifer Smith 2018.

77. Teaford 2000.

78. Moss 2017; Fullilove 2016.

79. Fullilove 2016.

80. Fullilove 2016.

81. Fullilove 2016.

82. Hackworth and Smith 2001.

83. See, for instance, Oldenburg 1989.

84. Jimenez and Huante 2023 define "gente-fication" as "the return of middle-class Latinxs to
the Latinx barrio with an eye toward investing and/or residing in the community" (22). See also
Huante 2021; Miranda 2018. Of course, some might wish to call this population movement something other than *gentrification*, for they may conceptualize literal gentrification as the movement
of affluent Whites into neighborhoods populated by poor and working-class people of color.

85. Jimenez and Huante 2023 suggest that *Gentefied* explores "a social and cultural anxiety
around home, Latinx community, and belonging in the United States" (23).

86. On cultural heterogeneity, migration, and families see, for instance, Van Beurden et al.
2019.

87. See, for instance, Ahrens 2015; Huante 2021; Sandoval 2021.

88. "Mapping LA: East Side: Boyle Heights," *Los Angeles Times*, www.maps.latimes.com
/neighborhoods/neighborhood/boyle-heights/.

89. "Mapping LA: East Side: Boyle Heights," *Los Angeles Times*, www.maps.latimes.com
/neighborhoods/neighborhood/boyle-heights/.

90. Median value of owner-occupied homes in Boyle Heights is from the American Community Survey, "Selected Housing Characteristics," DPOV 2023 5-year estimate; 2013 data is

from American Community Survey, "Selected Housing Characteristics," PDOV 2023 5-year estimate. The 2023 median household income figure is from the American Community Survey, 2023 5-year estimate, "Income in the Past Twelve Months [in 2023-Inflation Adjusted Dollars]," S1901. The 2010 figure is from American Community Survey, 2010 5-year estimate, "Income in the Past Twelve Months [in 2010-Inflation Adjusted Dollars]," S1901.

91. Jimenez and Huante 2023 propose that *Gentefied* explores "the significance of home for the Latinx protagonists against a backdrop of looming gentrification" (27).

92. The character is referencing the podcast *There Goes the Neighborhood*, WNYC Studios, www.wnycstudios.org/podcasts/neighborhood/about.

93. See, for instance, Spain 1993; Taylor 2002; Pattillo 2010.

94. On gente-fication see Delgado and Swanson 2021; Scorsone 2019; Huante 2021.

95. See, for instance, Wanzo 2021; Lawton 2018; Griffis 2022; Greenberg 2014. See also Wynn 2019; Brady 2019; Aspden 2019.

96. Zack Sharf, "'The Last Black Man in San Francisco' Trailer: A24's Sundance Winner Is a Must-See Summer Indie," *IndieWire*, March 21, 2019, www.indiewire.com/2019/03/the-last -black-man-in-san-francisco-trailer-a24-1202052546/.

97. Twenty-two percent of Black San Franciscans live in Bayview-Hunters Point (see San Francisco Municipal Transportation Agency, "Bayview Hunters Point Express," www.sfmta.com /projects/bayview-hunters-point-express#:~:text=Bayview's%20population%20is%20com-prised%20of,2%2F18%2F20). In 2000, more than 45 percent of Bayview-Hunters Point residents identified as African American (see San Francisco Mayor's Office of Housing and Community Development, "Bayview Hunters Point Neighborhood Profile," sfmohcd.org/sites/default/files /FileCenter/Documents/911-BayviewHuntersPoint.pdf), but by 2010 that percentage had dropped to 33 percent (see San Francisco Department of Public Health, link now defunct, www .sfdph.org/dph/files/hcsmp/hcsmp_datahandout_eng_03222012.pdf), and it dropped again, to 26.9 percent, in 2020 (See Jiyun Tsai, "One in Three Homes in This San Francisco Neighbor-hood Lives below the Poverty Line," San Francisco Standard, December 8, 2022, www.sfstandard .com/research-data/san-francisco-neighborhood-new-census-data-maps/). In general, San Francisco has lost Black population over time; from over 13 percent in 1970 to around 6 percent in 2019 (See US Census Bureau, search Black or African American/San Francisco County, www .data.census.gov/table?q=Black+or+African+American&g=010XX00US_050XX00US06075 &tid=ACSDT1Y2019.B02009&hidePreview=false).

98. Walker 1998; Pepin and Watts 2006. See Fillmore Activist Project.

99. Walker 1998; Pepin and Watts 2006. See Fillmore Activist Project.

100. Lai 2012; Jackson and Jones 2012.

101. Wanzo 2021.

102. Spain 1993.

103. Oldenburg 1999.

104. Williams 1975.

Chapter 3: The "Gentrification" of the Self

1. As is true throughout the book, I borrow the phrase "literal gentrification" from Sarah Schulman 2012.

2. For her part, Schulman 2012 advocates for resistance to the structural and cultural forces that encourage the "gentrification of the mind."

3. This facet of the parables most closely aligns with Schulman's concept of the "gentrification of the mind" (2012).

4. See, for instance, Craig and Richeson 2014; Bobo 2017.

5. See Bourdieu 1987.

6. On theories of racial capitalism, which would support this view, see Bhattacharyya 2018. See also Rucks-Ahidiana 2021.

7. On intersectionality see Crenshaw 1989; Hill Collins and Bilge 2016.

8. See, for instance, McCall 2005.

9. Trilling 2009.

10. On historic preservation tax credits see Ryberg-Webster & Kinahan (2017).

11. Cynthia Belmont writes of the period that Lawlor's book depicts as "a time when gay hedonism, lesbian feminism, punk anti-homonormativity, and LGBTQ responses to AIDS combined to make a complex heyday of queer culture" (2023:154).

12. See Schulman 2012. See also Myles 2020.

13. Duggan 2002.

14. Warner 2000; Stryker 2008.

15. Boym 2008.

16. See Ghaziani 2016; Orne 2020.

17. Glass 1964. The poet and memoirist Eileen Myles, quoted earlier in this section, presents 1970s New York as a refuge from oppressive suburbia in *Chelsea Girls*. Myles writes of returning from a trip to suburban Long Island: "By the time we got back to Manhattan we both felt sick. Sara wanted to get some heroin, I wanted a big glass of whiskey. We parked her car in her usual spot, the lot on 7th between C & D and just shook our heads and shuddered all the way west to First Avenue and her street, 9th, where we spent the night" (1994, 146).

18. This began as early as the early-twentieth-century Chicago School of Urban Sociology. See Zorbaugh 1929. On more recent bohemias see Lloyd 2010.

19. On the formation of LGBTQIA+ residential concentrations in cities in the twentieth century see D'Emilio 1983; Bérubé 1990.

20. Delany 1999; Stehlin 2016.

21. However, by 2000 Michael Warner had published his treatise, *The Trouble with Normal.* See Warner 2000.

22. On the emergence of queer identities and politics, and reflections thereon, see Cohen 2019; Macias 2022; Gamson 1995; Doan 2007; Browne 2011; Nash 2011; Stone 2013.

23. To be fair, for Schulman gentrification is not solely responsible for this "gentrification of the mind." Rather, the AIDS pandemic and a broader neoliberal turn that individualizes risk and responsibility set an important backdrop for this transformation. Schulman writes, "If I were an academic, I might describe my thesis this way: 'A certain urban ecology of queer subcultural existence has been wiped out, through both AIDS and gentrification'" (2012, 15). See also Peacock 2024.

24. Frank 2018; Butler 2007; Hammett and Cooper 2007. See also coverage in popular media, including a *Bloomberg* article by Richard Florida, "The Fading Distinction between City and

Suburb," October 6, 2014, www.bloomberg.com/news/articles/2014-10-06/the-fading
-distinction-between-city-and-suburb.

25. Of course, whether San Francisco or even the Mission was truly "ungentrified" in this
period is up for debate (see Brown-Saracino 2021). Indeed, it is reasonable to conclude that
LBQT+ San Franciscans played a role themselves in the gentrification of the neighborhood,
constituting a first wave of gentrification (Brown-Saracino 2021; Smith 1996). However, in contrast to the concentration of wealth found in the contemporary Mission District, the 1990s
version of the neighborhood may indeed appear "ungentrified" (Brown-Saracino 2021). For
media coverage see: Rae Alexandra, "Chloe Sherman's 'Renegade' Photography Captures '90s
Queer Culture in SF," KQED, June 21, 2022, www.kqed.org/arts/13915084/chloe-sherman
-renegade-san-francisco-1990s-schlomer-haus; Chloe Sherman, "Chloe Sherman's Photographs Bring Queer History to Light Just in Time for Pride 2022," *LGBTQ Nation*, June 6, 2022,
www.lgbtqnation.com/2022/06/chloe-shermans-photographs-bring-queer-history-light-just
-time-pride-2022; Heather Cassell, "Chloe Sherman's 'Renegades': Photo Exhibit Documents
SF's '90s Lesbian Scene," Edge Media Network, June 14, 2022, www.edgemedianetwork.com
/story.php?ch=entertainment&sc=fine_arts&id=316367&chloe_shermans_renegades_
_photo_exhibit_documents_sfs_90s_lesbian_scene.

26. Brown-Saracino 2021.

27. Chloe Sherman, "When We Were Renegades," *Gigantic*, www.giganticmagazine.com
/issue-4-chloe-sherman.

28. Of course, LBQT+ individuals' experiences of and relationship to lesbian identity politics varied by race, class, geography, and even precise sexual or gender identity (see Rupp and
Taylor 1999; Esterberg 1997; Brown-Saracino 2021; Moore 2011). See also Stein 1997.

29. On the radical-visibility politics of the Avengers, which emphasized displays of sexuality,
see Rand 2013.

30. On this transition from lesbian identity politics, see Farquhar 2000; Humphrey 1999.

31. On Portland's gentrification see Shaw and Sullivan 2011. See also Goodling, Green, and
McClintock 2015; Bates 2013. On shifts in LBQT+ identities in this period, see Podmore 2006.

32. On post–identity politics see Brown-Saracino 2011. See also Forstie 2019.

33. On how Subaru came to market itself to and become a symbol for queer women, see
"When Subaru Came Out," NPR, *Planet Money*, episode 729, October 14, 2016, www.npr.org
/sections/money/2016/10/14/497958151/episode-729-when-subaru-came-out.

34. Tea 2022.

35. See Lorde 1982; Myles 1994.

36. See, again, Warner 2000 and Schulman 2012.

37. Between 2010 and 2023, median household income nearly doubled in Boyle Heights and
the median value of owner-occupied homes in Boyle Heights more than doubled in the same
set of US Census tracts between 2013 and 2023 (Sources: American Community Survey, 2023
5-year estimate, "Income in the Past Twelve Months [in 2023-Inflation Adjusted Dollars]," S1901;
American Community Survey, 2010 5-year estimate, "Income in the Past Twelve Months [in
2010-Inflation Adjusted Dollars]," S1901). Just over 2 percent of Boyle Heights residents listed
their race as "White alone" on the 2000 Census (from US Census 2020, "Hispanic or Latino,
and not Hispanic or Latino by Race, p. 9). By contrast, over 20 percent of Boyle Heights

residents are listed as White on the 2023 American Community Survey. See www.planning.lacity
.gov/odocument/338ef37c-4d26-43f9-836e-78dcfbcc79eb/standard_report2022_BOYLE
_HTS_mail.pdf. These changes have produced protests, many of which have specifically targeted the role of arts institutions in neighborhood change. See, for instance, Miranda 2018;
Chang 2016.

38. *Vida* emphasizes economic gentrification by problematizing the upward mobility of the
series' two most affluent primary characters, Emma and Nelson. However, the series also draws
secondary attention to how the acquisition of cultural capital associated with upper-middle-
class tastes and practices can alienate one from one's community of origin. Given this, I use
"economic" and "class" gentrification interchangeably. In so doing, I mean to communicate how
the series primarily attends to economic mobility, and, secondarily, to the accumulation of
cultural capital (Bourdieu 1987). Of course, I recognize that economic and cultural capital often
intersect, but they are not interchangeable.

39. Covarrubias and Fryberg 2015, 424.

40. Research indicates that White gentrifiers continue to avoid majority-Black neighborhoods. For a summary of such research see Brown-Saracino 2017 and Ocejo 2023. See also
Hwang 2020.

41. The viewer also learns that Emma greatly resents her mother, as, after encountering evidence of Emma's attraction to women, Vidalia sent preteen Emma away to live with her grandmother. Thus, as an adult, Emma had minimal contact with Vidalia and therefore was unaware
that Vidalia was partnered with a woman.

42. Zimmer 2022; Butler and Lees 2006.

43. When Lyn eventually leaves the party, she finds herself on a bus traveling back to Boyle
Heights with Aurora. As they ride, each looking straight ahead, avoiding eye contact with one
another, a song, in Spanish, featuring the words, "She doesn't look up because her work is domestic," plays.

44. McCall 2005.

45. The one moment of homophobic reality occurs after Eddy intervenes when a cisgender
heterosexual man harasses one of her femme lesbian friends and the man then violently attacks
Eddy in the bar bathroom—landing her in the ICU. This violent attack is the only overt homophobia that *Vida*'s characters encounter across three seasons, and the violence serves as a
crucial point of contrast from the warmth and support that the other characters offer their
LGBTQIA+ friends, family, and neighbors. In fact, while there is much tension between and
among primary and secondary characters, none of it is based on sexuality (except for Emma's
recollections, from her youth, of how Vidalia sent her away in her early teens).

46. Saez and Zucman 2016; Gilbert 2017; Temin 2018.

47. Kraus and Tan 2015; Alesina et al. 2018.

48. Schulman 2012.

49. In point of fact, early-stage gentrifiers are often individuals with high cultural capital and
low economic capital, such as artists and students (see Zukin 1987; Smith 2004). However, *Vida*
does not present these characters in that light.

50. Sanchez and Masuoka 2010. See also Jones-Correa 2011.

51. See Rucks-Ahidiana 2021.

52. Rucks-Ahidiana 2021.

53. Becker 2023.

54. NYU Furman Center, "Central Harlem MN10: Neighborhood Indicators," www
.furmancenter.org/neighborhoods/view/central-harlem.

55. Jackson 2001.

56. See Jackson 2001; Taylor 2002; Hyra 2008.

57. "The concept 'Black middle class' is incompatible with some Black women's notions of
self, and that their ambivalence about the 'Black middle classes' is partly rooted in an emotional
need to remain connected to the wider Black community" (Maylor and Williams 2011, 345).

58. "Black racial authenticity, like authenticity in general, is a slippery concept. Broadly, black
authenticity can be defined as an ideological conceptualization of a 'true' or 'real' black identity,
encompassing the expectations of what it means to 'be black'" (Cox 2020, 173).

59. See Gates 2004.

60. See also Courtney Thomas 2015, 194.

61. See Landry and Marsh 2011; Hyra 2007, 89.

62. See Haynes 2008; Jackson 2001; Pattillo 2005.

63. See Jackson 2001.

64. See Jackson 2001; Taylor 2002. On these trends more generally, see also Pattillo 2005,
314; Haynes 2008.

65. See Jackson 2001, Taylor 2002, Pattillo 2008, Boyd 2008, Hyra 2008.

66. On "authenticity" see, among others, Lindholm 2007; Bendix 2009.

67. On the social construct of authenticity see Erickson 1995; Lindholm 2007; Trilling 2009.

68. Cox writes that "social class is often conflated with race such that authentic blackness is
attributed to blacks living in poverty or the ghetto" (2020, 175; see also Collins 2004; Lacy 2007).

69. See, for instance, *Class* (2017), by Lucinda Rosenfeld, which underlines the questionable
moral character of the gentrifier protagonist.

70. Rich 1980.

71. I do not believe that the presence of background narratives about sexuality, even in works
that are not principally about the "gentrification" of sexuality, is a coincidence. In my archive,
parables of the "gentrification" of the self tend to either celebrate "nonnormative" (read: queer)
sexualities or to express nostalgia for what we might think of, broadly speaking, as sexual liberation or sexual "authenticity." This ranges from nostalgia for a 1990s Mission District in which
queer women casually hooked up with one another, to Radha pursuing a man from a different
borough and walk of life, or Lyn and Emma, in *Vida*, freely and openly seeking sexual pleasure
with a variety of partners. While anxiety about the "gentrification" of the sexual self is most front
and center in the memoirs and novels with which this chapter opens, it is a background feature
of all of the works this chapter engages. Why is this the case? Perhaps sexual freedom—whether
the freedom to cross class lines or to challenge traditional, gendered, and racialized expectations
of sexual deportment—is part of what some fear dominant culture will "gentrify" out of existence. Do we worry not only about the purported "suburbanization" of the city (via literal
gentrification) but also about the "suburbanization" of our sexual lives (via personal "gentrification")? Do stories that evoke literal gentrification highlight anxieties about sexuality in part
because of long-standing cultural associations of cities with sexual freedom (particularly for

queer subjects, but also for single people and others)? And since men's sexual liberation is so often taken for granted, are we best able to convey the threat of sexual "gentrification" by featuring women (or nonbinary individuals, such as Paul/Polly), and, in the instances that I have highlighted, queer women and/or women of color? By posing these questions, I argue that the *Forty-Year-Old Version* and *Vida* reveal dual and partially overlapping anxieties about the "gentrification" of contemporary racial and sexual identities. It is perhaps not a coincidence that these areas of anxiety parallel some of the spaces in which literal gentrification has encroached in many contemporary cities, including the gayborhood and, even more recently, historically African American and Latinx neighborhoods such as Harlem, Bedford Stuyvesant, and Boyle Heights. This makes *gentrification* a particularly apt metaphor for encapsulating personal changes pertaining to sexual and racial identities.

Chapter 4: *Gentrification* as a Political Metaphor and Heuristic

1. As is true throughout the book, I borrow the term "literal gentrification" from Sarah Schulman (2012), who uses the term to differentiate brick-and-mortar gentrification from what she terms "the gentrification of the mind."

2. See Lolis Elie, "Gentrification Might Kill New Orleans Before Climate Change Does," *New York Times*, August 27, 2019, www.nytimes.com/2019/08/27/opinion/new-orleans.html ?searchResultPosition=1.

3. See "Conservative Christian Gentrification of the Rainbow Pride Flag Has Begun, Only Two More Causes to Go and They'll Be Flying Their 'Conservative Pride Flag,'" Reddit, posted by user RustyBarbedWireCactus on r/ Political Humor, www.reddit.com/r/PoliticalHumor /comments/pzfekt/conservative_christian_gentrification_of_the/.

4. See image posted on Reddit titled, "Here goes the gentrification of the term code switching by none other than amanda bucci," posted by user gymsnark, www.i.redd.it/sxla2wy6k7oa1 .jpg.

5. Lingel 2021.

6. On tech and gentrification see, for instance, Maharawal 2017 and Stehlin 2016.

7. Goldman (2021).

8. For arguments on behalf of the notion of suburban gentrification, see Markley 2018; Charles 2011; Markley and Sharma 2016; Lung-Amam 2024.

9. Goldman elaborates, "I call HGTV gentrification TV because of its insistence that the houses most suited to profitable renovations and flipping are those that are discounted to the market as a result of age, neglect, style, changing demographics, neighborhood or other markers of class" (2021, 81).

10. Zukin 1987.

11. Smith 1987.

12. Some reviews shared this view of Stein's book, as principally advancing understandings of literal gentrification. See: Annie Lloyd, "Samuel Stein's 'Capital City: Gentrification and the Real Estate State' and What It Means for LA," Knock LA, March 7, 2019, www.knock-la.com /samuel-steins-capital-city-gentrification-and-the-real-estate-and-what-it-means-for-la -a5766762f6a5/; Nick Licata, "What Does 'an AntiCcapitalist' City Look Like? In 'Capital City,'

an Urban Planner Investigates," *Seattle Times*, May 10, 2019, www.seattletimes.com /entertainment/books/what-does-an-anti-capitalist-city-look-like-in-capital-city-an-urban -planner-investigates/. As an example of how reviews interpreted the book as being about gentrification, an introduction to a set of reviews in *Society and Space* states, "In this well-written and accessible book, Sam Stein explains the role of the state in creating gentrification. In popular discourse, gentrification has often been seen as a 'private' phenomena" (see Eric Goldfischer, "Capital City by Samuel Stein," *Society and Space*, May 1, 2019, www.societyandspace.org/book -review-forums/capital-city-by-samuel-stein).

13. Of course, there is no singular gay male culture (see Greene 2024). The author gestures to a culture constituted primarily by White, gay men in New York City.

14. For a parallel argument, see Schulman 2012.

15. See, for instance, Moss 2017 and Stein 2019.

16. Duggan 2002.

17. Faderman 2015; Korte 2015; Belluck and Zezima 2003.

18. See Warner 2000; Duggan 2002; Schulman 2012.

19. See Sam Hall Kaplan, "Tough-Love Urbanism: On Jeremiah Moss's 'Vanishing New York: How a Great City Lost Its Soul,'" *LA Review of Books*, September 30, 2017, www .lareviewofbooks.org/article/tough-love-urbanism-on-jeremiah-mosss-vanishing-new-york -how-a-great-city-lost-its-soul/; Ginia Bellafonte, "Tracking the Hyper-Gentrification of New York, One Lost Knish Place at a Time," *New York Times*, September 27, 2017, www.nytimes.com /2017/09/27/books/review/vanishing-new-york-jeremiah-moss.html; Ronda Kaysen, "A Book from a Blogger about Disappearing New York," *New York Times*, August 11, 2017, www .nytimes.com/2017/08/11/realestate/a-book-from-a-blogger-about-disappearing-new-york .html.

20. Ganti 2014.

21. But see Gale 2021 for a different history of gentrification, one that starts much earlier.

22. On the exploitative character of unpaid internships, see Yamada 2016.

23. Dyndahl et al. 2021.

24. Peterson and Kern 1996.

25. See Tuck and Yang 2021.

26. Dyndahl et al. 2014.

27. Halnon and Cohen 2006.

28. Turnbull 2009. See also Grazian 2005.

29. Tolfo and Doucet 2022.

30. "Fire Fire Gentrifier," posted June 30, 2020, by BLAkkkMALE, YouTube, www.youtube .com/watch?v=vGbegWkmGi0; "Protesters Interrupt Louisville Mayor at Ribbon-cutting," posted July 10, 2020, by WHAS11, YouTube, www.youtube.com/watch?v=a7yt3r7GBOk.

31. Manissa Maharawal, "Shut It Down: Notes on the #blacklivesmatter Protests—Part 2," focaal blog, June 22, 2015, www.focaalblog.com/2015/06/22/manissa-maharawal-shut-it-down -part-2/.

32. Hart 2017.

33. Hart 2017.

34. Hart 2017.

35. Link is now inactive, but accessed on December 11, 2024: www.righttothecity.org/news /marching-for-housing-justice-at-the-peoples-climate-march.

36. One was NJNP. Their primary work is aimed at organizing for trans liberation/sex work decriminalization, but they also work for housing justice and have a housing collective with five safe houses for current and former trans sex workers. The other was ONE DC, which is a grass-roots housing justice and antidisplacement organization.

37. This assessment is based on media coverage and a YouTube video of the march. See Riddle 2019, and "DC Dyke March 2019: Raw Footage," posted June 7, 2019, by News2Share, www.youtube.com/watch?v=Nk8VBmESsVw.

38. Riddle 2019, and "DC Dyke March 2019: Raw Footage," posted June 7, 2019, by News-2Share, www.youtube.com/watch?v=Nk8VBmESsVw.

39. These are themes we might anticipate finding at any dyke march. On dyke marches see Brown-Saracino and Ghaziani 2009; Podmore 2015; Currans 2012.

40. Consider, for instance, antigentrification activism aimed at blocking the redevelopment of Brooklyn's Atalntic Yards, and for increased density in Boston's Washington Street corridor. See Thompson (2011), and Yawu Miller, "Jamaica Plain Activists Press Walsh on Affordability," *Bay State Banner*, June 15, 2016, www.baystatebanner.com/2016/06/15/jamaica-plain-activists -press-walsh-on-affordability/.

41. Brown-Saracino 2017.

42. Brown-Saracino 2017.

43. For work on how literal gentrification harms urbanites, see Glass 1964; Marcuse 1985; Gotham 2001; Slater 2006; Wacquant 2008.

44. For work on how gentrification produces less harm than one might expect, particularly pertaining to direct displacement, see Freeman 2011; Freeman and Braconi 2004; Vigdor 2002.

45. For work on how to define gentrification, see Wacquant 2008; Rose 1984; Lees 2002.

46. For work on gentrification beyond the central city, see Bell 1994; Brown-Saracino 2009; Macgregor 2010; Stiman 2016. For work on how gentrification takes shape outside of the Global North, see Centner 2012; Maloutas 2012.

47. Brown-Saracino 2017.

48. On how to measure displacement, see Slater 2006; Wacquant 2008; Wyly et al. 2010; Vigdor 2002; Freeman 2011.

49. See Brown-Saracino 2017.

50. On gentrification as politically charged see Lees et al. 2008.

Conclusion

1. As I have done throughout the book, I borrow the term "literal gentrification" from Sarah Schulman (2012), who uses the term to differentiate brick-and-mortar gentrification from what she terms "the gentrification of the mind."

2. Gale writes, "Gentrification has become the victim of a process of semantic transmutation that has appended layers of connotation diffusing the concept's meaning nearly to the point of opacity" (2008, 206).

3. Smith 1987.

4. Glass 1960.

5. Wacquant 2008; Vigdor 2002.

6. Hepburn et al. 2024.

7. On this type of circulation see Lamont 1987 and Hallett et al. 2019.

8. See McDonnell et al. 2017.

9. On the circularity of the meaning assigned to cultural objects, see Hallett et al. 2019 and McDonnell et al. 2017. See also Lamont 1987 on the reception of academic concepts. See Gale on early adoption of the term gentrification by US journalists—before US academics began using the term (2023).

10. In doing so, I borrow from and build off an *Annual Review of Sociology* article I wrote on the subject. See Brown-Saracino 2017.

11. Timberlake and Johns-Wolfe 2017.

12. Likewise, Hwang and Sampson 2014 excluded neighborhoods such as Lincoln Square, which has, in recent years, been popularly recognized as gentrifying.

13. See, for instance, Berrey 2005; Betancur 2011; Brown-Saracino 2004 and 2009; Johansson and Cornebise 2010; Levy et al. 2007; Maly 2011, Ghaziani 2011; Orne 2020; Doering 2020.

14. Owens 2012.

15. See bunten et al. 2024.

16. Wacquant 2008.

17. Freeman and Braconi 2004, for instance, consider educational attainment.

18. See Immergluck 2009 on mortgage lending patterns and Kreager et al. 2011 on mortgage lending patterns.

19. See Hwang and Sampson 2014; Papachristos et al. 2011.

20. See Hosman 2018 on intermittent/slow gentrification and see Lees 2002 on ascendant gentrification.

21. Barton 2016; Landis 2016, 2.

22. See Owens 2012.

23. See Knieriem 2023.

24. On rural gentrification see Bell 1994; Brown-Saracino 2009; Macgregor 2010; Stiman 2016; Smith 1998; Smith and Holt 2005. On applying gentrification beyond the United States, see Centner 2012 and Maloutas 2015.

25. Rose 1984.

26. On advanced gentrification, see also Gotham 2005; Lees 2002; Zukin 2009. On stalled gentrification see also Hosman 2018.

27. See Hwang and Sampson 2014; Maciag 2015; Owens 2012; Timberlake and Johns-Wolfe 2017.

28. See Goetz 2011.

29. On this theme, writing about New York's Highline, Halle and Tiso write that "gentrification" is often used "very loosely, conflating several issues that should be considered separately" (2014, 16). Indeed, they suggest that different versions of literal gentrification have occurred along different sections of Manhattan's Highline, including "classic," "commercial," and "super-commercial" gentrification (17). Thus some of the disjuncture in the literature results from the fact that what scholars term *gentrification* varies across times and places, perhaps even along a single stretch of Manhattan real estate.

30. See also Slater 2006; Wacquant 2008.

31. Freeman 2011; Freeman and Braconi 2004. But see Ding et al. 2016; Newman and Wyly 2006.

32. Desmond 2016.

33. See also Vigdor 2002 on involuntary displacement.

34. Ding et al. 2016; Newman and Wyly 2006; Freeman et al. 2024.

35. Glass 1964.

36. See Rose 1984 on literal gentrification's chaos.

37. Lewis 2017.

38. See Park 1915; Zorbaugh 1929; Weston 1995.

39. The geographer Neil Smith referred to gentrification as "a dirty word" in a 1996 book.

40. Smith 1987.

41. Brown-Saracino 2004.

42. See, for instance, Shaw and Sullivan 2011; Ocejo 2011; Boterman and Wouter van Gent. 2022; Curran and Hamilton 2012; Anguelovski 2015; Hwang 2016; Summers 2021; Tissot 2015.

43. For an argument in favor of starting the clock earlier, see Gale 2023.

44. See also Butler and Robson 2003.

45. On the state of socioeconomic inequalities in the United States see Mijs and Roe 2021.

46. Link is no longer active, but accessed on March 4, 2024, twitter.com/Buddyhead/status /1744405116533563447?s=20.

47. Link is no longer active, but accessed on March 4, 2024, twitter.com/KevOnStage/status /1293921359970459648. Thanks to Jordan Rogers for bringing this material to my attention.

48. See Andreas Hale (@AndreasHale), Twitter, August 13, 2020, www.twitter.com /AndreasHale/status/1294102683964456960?ref_src=twsrc%5Etfw%7Ctwcamp%5Etweet embed%7Ctwterm%5E1294102683964456960%7Ctwgr%5Efa53e1551003f8b876b00e4ac5 0a377f84d88b83%7Ctwcon%5Es1_&ref_url=https%3A%2F%2Ftheboxhouston .com%2F10039812%2Fmusic-heads-call-out-tiktok-user-over-slow-reverb-being-gentrified -chopped-screwed-music%2F. Many thanks to Jordan Rogers for alerting me to this material.

49. Of course, as I said at the outset, I do not have data on creators' or producers' intentions.

50. Golash-Boza 2023. See also Gale 2021 on the "misunderstood history of gentrification."

51. See Becher 2014.

52. See Slater 2006 on the reasons why scholars ought not to be wedded to the original formulation that Ruth Glass offered.

53. See also Duneier 2016 and Wacquant 2022.

BIBLIOGRAPHY

Aalbers, Manuel B. 2016. *The Financialization of Housing: A Political Economy Approach.* Routledge.

Ahrens, Mareike. 2015. "'Gentrify? No! Gentefy? Sí!': Urban Redevelopment and Ethnic Gentrification in Boyle Heights, Los Angeles." *Aspeers* 8.

Alba, Richard D. 2019. "The Twilight of Ethnicity among Americans of European Ancestry: The Case of Italians." In *Celebrating 40 Years of Ethnic and Racial Studies*, edited by Martin Bulmer and John Solomos, 50–74. Routledge.

————. 2023. *Italian Americans: Into the Twilight of Ethnicity.* Plunkett Lake Press.

Alesina, Alberto, Stefanie Stantcheva, and Edoardo Teso. 2018. "Intergenerational Mobility and Preferences for Redistribution." *American Economic Review* 108 (2): 521–54.

American Community Survey. US Census Bureau. 2017–2019.

Anderson, Benedict. 2006. *Imagined Communities: Reflections on the Origin and Spread of Nationalism.* Verso Books.

Anguelovski, Isabelle. 2015. "Healthy Food Stores, Greenlining and Food Gentrification: Contesting New Forms of Privilege, Displacement and Locally Unwanted Land Uses in Racially Mixed Neighborhoods." *International Journal of Urban and Regional Research* 39, no. 6: 1209–30.

Armstrong, Elizabeth A. 2002. *Forging Gay Identities: Organizing Sexuality in San Francisco, 1950–1994.* University of Chicago Press.

Armstrong, Elizabeth A., and Suzanna M. Crage. 2006. "Movements and Memory: The Making of the Stonewall Myth." *American Sociological Review* 71 (5): 724–51.

Aspden, Peter. 2019. "'It's Starting to Lose its Soul': 'The Last Black Man in San Francisco' Pays Haunting Homage to the City's Unique Character and Vanishing Minority. Meets Its Makers." *Financial Times*, October 19.

August, Martine. 2020. "The Financialization of Canadian Multi-family Rental Housing: From Trailer to Tower." *Journal of Urban Affairs* 42 (7): 975–97.

Bader, Michael D. M., and Maria Krysan. 2015. "Community Attraction and Avoidance in Chicago: What's Race Got to Do with It?" *Annals of the American Academy of Political and Social Science* 660 (1): 261–81.

Banks, Sandy. 2012. "Downtown Charter a Dream." *Los Angeles Times*, October 23.

Barton, Michael. 2016. "An Exploration of the Importance of the Strategy Used to Identify Gentrification." *Urban Studies* 53, no. 1: 92–111.

Bartram, Robin. 2022. *Stacked Decks: Building Inspectors and the Reproduction of Urban Inequality.* University of Chicago Press.

Bates, Lisa K. 2013. "Gentrification and Displacement Study: Implementing an Equitable Inclusive Development Strategy in the Context of Gentrification." City of Portland, Bureau of Planning and Sustainability. www.portland.gov/sites/default/files/2020-01/2 -gentrification-and-displacement-study-05.18.13.pdf.

Beauregard, Robert A. 2009. "Urban Population Loss in Historical Perspective: United States, 1820–2000." *Environment and Planning A* 41 (3): 514–28.

Becher, Deborah. 2014. *Private Property and Public Power: Eminent Domain in Philadelphia*. Oxford University Press.

Becker, Howard S. 2023. *Art Worlds: Updated and Expanded*. University of California Press.

Bell, Michael Mayerfield. 1994. *Childerley: The Moral Landscape of a Country Village*. University of Chicago Press.

———. 1997. "The Ghosts of Place." *Theory and Society* 26 (6): 813–36.

Belluck, Pam, and Katie Zezima. 2003. "Marriage by Gays Gains Big Victory in Massachusetts." *New York Times*, November 19.

Belmont, Cynthia. 2023. "Organic Transitioning and Queer Topophilia in Paul Takes the Form of a Mortal Girl." *Feminist Formations* 35 (2): 154–73.

Bendix, Regina. 2009. *In Search of Authenticity: The Formation of Folklore Studies*. University of Wisconsin Press.

Berrey, Ellen C. 2005. "Divided over Diversity: Political Discourse in a Chicago Neighborhood." *City & Community* 4, no. 2: 143–70.

Bérubé, Allan. 1990. *Coming Out Under Fire: The History of Gay Men and Women in World War II*. Free Press.

Betancur, John. 2011. "Gentrification and Community Fabric in Chicago." *Urban Studies* 48, no. 2: 383–406.

Bhattacharyya, Gargi. 2018. *Rethinking Racial Capitalism: Questions of Reproduction and Survival*. Rowman & Littlefield.

Bobo, L. D. 2017. "Racism in Trump's America: Reflections on Culture, Sociology, and the 2016 US Presidential Election." *British Journal of Sociology* 68: S85–S104.

Borrelli, Christopher. 2013. "'World's End' Stars Battle the Crawl to Sameness." *Chicago Tribune*, August 18.

———. 2014. "Why Chefs Obsess over Food Awards." *Chicago Tribune*, November 13.

———. 2015. "Ticket Resale Is Not Just Killing Deadheads, It's Killing Live Music." *Chicago Tribune*, June 28.

Boterman, William, and Wouter van Gent. 2022. "Making the Middle-Class City." In Making the Middle-Class City. Palgrave Macmillan New York.

Bourdieu, Pierre. 1987. *Distinction: A Social Critique of the Judgement of Taste*. Translated by Richard Nice. Cambridge: Harvard University Press.

Boyd, M. R. 2008. *Jim Crow Nostalgia: Reconstructing Race in Bronzeville*. University of Minnesota Press.

Boym, Svetlana. 2007. "Nostalgia and Its Discontents." *Hedgehog Review* 9 (2): 7–19.

BPDA Research Division. 2017. *Historical Trends in Boston Neighborhoods since 1950*, Boston Planning Department, December. www.bostonplans.org/getattachment/89e8d5ee-e7a0 -43a7-ab86-7f49a943eccb.

Brady, Tara. 2019. "Expelled from Your Own City: A Documentary-Fiction Hybrid Made by Childhood Friends Joe Talbot and Jimmie Fails, The Last Black Man in San Francisco Tells a Story of Displacement and Loss That Many People Will Find Familiar." *Irish Times*, October 26.

Brodeur, Michael A. 2015. "Onward and Outward: Does Gay Culture Risk Getting Swept away in the Mainstream?" *Boston Globe*, July 5.

Brown-Rose, Josie A. 2009. *Critical Nostalgia and Caribbean Migration*. Vol. 23. Peter Lang.

Brown-Saracino, Japonica. 2009. *A Neighborhood That Never Changes: Gentrification, Social Preservation, and the Search for Authenticity*. University of Chicago Press.

———. 2010. *The Gentrification Debates: A Reader*. Routledge.

———. 2011. "From the Lesbian Ghetto to Ambient Community: The Perceived Costs and Benefits of Integration for Community." *Social Problems* 58 (3): 361–88.

———. 2015. "How Places Shape Identity: The Origins of Distinctive LBQ Identities in Four Small US Cities." *American Journal of Sociology* 121 (1): 1–63.

———. 2017. "Explicating Divided Approaches to Gentrification and Growing Income Inequality." *Annual Review of Sociology* 43: 515–39.

———. 2018. *How Places Make Us: Novel LBQ Identities in Four Small Cities*. University of Chicago Press.

———. 2020. "From Situated Space to Social Space: Dyke Bar Commemoration as Reparative Action." *Journal of Lesbian Studies* 24 (3): 311–25.

———. 2021. "The Afterlife of Identity Politics: Gentrification, Critical Nostalgia, and the Commemoration of Lost Dyke Bars." *American Journal of Sociology* 126 (5): 1017–66.

Brown-Saracino, Japonica, and Amin Ghaziani. 2009. "The Constraints of Culture: Evidence from the Chicago Dyke March." *Cultural Sociology* 3 (1): 51–75.

Browne, Kath. 2011. "'By Partner We Mean . . .': Alternative Geographies of 'Gay Marriage.'" *Sexualities* 14 (1): 100–22

Brubaker, Rogers, and Frederick Cooper. 2000. "Beyond 'Identity.'" *Theory and society* 29 (1): 1–47.

bunten, devin michelle, Benjamin Preis, and Shifrah Aron-Dine. 2024. "Re-measuring Gentrification." *Urban Studies* 61, no. 1: 20–39.

Burke, Kenneth. 1966. *Language as Symbolic Action: Essays on Life, Literature, and Method*. University of California Press.

Butler, Tim. 2007. "Re-urbanizing London Docklands: Gentrification, Suburbanization or New Urbanism?" *International Journal of Urban and Regional Research* 31 (4): 759–81.

Butler, Tim, and Garry Robson. 2003. *London Calling: The Middle Classes and the Re-making of Inner London*. Berg Publishers.

Butler, Tim, and Loretta Lees. 2006. "Super-gentrification in Barnsbury, London: Globalization and Gentrifying Global Elites at the Neighbourhood Level." *Transactions of the Institute of British Geographers* 31 (4): 467–87.

Cain, Taylor. 2020. "'A Place for Families Like Us': Reproducing Gentrification and Gentrifiers in Two Boston Neighborhoods." PhD diss., Boston University.

Carmon, Naomi. 1999. "Three Generations of Urban Renewal Policies: Analysis and Policy Implications." *Geoforum* 30 (2): 145–58.

Cashman, Ray. 2006. "Critical Nostalgia and Material Culture in Northern Ireland." *Journal of American Folklore* 119 (472): 137–60

Centner, Ryan. 2012. "Microcitizenships: Fractious Forms of Urban Belonging after Argentine Neoliberalism." *International Journal of Urban and Regional Research* 36 (2): 336–62.

Chandrasekaran, Rajiv. 2013. "How the Pentagon Got in a Food Fight." *Chicago Tribune*, July 7.

Chang, Cindy. 2016. "Boyle Heights Activists Protest Art Galleries, Gentrification." *Los Angeles Times*, November 5. www.latimes.com/local/lanow/la-me-ln-boyle-heights-protest-20161104-story.html.

Charles, Suzanne Lanyi. 2011. *Suburban Gentrification: Understanding the Determinants of Single-Family Residential Redevelopment, a Case Study of the Inner-Ring Suburbs of Chicago, IL, 2000–2010.* Joint Center for Housing Studies of Harvard University.

Chauncey, George. 2008. *Gay New York: Gender, Urban Culture, and the Making of the Gay Male World, 1890–1940.* Hachette UK.

Childress, Clayton. 2017. *Under the Cover: The Creation, Production, and Reception of a Novel.* Princeton University Press.

Cohen, Cathy. 2019. "The Radical Potential of Queer? Twenty Years Later." *GLQ* 25 (1): 140–44.

Cohen, Lizabeth. 2007. "Buying into Downtown Revival: The Centrality of Retail to Postwar Urban Renewal in American Cities." *Annals of the American Academy of Political and Social Science* 611 (1): 82–95

———. 2019. *Saving America's Cities: Ed Logue and the Struggle to Renew Urban America in the Suburban Age.* Farrar, Straus and Giroux.

Collins, Patricia Hill. 2004. *Black Sexual Politics: African Americans, Gender, and the New Racism.* Routledge.

———. 2015. "Intersectionality's Definitional Dilemmas." *Annual Review of Sociology* 41: 1–20.

Conforti, Joseph M. 1996. "Ghettos as Tourism Attractions." *Annals of Tourism Research* 23 (4): 830–42

Cotter, Holland. 2012. "On an Island, Worker Bees Fill a Long White Hive." *New York Times*, May 5.

Covarrubias, Rebecca, and Stephanie A. Fryberg. 2015. "Movin'on up (to College): First-Generation College Students' Experiences with Family Achievement Guilt." *Cultural Diversity and Ethnic Minority Psychology* 21 (3): 420.

Covarrubias, Rebecca, Fabiana De Lima, Isidro Landa, Ibette Valle, and Wilfrido Hernandez Flores. 2021. "Facets of Family Achievement Guilt for Low-Income, Latinx and Asian First-Generation Students." *Cultural Diversity and Ethnic Minority Psychology* 27 (4): 696–704.

Cox, Jonathan M. 2020. "On Shaky Ground: Black Authenticity at Predominantly White Institutions." *Social Currents* 7 (2): 173–89.

Craig, Maureen A., and Jennifer A. Richeson. 2014. "On the Precipice of a 'Majority-Minority' America: Perceived Status Threat from the Racial Demographic Shift Affects White Americans' Political Ideology." *Psychological Science* 25 (6): 1189–97.

Crenshaw, Kimberlé. 1989. "Demarginalizing the Intersection of Race and Sex: A Black Feminist Critique of Antidiscimination Doctrine, Feminist Theory and Antiracist Politics." *University of Chicago Legal Forum* (1): 139–67.

Curran, Winifred, and Trina Hamilton, eds. 2017. *Just Green Enough: Urban Development and Environmental Gentrification*. Routledge.

Currans, Elizabeth. 2012. "Claiming Deviance and Honoring Community: Creating Resistant Spaces in US Dyke Marches." *Feminist Formations* 24 (1): 73–101.

D'Emilio, John. 1983. *Sexual Politics, Sexual Communities: The Making of a Homosexual Minority in the United States, 1940–1970*. University of Chicago Press.

Davis, Tim. 2003. "The Diversity of Queer Politics and the Redefinition of Sexual Identity and Community in Urban Spaces." In *Mapping Desire: Geographies of Sexuality*, edited by David Bell and Gill Valentine, 259–77. Routledge.

Delany, Samuel R. 1999. *Times Square Red, Times Square Blue*. NYU Press.

Delgado, Emanuel, and Kate Swanson. 2021. "Gentefication in the Barrio: Displacement and Urban Change in Southern California." *Journal of Urban Affairs* 43 (7): 925–40.

Desmond, Matthew. 2016. *Evicted: Poverty and Profit in the American City*. Crown.

Doan, Petra L. 2007. "Queers in the American City: Transgendered Perceptions of Urban Space." *Gender, Place and Culture* 14 (1): 57–74.

Doering, Jan. 2020. *Us Versus Them: Race, Crime, and Gentrification in Chicago Neighborhoods*. Oxford University Press.

Duggan, Lisa. 2002. "The New Homonormativity: The Sexual Politics of Neoliberalism." *Materializing Democracy: Toward a Revitalized Cultural Politics* 10: 175–94.

Duneier, Mitchell. 2016. *Ghetto: The Invention of a Place, the History of an Idea*. Macmillan.

Dunn, Thomas R. 2016. *Queerly Remembered: Rhetorics for Representing the GLBTQ Past*. University of South Carolina Press.

Dyndahl, Petter, Sidsel Karlsen, and Ruth Wright. 2021. *Musical Gentrification: Popular Music, Distinction and Social Mobility*. Taylor & Francis.

Dyndahl, Petter, Sidsel Karlsen, Odd Skårberg, and Siw Graabræk Nielsen. 2014. "Cultural Omnivorousness and Musical Gentrification: An Outline of a Sociological Framework and Its Applications for Music Education Research." *Action, Criticism & Theory for Music Education* 13 (1).

Eaton, Susan E. 2001. *The Other Boston Busing Story: What's Won and Lost across the Boundary Line*. Yale University Press.

Edel, Matthew, and Eliot Sclar. 1975. "The Distribution of Real Estate Value Changes: Metropolitan Boston, 1870–1970." *Journal of Urban Economics* 2 (4): 366–87.

Edel, Matthew, Elliott D. Sclar, and Daniel Luria. 1984. *Shaky Palaces: Homeownership and Social Mobility in Boston's Surburbanization*. Columbia University Press.

Erickson, Rebecca J. 1995. "The Importance of Authenticity for Self and Society." *Symbolic interaction* 18 (2): 121–44.

Esterberg, Kristin. 1997. *Lesbian & Bisexual Identities*. Temple University Press.

Exposito, Suzy. 2022. "Bad Bunny Committed to Being Total Oddball." *Chicago Tribune*, May 23.

Faderman, Lillian. 1991. *Odd Girls and Twilight Lovers: A History of Lesbian Life in Twentieth-Century America*. Columbia University Press.

———. 2015. *The Gay Revolution: The Story of the Struggle*. Simon and Schuster.

Farquhar, Clare. 2000. "'Lesbian' in a Post-Lesbian World? Policing Identity, Sex and Image." *Sexualities* 3 (2): 219–36.

Faughnder, Ryan. 2021. "How Taylor Sheridan's 'Yellowstone' Franchise Could Solve a Big Problem for Paramount+." *Los Angeles Times*, November 3.

Fillmore Activist Project. "History of Fillmore: Disparities & Activism." University of San Francisco blogs network. www.usfblogs.usfca.edu/fillmoreactivistproject/about/history-of-fillmore-activism/.

Fine, Gary Alan, and Sherryl Kleinman. 1979. "Rethinking Subculture: An Interactionist Analysis." *American Journal of Sociology* 85 (1): 1–20.

Fine, Gary Alan, and Ugo Corte. 2017. "Group Pleasures: Collaborative Commitments, Shared Narrative, and the Sociology of Fun." *Sociological Theory* 35 (1): 64–86.

Fischer, Claude S. 1975. "Toward a Subcultural Theory of Urbanism." *American Journal of Sociology* 80 (6): 1319–41.

Fisher, Sean M., and Carolyn Hughes, eds. 1992. *The Last Tenement: Confronting Community and Urban Renewal in Boston's West End*. Bostonian Society.

Florida, Richard. 2002. *The Rise of the Creative Class*. Basic Books.

Formisano, Ronald P. 2004. *Boston against Busing: Race, Class, and Ethnicity in the 1960s and 1970s*. University of North Carolina Press.

Forstie, Clare. 2019. "Disappearing Dykes? Post-Lesbian Discourse and Shifting Identities and Communities." *Journal of Homosexuality* 67 (12): 1760–78.

Frank, Susanne. 2018. "Inner-City Suburbanization—No Contradiction in Terms. Middle-Class Family Enclaves are Spreading in the Cities." *Raumforschung und Raumordnung, Spatial Research and Planning* 76 (2): 123–32.

Freeman, Lance. 2005. Displacement or Succession? Residential Mobility in Gentrifying Neighborhoods. *Urban Affairs Review* 40, no. 4: 463–91.

———. 2011. *The Impact of Source of Income Laws on Voucher Utilization and Locational Outcomes*. US Department of Housing and Urban Development, Office of Policy Development and Research.

Freeman, Lance, and Frank Braconi. 2004. "Gentrification and Displacement: New York City in the 1990s." *Journal of the American Planning Association* 70 (1): 39–52.

Freeman, Lance, Jackelyn Hwang, Tyler Haupert, and Iris Zhang. 2023. "Where Do They Go? The Destinations of Residents Moving from Gentrifying Neighborhoods." *Urban Affairs Review* 60 (1).

Fullilove, Mindy Thompson. 2001. "Root Shock: The Consequences of African American Dispossession." *Journal of Urban Health* 78: 72–80.

———. 2016. *Root Shock: How Tearing up City Neighborhoods Hurts America, and What We Can Do about It*. New Village Press.

Gale, Dennis E. 2021. *The Misunderstood History of Gentrification: People, Planning, Preservation, and Urban Renewal, 1915–2020*. Temple University Press.

Gamson, Joshua. 1995. "Must Identity Movements Self-Destruct? A Queer Dilemma." *Social Problems* 42 (3): 390–407.

Gans, Herbert J. 1982. *Urban Villagers*. Simon and Schuster.

Ganti, Tejaswini. 2014. "Neoliberalism." *Annual Review of Anthropology* 43: 89–104.

Gates, Gary J., and Jason Ost. 2004. *The Gay & Lesbian Atlas*. The Urban Institute.

Gay, Claudine, Jennifer Hochschild, and Ariel White. 2016. "Americans' Belief in Linked Fate: Does the Measure Capture the Concept?" *Journal of Race, Ethnicity, and Politics* 1 (1): 117–44.

Geismer, Lily. 2013. "Good Neighbors for Fair Housing: Suburban Liberalism and Racial Inequality in Metropolitan Boston." *Journal of Urban History* 39 (3): 454–77.

Gerstle, Gary. 2022. *The Rise and Fall of the Neoliberal Order: America and the World in the Free Market Era.* Oxford University Press.

Ghaziani, Amin. 2016. *There Goes the Gayborhood?* Princeton University Press.

Ghertner, D. Asher. 2015. "Why Gentrification Theory Fails in 'Much of the World.'" *City* 19 (4): 552–63.

Gilbert, Dennis L. 2017. *The American Class Structure in an Age of Growing Inequality.* SAGE Publications.

Glass, Ruth. 1964. "Introduction." In *London: Aspects of Change* No. 3, edited by Centre for Urban Studies, xiii–xlii, MacGibbon & Kee.

"Globe North Commentary." 2016. *Boston Globe,* February 19.

Goetz, Edward. 2011. "Gentrification in Black and White: The Racial Impact of Public Housing Demolition in American Cities." *Urban Studies* 48 (8): 1581–1604.

Golash-Boza, Tanya Maria. 2023. *Before Gentrification: The Creation of DC's Racial Wealth Gap.* University of California Press.

Gold, Jonathan. 2013. "A Hearty Blend of Smoke, Swank." *Los Angeles Times,* June 22.

Goldman, Robert. 2021. *Renovating Value: HGTV and the Spectacle of Gentrification.* Temple University Press.

Goodling, Erin, Jamaal Green, and Nathan McClintock. 2015. "Uneven Development of the Sustainable City: Shifting Capital in Portland, Oregon." *Urban Geography* 36 (4): 504–52.

Gonzalez, Erualdo R. 2017. *Latino City: Urban Planning, Politics, and the Grassroots.* Routledge.

Gorel, Amy. 2019. "This Artist Put a Mock-Up of a Triple-Decker in the Seaport to Make Us Think about the Housing Crisis." WBUR, October 3. www.wbur.org/news/2019/10/03/pat-falco-mock-up-triple-decker-housing-crisis-seaport.

Gotham, Kevin Fox. 2001. "A City without Slums: Urban Renewal, Public Housing, and Downtown Revitalization in Kansas City, Missouri." *American Journal of Economics and Sociology* 60 (1): 285–316.

———. 2007. "(Re)branding the Big Easy: Tourism Rebuilding in Post-Katrina New Orleans." *Urban Affairs Review* 42 (6): 823–50.

Gotham, Kevin Fox, and Miriam Greenberg. 2014. *Crisis Cities: Disaster and Redevelopment in New York and New Orleans.* Oxford University Press.

Grazian, David. 2005. *Blue Chicago: The Search for Authenticity in Urban Blues Clubs.* University of Chicago Press.

Greenberg, Miriam. 2014. "Films on Gentrification." *City & Community* 13 (4): 403–11.

Greene, Theodore. 2014. "Gay Neighborhoods and the Rights of the Vicarious Citizen." *City & Community* 13 (2): 99–118.

Griffin, F. Hollis. 2017. *Feeling Normal: Sexuality and Media Criticism in the Digital Age.* Indiana University Press.

Griffis, Noelle. 2022. "'What Am I Supposed to Do with All These White People?': Fifty Years of Gentrification Anxiety on Screen." In *The Routledge Companion to Media and the City,* edited by Erica Stein, Germaine R. Halegoua, and Brendan Kredell, 284–94. Routledge.

Griswold, Wendy. 1987. "A Methodological Framework for the Sociology of Culture." *Sociological Methodology* 17 (1): 1–35.

———. December 1992. "The Writing on the Mud Wall: Nigerian Novels and the Imaginary Village." *American Sociological Review*: 709–24.

———. 2001. "The Ideas of the Reading Class." *Contemporary Sociology* 30 (1): 4–6.

———. 2012. *Cultures and Societies in a Changing World*. Sage.

Hackworth, Jason, and Neil Smith. 2001. "The Changing State of Gentrification." *Tijdschrift voor economische en sociale geografie* 92 (4): 464–77.

Halle, David, and Elisabeth Tiso. 2014. *New York's New Edge: Contemporary Art, the High Line, and Urban Megaprojects on the Far West Wide*. University of Chicago Press.

Hallett, Tim, Orla Stapleton, and Michael Sauder. 2019. "Public Ideas: Their Varieties and Careers." *American Sociological Review* 84 (3): 545–76.

Halnon, Karen, and Saundra Cohen. 2006. "Muscles, Motorcycles and Tattoos: Gentrification in a New Frontier." *Journal of Consumer Culture* 6 (1): 33–56.

Hammett, Jerilou, and Kingsley Hammett, eds. 2007. *Suburbanization of New York: Is the World's Greatest City Becoming Just Another Town?* Princeton Architectural Press.

Hannon, James T. 1984. "The Influence of Catholic Schools on the Desegregation of Public School Systems: A Case Study of White Flight in Boston." *Population Research and Policy Review* 3: 219–37.

Hart, Benji. 2017. "Happening Now: Trans-Led Coalition Shuts Down Chicago Pride Parade." *Radical Faggot*, June 25. radfag.com/2017/06/25/happening-now-trans-led-coalition-shuts-down-chicago-pride-parade/.

Hartman, Chester. 1963. "The Limitations of Public Housing: Relocation Choices in a Working-Class Community." *Journal of the American Institute of Planners* 29 (4): 283–96.

Haynes, Bruce D. 2008. *Red Lines, Black Spaces: The Politics of Race and Space in a Black Middle-Class Suburb*. Yale University Press.

Heise, Thomas. 2021. *The Gentrification Plot: New York and the Postindustrial Crime Novel*. Columbia University Press.

Henryson, Hanna, and Davy Knittle. 2023. "Representing a Long Emergency: New Approaches to Urban Change in Literary and Cultural Studies." *Journal of Urban Cultural Studies* 10 (1): 15–30.

Hepburn, Peter, Renee Louis, and Matthew Desmond. 2024. "Beyond Gentrification: Housing Loss, Poverty, and the Geography of Displacement." *Social Forces* 102 (3): 880–901.

Hill Collins, Patricia, and Sirma Bilge. 2016. *Intersectionality*. Polity.

Hillier, Amy E. 2003. "Redlining and the Home Owners' Loan Corporation." *Journal of Urban History* 29 (4): 394–420.

Hirsch, Marianne. 1997. *Family Frames: Photography, Narrative, and Postmemory*. Harvard University Press.

Hochstenbach, C. 2017. "Hoe Gentrificatie Mainstream is Geworden (How Gentrification Has Become Mainstream)." *Geografie*.

Holland, Gale. 2013. "Bullish on an Iconic Market." *Los Angeles Times*, January 8.

Hosman, Sarah. 2018. "From 'Street Car Suburb' to 'Student Ghetto': Allston and Urban Change." PhD diss., Boston University.

Huante, Alfredo. 2021. "A Lighter Shade of Brown? Racial Formation and Gentrification in Latino Los Angeles." *Social Problems* 68 (1): 63–79.

Humphrey, Jill C. 1999. "To Queer or Not to Queer a Lesbian and Gay Group? Sexual and Gendered Politics at the Turn of the Century." *Sexualities* 2 (20: 223–46.

Hunter, Marcus Anthony. 2010. "All the Gays Are White and All the Blacks are Straight: Black Gay Men, Identity, and Community." *Sexuality Research and Social Policy* 7: 81–92.

Hwang, Jackelyn. 2020. "Gentrification without Segregation? Race, Immigration, and Renewal in a Diversifying City." *City & Community* 19 (3): 538–72

Hwang, Jackelyn, and Robert J. Sampson. 2014. "Divergent Pathways of Gentrification: Racial Inequality and the Social Order of Renewal in Chicago Neighborhoods." *American Sociological Review* 79 (4): 726–51.

Hwang, Jackelyn, and Lei Ding. 2020. "Unequal Displacement: Gentrification, Racial Stratification, and Residential Destinations in Philadelphia." *American Journal of Sociology* 126 (2): 354–406.

Hyra, Derek S. 2006. "Racial uplift? Intra-racial Class Conflict and the Economic Revitalization of Harlem and Bronzeville." *City & Community* 5 (1): 71–92.

———. 2008. *The New Urban Renewal: The Economic Transformation of Harlem and Bronzeville.* University of Chicago Press.

———. 2012. "Conceptualizing the New Urban Renewal: Comparing the Past to the Present." *Urban Affairs Review* 48 (4): 498–527.

Immergluck, Dan. 2009. "Large Redevelopment Initiatives, Housing Values and Gentrification: The Case of the Atlanta Beltline." *Urban Studies* 46, no. 8: 1723–45.

Jackson Jr., John L. 2001. *Harlemworld: Doing Race and Class in Contemporary Black America.* University of Chicago Press.

Jackson, Christina, and Nikki Jones. 2012. "Remember the Fillmore: The Lingering History of Urban Renewal in Black San Francisco." In *Black California Dreamin': The Crises of California's African-American Communities,* 57.

Jackson, Kenneth T. 1987. *Crabgrass Frontier: The Suburbanization of the United States.* Oxford University Press.

Jacobs, Jane. 1961. *The Death and Life of Great American Cities.* Random House.

Jimenez, Carlos, and Alfredo Huante. 2023. "Home in Vida and Gentefied: The Politics of Representation in Gente-fication Narratives." *Aztlán: A Journal of Chicano Studies* 48 (1): 21–52.

Johansson, Ola, and Michael Cornebise. 2010. "Place Branding Goes to the Neighbourhood: The Case of Pseudo-Swedish Andersonville." *Geografiska Annaler: Series B, Human Geography* 92, no. 3: 187–204.

Jones-Correa, Michael. 2011. "Commonalities, Competition, and Linked Fate." In *Just Neighbors?: Research on African American and Latino Relations in the United States,* 63–95.

Kennedy, Elizabeth Lapovsky, and Madeline D. Davis. 2014. *Boots of Leather, Slippers of Gold: The History of a Lesbian Community.* Routledge.

Kent-Stoll, Peter. 2020. "The Racial and Colonial Dimensions of Gentrification." *Sociology Compass* 14 (12): 1–17.

Kirkland, Elizabeth. 2008. "What's Race Got to Do With it? Looking for the Racial Dimensions of Gentrification." *Western Journal of Black Studies* 32 (2).

Knieriem, Marijn. 2023. "Why Can't We Grasp Gentrification? Or: Gentrification as a Moving Target." *Progress in Human Geography* 47 (1): 3–23.

Knittle, Davy. 2019. "Public Sexuality and the Feminist Poetics of Redevelopment in Leslie Scalapino and Adrienne Rich." *Women's Studies Quarterly* 47 (3/4): 232–50.

Kofman, Ava. 2023. "Measure for Measure: On the Frontiers of Penile Enhancement, Competition for Patients Grows Cutthroat." *New Yorker*, July 3.

Korte, Gregory. 2015. "Obama: Gay Marriage Ruling Is 'a Victory for America.'" *USA Today*.

Kosta, Ervin B. 2019. "Becoming Italian, Becoming American: Ethnic Affinity as a Strategy of Boundary Making." *Ethnic and Racial Studies* 42 (5): 801–19.

Krase, Jerome. 1990. "America's Little Italies: Past, Present and Future." In *Their Languages, Literature, and Lives: Proceedings of the 20th Annual Conference of the American Italian Historical Association, Chicago, Illinois, November 11–13, 1987*, 169–84). The American Italian Historical Association.

Kraus, Michael W., and Jacinth JX Tan. 2015. "Americans Overestimate Social Class Mobility." *Journal of Experimental Social Psychology* 58: 101–11.

Krause, Monika. 2019. "What Is Zeitgeist? Examining Period-Specific Cultural Patterns." *Poetics* 76.

Kreager, D. A., C. J. Lyons, and Z. R. Hays. 2011. "Urban Revitalization and Seattle Crime, 1982–2000." *Social Problems* 58, no. 4: 615–39.

Lacy, Karyn R. 2007. *Blue-Chip Black: Race, Class, and Status in the New Black Middle Class.* University of California Press.

Lai, Clement. 2012. "The Racial Triangulation of Space: The Case of Urban Renewal in San Francisco's Fillmore District." *Annals of the Association of American Geographers* 102 (1): 151–70.

Lamont, Michèle. 1987. "How to Become a Dominant French Philosopher: The Case of Jacques Derrida." *American Journal of Sociology* 93 (3): 584–622.

Landis, John D. 2016. "Tracking and Explaining Neighborhood Socioeconomic Change in US Metropolitan Areas Between 1990 and 2010." *Housing Policy Debate* 26, no. 1: 2–52.

Landry, Bart, and Kris Marsh. 2011. "The Evolution of the New Black Middle Class." *Annual Review of Sociology* 37: 373–94.

Lapidos, Juliet. 2013. 2013. "Stars with Their Hands Out." *New York Times*, September 15.

Lawlor, Andrea. 2019. *Paul Takes the Form of a Mortal Girl.* Vintage.

Lawton, Philip. 2018. "Culture, Capital and the Big Screen: Tracing the Changing Dynamics of Gentrification in the Films of Woody Allen." *Urban Geography* 39 (3): 367–87.

Lees, Loretta. 2002. "Rematerializing Geography: The 'New' Urban Geography." *Progress in Human Geography* 26 (1): 101–12.

———. 2003. "Super-gentrification: The Case of Brooklyn Heights, New York City." *Urban studies* 40 (12): 2487–2509.

———. 2014. "Gentrification in the Global South?" In *The Routledge Handbook on Cities of the Global South*, edited by Susan Parnell and Sophie Oldfield, 506–21. Routledge.

Lees, Loretta, Tom Slater, and Elvin Wyly. 2008. *Gentrification.* Routledge.

Lefebvre, Henri. 1968. "The Right to the City [Le Droit à la Ville]." *Anthropos: Paris, France.*

Levy, Brian L., and Denise L. Levy. 2017. "When Love Meets Hate: The Relationship between State Policies on Gay and Lesbian Rights and Hate Crime Incidence." *Social Science Research* 61: 142–59.

Lewis, Nathaniel M. 2017. "Canaries in the Mine? Gay Community, Consumption and Aspiration in Neoliberal Washington, DC." *Urban Studies* 54 (3): 695–712.

Lindholm, Charles. 2007. *Culture and Authenticity*. John Wiley & Sons.

Lingel, Jessa. 2021. *The Gentrification of the Internet: How to Reclaim our Digital Freedom*. University of California Press.

Lloyd, Richard. 2010. *Neo-Bohemia: Art and Commerce in the Postindustrial City*. Routledge.

Lloyd, Robert. 2019. "Feeding His LA Love." *Los Angeles Times*, June 2.

Lorde, Audre. 1982. *Zami: A New Spelling of My Name*. Crossing Press.

Lung-Amam, Willow S. 2024. *The Right to Suburbia: Combating Gentrification on the Urban Edge*. University of California Press.

Macgregor, Lyn C. 2013. *Habits of the Heartland: Small-Town Life in Modern America*. Cornell University Press.

Maciag, Michael. 2015. *Gentrification in America Report. Governing*, January 23.

Macias, Stacy I. 2021. "'Somos contra la queer-ificacíon'/'We reject the queer-ification of lesbianism'": Lesbian Political Identity and Anti-Queer Politics among Mexican Lesbians and Queer Chicanas-Latinas." *Journal of Lesbian Studies* 26 (1): 73–88.

Magagnoli, Paolo. 2011. "Critical Nostalgia in the Art of Joachim Koester." *Oxford Art Journal* 34 (1): 97–121.

Maharawal, Manissa M. 2017. "San Francisco's Tech-Led Gentrification: Public Space, Protest, and the Urban Commons." In *City Unsilenced: Urban Resistance and Public Spaces in the Age of Shrinking Democracy*, edited by Jeffrey Hou and Sabine Knierbein, 30–43. Routledge.

Maloutas, Thomas. 2012. "Contextual Diversity in Gentrification Research." *Critical Sociology* 38 (1): 33–48.

Maly, Michael. 2011. *Beyond Segregation: Multiracial and Multiethnic Neighborhoods*. Temple University Press.

Marcuse, Peter. 1985. "Gentrification, Abandonment, and Displacement: Connections, Causes, and Policy Responses in New York City." *Washington University Journal of Urban & Contemporary Law* 28: 195.

Markley, Scott. 2018. "Suburban Gentrification? Examining the Geographies of New Urbanism in Atlanta's Inner Suburbs." *Urban Geography* 39 (4): 606–30.

Markley, Scott, and Madhuri Sharma. 2016. "Gentrification in the Revanchist Suburb: The Politics of Removal in Roswell, Georgia." *Southeastern Geographer* 56 (1): 57–80.

Massey, Douglas S., and Nancy A. Denton. 1988. "Suburbanization and Segregation in US Metropolitan Areas." *American Journal of Sociology* 94 (3): 592–626.

Masur, Louis P. 2008. *The Soiling of Old Glory: The Story of a Photograph That Shocked America*. Bloomsbury Publishing USA.

Mattson, Greggor. 2019. "Are Gay Bars Closing? Using Business Listings to Infer Rates of Gay Bar Closure in the United States, 1977–2019." *Socius* 5.

———. 2020. "Small-City Gay Bars, Big-City Urbanism." *City & Community* 19 (1): 76–97.

Maylor, Uvanney, and Katya Williams. 2011. "Challenges in Theorising 'Black Middle-Class' Women: Education, Experience and Authenticity." *Gender and Education* 23 (3): 345–56.

McCall, Leslie. 2005. "The Complexity of Intersectionality." *Signs: Journal of Women in Culture and Society* 30 (3): 1771–1800.

McDermott, Sinead. 2002. "Memory, Nostalgia, and Gender in A Thousand Acres." *Signs: Journal of Women in Culture and Society* 28 (1): 389–407.

McDonnell, Terence E. 2023. "Cultural Objects, Material Culture, and Materiality." *Annual Review of Sociology* 49 (1): 195–220.

McDonnell, Terence E., Christopher A. Bail, and Iddo Tavory. 2016. "A Theory of Resonance." *Sociological Theory* 35 (1): 1–14.

Meyer, Ilan H., Lindsay Rossano, James M. Ellis, and Judith Bradford. 2002. "A Brief Telephone Interview to Identify Lesbian and Bisexual Women in Random Digit Dialing Sampling." *Journal of Sex Research* 39 (2): 139–44.

Mijs, Jonathan J. B., and Elizabeth L. Roe. 2021. "Is America Coming Apart? Socioeconomic Segregation in Neighborhoods, Schools, Workplaces, and Social Networks, 1970–2020." *Sociology Compass* 15 (6).

Miranda, Carolina. 2018. "The Art Gallery Exodus from Boyle Heights and Why More Anti Gentrification Battles Loom on the Horizon." *Los Angeles Times*, August 8. www.latimes.com /entertainment/arts/miranda/la-et-cam-gentrification-protests-future-of-boyle-heights -20180808-story.html.

Montero, David. 2018. "Betting Big on Legal Weed." *Los Angeles Times*, November 24.

Moore, Mignon. 2011. *Invisible Families: Gay Identities, Relationships, and Motherhood among Black Women*. University of California Press.

Moran, Robyn, and Lisbeth Berbary. 2022. "Placemaking as Unmaking: Settler Colonialism, Gentrification, and the Myth of 'Revitalized' Urban Spaces." In *Leisure Myths and Mythmaking*, edited by Brett Lashua, Simon Baker, and Troy Glover, 106–20. Routledge.

Moss, Jeremiah. 2017. *Vanishing New York: How a Great City Lost Its Soul*. HarperCollins.

Myles, Eileen. 1994. *Chelsea Girls*. Reprint, 2015. Ecco.

———. 2020. *For Now*. Yale University Press.

Nanos, Janelle. 2018. "What Are Dunkin's New Treats Like?" *Boston Globe*, April 11.

Nash, Catherine Jean. 2011. "Trans Experiences in Lesbian and Queer Space." *Canadian Geographer/Le Géographe Canadien* 55 (2): 192–207.

Neculai, Catalina. 2014. *Urban Space and Late Twentieth-Century New York Literature: Reformed Geographies*. Springer.

Newman, Kathe, and Elvin Wyly. 2006. "The Right to Stay Put, Revisited: Gentrification and Resistance to Displacement in New York City." *Urban Studies* 43, no. 1: 23–57.

O'Connor, Thomas H. 1995. *Building a New Boston: Politics and Urban Renewal, 1950–1970*. Northeastern University Press.

Ocejo, Richard E. 2024. *Sixty Miles Upriver: Gentrification and Race in a Small American City*. Princeton University Press.

Oldenburg, Ray. 1999. *The Great Good Place: Cafes, Coffee Shops, Bookstores, Bars, Hair Salons, and Other Hangouts at the Heart of a Community*. Da Capo Press.

Orne, Jason. 2020. *Boystown: Sex and Community in Chicago*. University of Chicago Press.

Osman, Suleiman. 2016. "What time Is Gentrification?" *City & Community* 15 (3): 215–19.

Page, Clarence. 2014. "The Gentrification of Collard Greens." *Chicago Tribune*, October 15.

Papachristos, Andrew V., Chris M. Smith, Mary L. Scherer, Melissa A. Fugiero. 2011. "More Coffee, Less Crime? The Relationship Between Gentrification and Neighborhood Crime Rates in Chicago, 1991 to 2005." *City & Community* 10, no. 3: 215–40.

Park, Robert E. 1915. "The City: Suggestions for the Investigation of Human Behavior in the City Environment." *American Journal of Sociology* 20 (5): 577–612.

Pasto, James. 2010. "Streets of Fear: Drugs and Violence in Boston's North End." In *Small Towns, Big Cities: The Urban Experience of Italian Americans*, 165–85. Italian American Studies Association.

———. 2017. "Immigrants and Ethnics: Post-World War II Italian Immigration and Boston's North End (1945–2016)." In *New Italian Migrations to the United States. Vol. 1: History and Politics Since 1945*, edited by Laura E. Ruberto and Joseph Sciorra, 105–31. University of Illinois Press.

Pattillo, Mary. 2005. "Black Middle-Class Neighborhoods." *Annual Review of Sociology* 31: 305–29.

———. 2008. "Race, Class, and Neighborhoods." In *Social Class: How Does It Work?* edited by Annette Lareau and Dalton Conley. Russell Sage Foundation.

———. 2010. *Black on the Block: The Politics of Race and Class in the City*. University of Chicago Press.

Peacock, James. 2019. "Those the Dead Left Behind: Gentrification and Haunting in Contemporary Brooklyn Fictions." *Studies in American Fiction* 46 (1): 131–56.

———. 2023. "Other Neighbourhoods, Other Worlds: Gentrification and Contemporary Speculative Fictions." *Journal of Urban Cultural Studies* 10 (1): 113–34.

Pepin, Elizabeth, and Lewis Watts. 2006. *Harlem of the West: The San Francisco Fillmore Jazz Era*. Chronicle Books.

Peterson, Richard A., and Roger M. Kern. 1996. "Changing Highbrow Taste: From Snob to Omnivore." *American Sociological Review* 61 (5): 900–7.

Plett, Casey. 2023. *On Community*. Biblioasis.

Podmore, Julie A. 2006. "Gone 'Underground'? Lesbian Visibility and the Consolidation of Queer Space in Montréal." *Social & Cultural Geography* 7 (4).

———. 2015. "Contested Dyke Rights to the City: Montreal's 2012 Dyke Marches in Time and Space." In *Lesbian Geographies: Gender, Place, and Power*, edited by Kath Browne and Eduarda Ferreira, 71–90. Routledge.

Putnam, Robert D. 2000. *Bowling Alone: The Collapse and Revival of American Community*. Simon & Schuster.

Rafail, Patrick. 2018. "Nonprobability Sampling and Twitter: Strategies for Semibounded and Bounded Populations." *Social Science Computer Review* 36 (2): 195–211.

Rand, Erin J. 2013. "An Appetite for Activism: The Lesbian Avengers and the Queer Politics of Cisibility." *Women's Studies in Communication* 36 (2): 121–41.

Riccio, Anthony V. 2022. *Stories, Streets, and Saints: Photographs and Oral Histories from Boston's North End*. State University of New York Press.

Rich, Adrienne Cecile. 1980. "Compulsory Heterosexuality and Lesbian Existence." *Journal of Women's History* 15 (3): 11–48.

Richards, David A. J. 1999. *Italian American: The Racializing of an Ethnic Identity*. NYU Press.

Riddle, Natasha. 2019. "Housing Is a Queer Issue: DC Dykes Plan to March against Displacement." *Greater Greater Washington,* May 15. www.ggwash.org/view/72081/dc-dykes-march-against-displacement-lgbtq-housing-washington.

Roller, Emma. 2016. "Just Saying Yes to the Politics of Drugs." *New York Times,* January 19.

Rose, Damaris. 1984. "Rethinking Gentrification: Beyond the Uneven Development of Marxist Urban Theory." *Environment and Planning D: Society and Space* 2 (1): 47–74.

Rosenberg, Eli. 2016. "A Sandwich's Sharp-Edge Rise to Fame." *New York Times,* November 8.

Rosenfeld, Lucinda. 2017. *Class.* Little, Brown & Company.

Rossell, Christine H. 1975. "School Desegregation and White Flight." *Political Science Quarterly* 90 (4): 675–95.

———. 1977. "Boston's Desegregation and White Flight." *Integrated Education* 15 (1): 36–39.

Rothstein, Richard. 2017. *The Color of Law: A Forgotten History of How Our Government Segregated America.* Liveright Publishing.

Rucks-Ahidiana, Zawadi. 2021. "Racial Composition and Trajectories of Gentrification in the United States." *Urban Studies* 58 (13): 2721–41

———. 2022. "Theorizing Gentrification as a Process of Racial Capitalism." *City & Community* 21 (3): 173–92.

———. 2024. "Controlling Images of Neighborhoods in Gentrification Coverage." *Social Problems.*

Ryberg-Webster, Stephanie, and Kelly L. Kinahan. 2017. "Historic Preservation in Declining City Neighbourhoods: Analysing Rehabilitation Tax Credit Investments in Six US Cities." *Urban Studies* 54 (7): 1673–91.

Rupp, Leila J., and Verta Taylor. 1999. "Forging Feminist Identity in an International Movement: A Collective Identity Approach to Twentieth-Century Deminism." *Signs: Journal of Women in Culture and Society* 24 (2): 363–86.

Saez, Emmanuel, and Gabriel Zucman. 2016. "Wealth Inequality in the United States since 1913: Evidence from Capitalized Income Tax Data." *Quarterly Journal of Economics* 131 (2): 519–78.

Sanchez, Gabriel R., and Natalie Masuoka. 2010. "Brown-Utility Heuristic? The Presence and Contributing Factors of Latino Linked Fate." *Hispanic Journal of Behavioral Sciences* 32 (4): 519–31.

Sandoval, Gerardo Francisco. 2021. "Planning the Barrio: Ethnic Identity and Struggles over Transit-Oriented, Development-Induced Gentrification." *Journal of Planning Education and Research* 41 (4): 410–24.

Schulman, Sarah. 2012. *The Gentrification of the Mind: Witness to a Lost Imagination.* University of California Press.

Scorsone, Kristyn. 2019. "Invisible Pathways: Public History by Queer Black Women in Newark." *The Public Historian* 41 (2): 190–217.

Shaw, Samuel, and Daniel Monroe Sullivan. 2011. "'White Night': Gentrification, Racial Exclusion, and Perceptions and Participation in the Arts." *City & Community* 10 (3): 241–64.

Sicha, Choire. 2015. "Farewell, My Lovely Cigarettes." *New York Times,* June 3. /www.nytimes.com/2015/06/05/fashion/mens-style/farewell-my-lovely-cigarettes.html.

Slater, Tom. 2006. "The Eviction of Critical Perspectives from Gentrification Research." *International Journal of Urban and Regional Research* 30 (4): 737–57.

Smajda, Jon, and Joseph Gerteis. 2012. "Ethnic Community and Ethnic Boundaries in a 'Sauce-Scented Neighborhood.'" *Sociological Forum* 27 (3): 617–40.

Small, Mario Luis. 2004. *Villa Victoria: The Transformation of Social Capital in a Boston Barrio.* University of Chicago Press.

Smith, Darren P., and Louise Holt. 2005. "'Lesbian Migrants in the Gentrified Valley' and 'Other' Geographies of Rural Gentrification." *Journal of Rural Studies* 21, no. 3: 313–22.

Smith, Jennifer. 2018. "Profiling the Still Ubiquitous—and Profitable—Boston Three-Decker," *Dorchester Reporter*, June 4. www.dotnews.com/2018/profiling-still-ubiquitous-and -profitable-boston-three-decker

Smith, Neil. 1987. "Gentrification and the Rent Gap." *Annals of the Association of American geographers* 77 (3): 462–65.

———. 1996. *The New Urban Frontier: Gentrification and the Revanchist City.* Routledge.

———. 2002. "New Globalism, New Urbanism: Gentrification as Global Urban Strategy." *Antipode* 34 (3): 427–50.

Spain, Daphe. 1993. "Been-Heres versus Come-Heres Negotiating Conflicting Community Identities." *Journal of the American Planning Association* 59 (2): 156–71.

Stehlin, John. 2016. "The Post-Industrial 'Shop Floor': Emerging Forms of Gentrification in San Francisco's Innovation Economy." *Antipode* 48 (20): 474–93.

Stein, Arlene. 1997. *Sex and Sensibility: Stories of a Lesbian Generation.* University of California Press.

Stein, Marc. 2022. *Rethinking the Gay and Lesbian Movement.* Routledge.

Stein, Samuel. 2019. *Capital City: Gentrification and the Real Estate State.* Verso Books.

Stiman, Meaghan. 2020. "Second Homes in the City and the Country: A Reappraisal of Vacation Homes in the Twenty-First Century." *International Journal of Housing Policy* 20 (1): 53–74.

Stone, Amy L. 2013. "Flexible Queers, Serious Bodies: Transgender Inclusion in Queer Spaces." *Journal of Homosexuality* 60 (12): 1647–65.

Stryker, Susan. 2008. "Transgender History, Homonormativity, and Disciplinarity." *Radical History Review* (100): 145–57.

Sulimma, Maria. 2023. "'To Live in a City Is to Consume Its Offerings': Speculative Fiction and Gentrification in Ling Ma's Severance (2018)." *Journal of Urban Cultural Studies* 10 (1): 95–112.

Summers, Brandi T. 2021. "Reclaiming the Chocolate City: Soundscapes of Gentrification and Resistance in Washington, DC." *Environment and Planning D: Society and Space* 39, no. 1: 30–46.

Suttles, Gerald D. 1968. *The Social Order of the Slum: Ethnicity and Territory in the Inner City.* University of Chicago Press.

Tabak, Lauren, and Susie Smith, dirs. 2015. *Never a Cover: A Short Film about the Lexington Club.*

Taylor, Monique M. 2002. *Harlem: Between Heaven and Hell.* University of Minnesota Press.

Tea, Michelle. 2010. *Valencia.* Hachette UK.

———. 2022. *Knocking Myself Up: A Memoir of My (In)fertility.* Harper Collins.

Teaford, Jon C. 2000. "Urban Renewal and Its Aftermath." *Housing Policy Debate* 11 (2): 443–65.

Temin, Peter. 2018. *The Vanishing Middle Class, New Epilogue: Prejudice and Power in a Dual Economy.* MIT Press.

Teresa, Benjamin F. 2019. "New Dynamics of Rent Gap Formation in New York City Rent-Regulated Housing: Privatization, Financialization, and Uneven Eevelopment." *Urban Geography* 40 (10): 1399–1421.

Theoharis, Jeanne F. 2001. "'We Saved the City': Black Struggles for Educational Equality in Boston, 1960–1976." *Radical History Review* 81 (1): 61–93.

Thomas, Courtney S. 2015. "A New Look at the Black Middle Class: Research Trends and Challenges." *Sociological Focus* 48: 191–207.

Thompson, Carolyn. 2011. "Discourses of Community Contestation: The Fight over the Atlantic Yards in Brooklyn, New York." *Urban Geography* 32 (8): 1189–1207.

Timberlake, Jeffrey M., and Elaina Johns-Wolfe. 2017. "Neighborhood Ethnoracial Composition and Gentrification in Chicago and New York, 1980 to 2010." *Urban Affairs Review* 53 (2): 236–72.

Tingwall, Eric. 2013. "Expires 2013: Models that Won't Return." *New York Times*, September 29.

Tissot, Sylvie. 2015. *Good Neighbors: Gentrifying Diversity in Boston's South End*. Verso Books.

Tolfo, Giuseppe, and Brian Doucet. 2021. "Gentrification in the media: the eviction of critical class perspective." *Urban Geography* 42, no. 10 (2021): 1418–1439.

———. 2022. "Livability for Whom?: Planning for Livability and the Gentrification of Memory in Vancouver." *Cities* 123: 103564.

Trilling, Lionel. 2009. *Sincerity and Authenticity*. Harvard University Press.

Tuck, Eve, and K. Wayne Yang. 2012. "Decolonization Is Not a Metaphor." *Decolonization: Indigeneity, Education & Society* 1 (1): 1–40.

———. 2021. "Decolonization Is Not a Metaphor." *Tabula Rasa* 38: 61–111.

Turnbull, Gillian. 2009. "'Land of the In Between': Nostalgia and the Gentrification of Calgarian Roots Music." *MusiCultures*.

Valle, Melissa M. 2021. "Globalizing the Sociology of Gentrification." *City & Community* 20 (1): 59–70.

Van Beurden, Spark L., and Mariëtte de Haan. 2019. "How Do Moroccan-Dutch Parents (Re) Construct Their Parenting Practices? Post-Migration Parenthood as a Social Site for Learning and Identity." *Learning, Culture and Social Interaction* 21: 1–9.

Vigdor, Jacob L. 2002. "Locations, Outcomes, and Selective Migration." *Review of Economics and Statistics* 84 (4): 751–55.

Vigdor, Jacob L., Douglas S. Massey, and Alice M. Rivlin. 2002. "Does Gentrification Harm the Poor?" *Brookings-Wharton Papers on Urban Affairs*: 133–82.

Wacquant, Loïc. 2008. "Relocating Gentrification: The Working Class, Science and the State in Recent Urban Research." *International Journal of Urban and Regional Research* 32 (1): 198–205.

———. 2008. *Urban Outcasts: A Comparative Sociology of Advanced Marginality*. Polity.

———. 2022. *The Invention of the "Underclass": A Study in the Politics of Knowledge*. John Wiley & Sons.

Wacquant, Loïc, Tom Slater, and Virgílio Borges Pereira. 2014. "Territorial Stigmatization in Action." *Environment and Planning A* 46 (6): 1270–80.

Walker, Richard. 1998. "An Appetite for the City." In *Reclaiming San Francisco: History, Politics, Culture*, edited by James Brook, Chris Carlsson, and Nancy Peters, 1–19.

Wanzo, Rebecca. 2021. "Black Obliteration around the Corner: The Gentrification Film." *Film Quarterly* 75 (1): 79–83

Warner, Michael. 2000. *The Trouble with Normal: Sex, Politics, and the Ethics of Queer Life*. Harvard University Press.

Waters, Mary C. 1990. *Ethnic Options: Choosing Identities in America*. University of California Press.

Weston, Kath. 1995. "Get Thee to a Big City: Sexual Imaginary and the Great Gay Migration." *GLQ: A Journal of Lesbian and Gay Studies* 2 (3): 253–77.

Wharton, J. L. 2008. "Gentrification: The New Colonialism in the Modern Era." In *Forum on Public Policy: A Journal of the Oxford Round Table*. Forum on Public Policy.

Whyte, William Foote. 1943. *Street Corner Society: The Social Structure of an Italian Slum*. University of Chicago Press.

Williams, Raymond. 1975. *The Country and the City*. Vol. 423. Oxford University Press USA.

Wirth, Louis. 1938. "Urbanism as a Way of Life." *American Journal of Sociology* 44, no. 1: 1–24.

Wyatt-Nichol, Heather. 2011. "The Enduring Myth of the American Dream: Mobility, Marginalization, and Hope." *International Journal of Organization Theory & Behavior* 14 (2): 258–79.

Wyly, Elvin K., and Daniel J. Hammel. 1999. "Islands of Decay in Seas of Renewal: Housing Policy and the Resurgence of Gentrification." *Housing Policy Debate* 10 (4): 711–71.

Wynn, Ron. 2019. "'Last Black Man in San Francisco' Tells Somber Story." *Tennessee Tribune*, July 4.

Yamada, David C. 2016. "Mass Exploitation Hidden in Plain Sight: Unpaid Internships and the Culture of Uncompensated Work." *Idaho Law Review* 52 (3): 937.

Zarrelli, Natalie. 2016. "The Lost Lesbian Bars of New Orleans." *Atlas Obscura*, September 14. www.atlasobscura.com/articles/the-lost-lesbian-bars-of-new-orleans.

Zimmer, Tyler J. 2022. "Gentrification and the Racialization of Space." *Philosophy & Social Criticism* 48 (2): 268–88.

Zorbaugh, Harvey Warren. 1929. *The Gold Coast and the Slum: A Sociological Study of Chicago's Near North Side*. University of Chicago Press.

Zukin, Sharon. 1987. "Gentrification: Culture and Capital in the Urban Core." *Annual Review of Aociology* 13 (1): 129–47.

———. 1993. *Landscapes of Power: From Detroit to Disney World*. University of California Press.

INDEX

affordable housing, 3, 26; neoliberalism and, 239, 242; public support for, 32–33, 175

AIDS pandemic, 33, 122–23, 266n11; Eubanks on, 196–97, 200; Schulman on, 266n23

alcoholism, 44, 48. *See also* substance abuse

anti-gentrification art installations, 7

"authenticity," 18, 23, 128, 173, 236; metaphorical *gentrification* and, 131; of urban life, 219

Bad Bunny (musician), 15–16

Balcom, John, 81

Barnett, Courtney (musician), 118

Bartram, Robin, 180, 211

Beirut, Lebanon, 68

Bellafante, Ginia, 15

Belmont, Cynthia, 266n11

Big Chill, The (film), 124

Black Lives Matter, 8, 182, 208–9, 211

Blank, Radha, 130, 164–74

bookstores, 49, 53, 72, 137, 141

Boston, 3, 44, 81–92, 239; demographics of, 82, 83; school desegregation in, 84; triple-decker houses of, 78–79, 92–102, 223

Boston's North End (film), 83, 85–92, 100, 101

Boyle Heights neighborhood (Los Angeles), 35, 109, 148–63, 168, 231; demographics of, 267n37; home prices in, 106

brick-and-mortar gentrification. *See* literal gentrification

Burning Man festival, 1

Calgary (Alberta), 206–7

Charlene's bar (New Orleans), 39–40, 42

Chávez, Linda Yvette, 104–5

Chicago, 64–65, 67–68, 225–26; Andersonville neighborhood of, 42, 60, 65, 225; dyke bar commemorators on, 37–38; North Side neighborhoods, 224–25; West Side neighborhoods, 226–27

Chicago School of Sociology, 266n18

Childress, Clayton, 30

class distinctions, 149–50, 155–58, 169, 268n38

Clements, Alexis, 50, 56

climate change, 179, 182, 210

Clinton Foundation, 165

Clybourne Park (Norris), 222, 255n32

coffee shops, 41, 104, 118, 137, 146, 149

Cogswell, Kelly, 144–46

Cohen, Saundra, 24, 206

colonization, 205, 244; decolonization and, 21–22; displacement as, 11; recolonization and, 149

Columbia University, 165

Cottrell, Honey Lee, 259n30

Covid pandemic, 51, 208

Cox, Jonathan M., 269n68

critical race theory, 224

Cubby Hole bar (NYC), 57

cultural appropriation, 35, 205–8

cultural capital (Bourdieu), 63; economic mobility and, 128–29, 149–50, 154, 158, 268n38; of elite education, 66; low economic capital and, 160–61, 268n49

A NOTE ON THE TYPE

This book has been composed in Arno, an Old-style serif typeface in the classic Venetian tradition, designed by Robert Slimbach at Adobe.